CATALOGUE

OF THE

CABINET OF NATURAL HISTORY

OF THE STATE OF NEW-YORK,

AND OF THE

Historical and Antiquarian Collection

ANNEXED THERETO.

Printed by Order of the Regents of the University.

ALBANY:

C. VAN BENTHUYSEN, PRINTER TO THE LEGISLATURE.

1853.

REGENTS OF THE UNIVERSITY, 1853.

HORATIO SEYMOUR, Governor, *ex officio.*
SANFORD E. CHURCH, Lieutenant-Governor, *ex officio.*
HENRY S. RANDALL, Secretary of State, *ex officio.*
GERRIT Y. LANSING, *Chancellor.*
JOHN GREIG, *Vice-Chancellor.*

GULIAN C. VERPLANCK, LL.D.
JOHN K. PAIGE.
ERASTUS CORNING.
PROSPER M. WETMORE.
JOHN L. GRAHAM.
JOHN M'LEAN.
GIDEON HAWLEY, LL.D.
DAVID BUEL.
JAMES S. WADSWORTH.

JOHN V. L. PRUYN, LL.D.
JABEZ D. HAMMOND, LL.D.
JOHN L. O'SULLIVAN.
ROBERT CAMPBELL.
Rev. SAMUEL LUCKEY, D.D.
ROBERT G. RANKIN.
PHILIP S. VAN RENSSELAER.
Rev. JOHN N. CAMPBELL, D.D.

T. ROMEYN BECK, *Secretary.*

STANDING COMMITTEE OF THE REGENTS,

SPECIALLY CHARGED WITH THE CARE OF THE STATE CABINET.

HORATIO SEYMOUR, *Governor.*
HENRY S. RANDALL, *Secretary of State.*
ERASTUS CORNING.
JOHN M'LEAN.
JAMES S. WADSWORTH.

JOHN GEBHARD JUNIOR, *Curator.*

JAMES HURST, *Taxidermist.*

MEMORANDUM.

The Regents of the University have directed the publication of the accompanying Catalogue, with the double object of showing the contents and the wants of the Collection.

When received under their charge in 1848, it was found to be in an extremely imperfect condition; and most, indeed, of the quadrupeds and birds have been replaced by better specimens.

As the Catalogue is intended as an accompaniment to the "Natural History of New-York," the nomenclature there used has been preserved.

A portion only of the Collection is contained in this volume. The Fishes, Insects, Shells, etc. are for the present omitted, in the hope that they may soon be increased in number, and duly arranged and named. The various divisions are accordingly so paged, that additions can be readily made, and new parts inserted. The attention of Naturalists is invited to the deficiencies in the Cabinet, in the hope that, through their aid and advice, these may be supplied.

The building at present appropriated for this Collection has become of too small capacity for properly exhibiting its contents; and the Regents can only rely on the liberality of the Legislature, to furnish them with accommodations worthy of what in a few years may be made a Museum of the animal, vegetable, and mineral products of the State of New-York. T. R. B.

CONTENTS.

ZOOLOGY OF NEW-YORK,

OR THE

New-York Fauna.

BY JAMES E. DE KAY.

PART I. MAMMALIA.

2

N. B. If there be a specimen of any animal named in the Collection, it is so stated in the third column.

ZOOLOGY.

CLASS I. MAMMALIA.

ORDER I. QUADRUMANA.

ORDER II. MARSUPIATA.

FAMILY DIDELPHIDÆ.

	Latin Name.	English Name.	In the
1	Didelphis virginiana,	*American Opossum.* - - -	Cabinet.

ORDER III. CARNIVORA.

FAMILY VESPERTILIONIDÆ.

2	Vespertilio noveboracensis,	*New-York Bat* (m. & f.). -	Cabinet.
3	Vespertilio pruinosus,	*Hoary Bat.*	
4	Vespertilio subulatus,	*Little Brown Bat.* - - -	Cabinet.
5	Vespertilio noctivagans,	*Silver-haired Bat* (m. & f.).	Cabinet.
6	Vespertilio carolinensis,	*Carolina Bat* (m. f. & y.). -	Cabinet.

FAMILY SORECIDÆ.

7	Condylura cristata,	*Common Starnose* (two). -	Cabinet.
8	Scalops aquaticus,	*Common Shrew Mole.* - -	Cabinet.
9	Sorex dekayi,	*Dekay's Shrew.* - - - -	Cabinet.
10	Sorex brevicaudus,	*Short-tailed Shrew.*	
11	Sorex parvus,	*Small Shrew.*	
12	Sorex forsteri,	*Forster's Shrew.*	
13	Sorex carolinensis,	*Carolina Shrew.*	
14	Otisorex platyrhinus,	*Broad-nosed Shrew.*	

FAMILY URSIDÆ.

	Latin Names.	English Names.	
15	URSUS AMERICANUS,	*American Black Bear.* - -	Cabinet.
16	PROCYON LOTOR,	*Raccoon* (m. & f.). - - -	Cabinet.
17	GULO LUSCUS,	*Wolverene.*	

FAMILY MUSTELIDÆ.

18	MEPHITIS AMERICANA,	*Skunk.* - - - - - - - -	Cabinet.
19	MUSTELA CANADENSIS,	*Fisher.* - - - - - - - -	Cabinet.
20	MUSTELA MARTES,	*American Sable.*	
21	MUSTELA PUSILLA,	*Small Weasel.*	
22	MUSTELA FUSCA,	*Brown Weasel.* - - - - -	———
23	PUTORIUS NOVEBORACENSIS,	*New-York Ermine* (m. & f.).	Cabinet.
24	PUTORIUS VISON,	*Mink.* - - - - - - - -	Cabinet.

FAMILY LUTRIDÆ.

25	LUTRA CANADENSIS,	*North-American Otter.* - -	Cabinet.

FAMILY CANIDÆ.

26	CANIS FAMILIARIS,	*Domestic Dog* (domesticated).	
27	LUPUS OCCIDENTALIS,	*Common American Wolf.*	
28	VULPES FULVUS,	*Red Fox.* - - - - - - -	Cabinet.
29	VULPES VIRGINIANUS,	*Grey Fox.* - - - - - - -	Cabinet.

FAMILY FELIDÆ.

30	FELIS CONCOLOR,	*Northern Panther* (2 m. & f.).	Cabinet.
31	LYNCUS BOREALIS,	*Northern Lynx.* - - - -	Cabinet.
32	LYNCUS RUFUS,	*Wildcat*, or *Bay Lynx.* - -	Cabinet.

FAMILY PHOCIDÆ.

33	PHOCA CONCOLOR,	*American Seal.* - - - -	Cabinet.
34	STEMMATOPUS CRISTATUS,	*Hooded Seal.*	

ORDER IV. RODENTIA.

FAMILY SCIURIDÆ.

35	SCIURUS LEUCOTIS,	*Little Grey Squirrel.* - -	Cabinet.
36	SCIURUS VULPINUS,	*Fox Squirrel* (m. & f.). - -	Cabinet.
37	SCIURUS NIGER,	*Black Squirrel.* - - - -	Cabinet.
38	SCIURUS HUDSONICUS,	*Red Squirrel* (m. & f.). - -	Cabinet.
39	SCIURUS STRIATUS,	*Striped Squirrel.* - - - -	———
40	PTEROMYS VOLUCELLA,	*Small American Flying Squirrel* (m. & f.).	Cabinet.

FAMILY ARCTOMIDÆ.

	Latin Names.	English Names.	
41	Arctomys monax,	*Woodchuck* (m. & f.). - -	Cabinet.

FAMILY GERBILLIDÆ.

42	Meriones americanus,	*Deer Mouse* (f.). - - - -	Cabinet.

FAMILY CASTORIDÆ.

43	Castor fiber,	*Beaver.* - - - - - - - -	Cabinet.
44	Fiber zibethicus,	*Musquash* (2 m. & f.). - -	Cabinet.

FAMILY HYSTRICIDÆ.

45	Hystrix hudsonius,	*North-American Porcupine*(f.).	Cabinet.

FAMILY MURIDÆ.

46	Mus decumanus,	*Brown Rat* (introduced. m. & f.).	Cabinet.
47	Mus rattus,	*Black Rat* (introduced).	
48	Mus americanus,	*American Black Rat.* - -	Cabinet.
49	Mus musculus,	*Common Mouse* (m. & f.). -	Cabinet.
50	Mus leucopus,	*Jumping Mouse* (f.). - - -	Cabinet.
51	Arvicola riparius,	*Marsh Meadow Mouse.*	
52	Arvicola rufescens,	*Tawny Meadow Mouse.* - -	Cabinet.
53	Arvicola hirsutus,	*Beaver Field Mouse.* - -	Cabinet.
54	Arvicola oneida,	*Oneida Meadow Mouse.*	
55	Arvicola albo-rufescens,	*Light-colored Meadow Mouse.*	
56	Arvicola xanthognathus,	*Yellow-cheeked Meadow Mouse.*	

FAMILY LEPORIDÆ.

57	Lepus nanus,	*American Gray Rabbit* (two).	Cabinet.
58	Lepus americanus,	*Northern Hare.* - - - -	Cabinet.

ORDER V. EDENTATA.

ORDER VI. UNGULATA.

FAMILY ELEPHANTIDÆ.

59	Elephas primigenius,	*Fossil Elephant.*	
60	Elephas americanus,	*American Elephant* (fossil).	
61	Mastodon maximus,	*Great Mastodon* (fossil).	

FAMILY SUIDÆ.

	Latin Names.	English Names.	
62	Sus scrofa, *var.* domesticus,	*Common Hog* (introduced).	

FAMILY EQUIDÆ.

63	Equus caballus,	*Horse* (introduced).	
64	Equus asinus,	*Ass* (introduced).	
65	Equus major,	*Fossil Horse.*	

FAMILY BOVIDÆ.

66	Bos taurus,	*Common Ox* (introduced).	

FAMILY CAPRIDÆ.

67	Ovis aries,	*Domestic Sheep* (introduced).	

FAMILY CERVIDÆ.

68	Cervus virginianus,	*American Deer.* - - - -	Cabinet.
96	Cervus alces,	*Moose.* - - - - - - - -	Cabinet.
70	Elaphus canadensis,	*American Stag*, or *Elk* (horns).	Cabinet.
71	Elaphus americanus,	*Fossil Stag.*	
72	Rangifer tarandus,	*Reindeer* (extirpated?).	

ORDER VII. CETACEA.

FAMILY MANATIDÆ.

FAMILY BALÆNIDÆ.

73	Balæna mysticetus,	*Right Whale.*	
74	Physeter macrocephalus,	*Sperm Whale.*	
75	Rorqualus rostratus,	*Beaked Rorqual.*	
76	Rorqualus borealis,	*Northern Rorqual.*	

FAMILY DELPHINIDÆ.

77	Globicephalus melas,	*Social Whale.*	
78	Phocæna communis,	*Common Porpoise.*	
79	Phocæna orca,	*Grampus.*	
80	Delphinus delphis,	*Sea Porpoise.*	

Castoroides ohioensis, *Fossil Beaver* (cast of skull & lower jaw).* Cabinet.

* De Kay, in his Zoology of New-York, describes the Fossil Beaver as *extra-limital.* The original specimen from which the casts in the collection were taken was found near Clyde in Wayne county, N. York. We therefore place the Fossil Beaver in the catalogue of the New-York Mammalia.

ZOOLOGY OF NEW-YORK,

OR THE

New-York Fauna.

BY JAMES E. DE KAY.

PART II. BIRDS.

ZOOLOGY.

CLASS II. BIRDS.

ORDER I. ACCIPITRES.

FAMILY VULTURIDÆ.

	Latin Name.	English Name.	In the
1	Cathartes aura,	*Turkey Buzzard.* . - - - -	———

FAMILY FALCONIDÆ.

2	Aquila chrysaetos,	*Golden Eagle.* - - - -	Cabinet.
3	Haliaetos leucocephalus,	*Brown* or *Bald Eagle* (m. & 2 f.).	Cabinet.
4	Pandion carolinensis,	*American Fish Hawk.* - -	Cabinet.
5	Buteo sancti-johannis,	*Rough-legged Buzzard* (m. & f.).	Cabinet.
6	Buteo borealis,	*Red-tailed Buzzard* (m. & f.).	Cabinet.
7	Buteo hyemalis,	*Red-shouldered Buzzard.* -	Cabinet.
8	Buteo pennsylvanicus,	*Broad-winged Buzzard* (m. & f.).	Cabinet.
9	Nauclerus furcatus,	*Swallow-tailed Hawk.* - -	———
10	Falco anatum,	*Duck Hawk* (m. & f.). - -	Cabinet.
11	Falco columbarius,	*Pigeon Hawk.* - - - -	Cabinet.
12	Falco sparverius,	*American Sparrowhawk* (m. & f.).	Cabinet.
13	Astur fuscus,	*Slate-colored Hawk* (m. & f.).	Cabinet.
14	Astur cooperi,	*Cooper's Hawk.* - - - -	Cabinet.
15	Astur atricapillus,	*American Goshawk* (m. & f.).	Cabinet.
16	Circus uliginosus,	*Marsh Harrier.* - - - -	Cabinet.

FAMILY STRIGIDÆ.

	Latin Names.	English Names.	
17	Surnia funerea,	*Hawk Owl.* - - - - -	Cabinet.
18	Surnia nyctea,	*Snowy Owl* (m. & f.). - -	Cabinet.
19	Bubo virginianus,	*Great Horned Owl* (m. & f.).	Cabinet.
20	Bubo asio,	*Little Screechowl* (m. f. & y.).	Cabinet.
21	Syrnium cinereum,	*Great Grey Owl* (m. & f.). -	Cabinet.
22	Otus americanus,	*Long-Eared Owl* (m. & f.). -	Cabinet.
23	Otus palustris,	*Short-eared Owl* (m. & f.). -	Cabinet.
24	Ulula nebulosa,	*Barred Owl* (2 m.). - - -	Cabinet.
25	Ulula acadica,	*Acadian Owl* (m. & f.). - -	Cabinet.
26	Strix pratincola,	*American Barn Owl.* - -	Cabinet.

ORDER II. PASSERES.

FAMILY CAPRIMULGIDÆ.

27	Caprimulgus vociferus,	*Whippoorwill.* - - - -	Cabinet.
28	Chordeiles americanus,	*Nighthawk.* - - - - -	Cabinet.

FAMILY HIRUNDINIDÆ.

29	Chætura pelasgia,	*Chimney Swallow* (m. & f.).	Cabinet.
30	Hirundo purpurea,	*Purple Martin* (m. & f.). -	Cabinet.
31	Hirundo bicolor,	*White-bellied Swallow.* - -	Cabinet.
32	Hirundo riparia,	*Bank Swallow.* - - - -	Cabinet.
33	Hirundo rufa,	*Barn Swallow.* - - - -	Cabinet.
34	Hirundo fulva,	*Cliff Swallow* (m. & f.). - -	Cabinet.

FAMILY AMPELIDÆ.

35	Bombycilla garrula,	*Black-throated Waxwing.* -	Cabinet.
36	Bombycilla carolinensis,	*Cedarbird* (m. & f.). - - -	Cabinet.

FAMILY ALCEDINIDÆ.

37	Alcedo alcyon,	*Belted Kingfisher* (two). -	Cabinet.

FAMILY TROCHILIDÆ.

38	Trochilus colubris,	*Red-throated Hummingbird* (m. & f.).	Cabinet.

FAMILY CERTHIDÆ.

	Latin Names.	English Names.	
39	Sitta carolinensis,	*White-breasted Nuthatch.* -	Cabinet.
40	Sitta canadensis,	*Red-bellied Nuthatch* (m. & f.).	Cabinet.
41	Certhia americana,	*Brown Creeper* (f.). - - -	Cabinet.
42	Mniotilta varia,	*Varied Creeping Warbler* (m. & f.).	Cabinet.
43	Troglodytes ædon,	*House Wren* (three). - - -	Cabinet.
44	Troglodytes americanus,	*Wood Wren.* - - - - -	———
45	Troglodytes ludovicianus,	*Mocking Wren* (m. & f.). -	Cabinet.
46	Troglodytes palustris,	*Marsh Wren* (m. & f.). - -	Cabinet.
47	Troglodytes hyemalis,	*Winter Wren* (m. & f.). - -	Cabinet.
48	Troglodytes brevirostris,	*Short-billed Wren.* - - -	Cabinet.

FAMILY PARIDÆ.

49	Parus bicolor,	*Crested Tit.* - - - - -	Cabinet.
50	Parus atricapillus,	*Black-cap Tit.* - - - -	Cabinet.
51	Parus carolinensis,	*Carolina Tit.* - - - - -	Cabinet.

FAMILY SYLVIADÆ.

52	Regulus satrapa,	*Golden-crested Kinglet.* - -	Cabinet.
53	Regulus calendula,	*Ruby-crowned Kinglet.* - -	Cabinet.
54	Sialia wilsoni,	*Bluebird* (m. & f.). - - -	Cabinet.

FAMILY MERULIDÆ.

55	Orpheus polyglottus,	*Common Mockingbird.* - -	Cabinet.
56	Orpheus rufus,	*Brown Thrush* (m. & f.). -	Cabinet.
57	Orpheus carolinensis,	*Catbird* (m. & f.). - - -	Cabinet.
58	Merula migratoria,	*American Robin* (m. & f. and an albino).	Cabinet.
59	Merula mustelina,	*Wood Thrush* (m. & f.). - -	Cabinet.
60	Merula solitaria,	*Hermit Thrush.* - - - -	Cabinet.
61	Merula olivacea,	*Olive-backed Thrush.* - -	Cabinet.
62	Merula wilsoni,	*Wilson's Thrush* (f.). - -	Cabinet.

FAMILY MOTACILLIDÆ.

63	Anthus ludovicianus,	*American Titlark* (f.). - -	Cabinet.
64	Seiurus noveboracensis,	*New-York Water Thrush* (m. & f.).	Cabinet.
65	Seiurus aurocapillus,	*Ovenbird.* - - - - - -	Cabinet.

FAMILY SYLVICOLIDÆ.

	Latin Names.	English Names.	
66	Trichas marilandica,	*Yellowthroat* (m. & f.). - -	Cabinet.
67	Trichas philadelphia,	*Mourning Warbler.* - - -	———
68	Vermivora pennsylvanica,	*Worm-eating Warbler.* - -	Cabinet.
69	Vermivora swainsoni,	*Whistling Warbler.*	
70	Vermivora solitaria,	*Blue-winged Warbler* (m. & f.).	Cabinet.
71	Vermivora chrysoptera,	*Golden-winged Warbler.* -	Cabinet.
72	Vermivora peregrina,	*Tennessee Warbler.* - - -	———
73	Vermivora rubricapilla,	*Nashville Warbler.* - - -	Cabinet.
74	Vermivora celata,	*Orange-crowned Warbler* (m. & f.).	Cabinet.
75	Sylvicola coronata,	*Myrtlebird.* - - - - -	Cabinet.
76	Sylvicola ruficapilla,	*Redpoll Warbler* (m. & f.). -	Cabinet.
77	Sylvicola maculosa,	*Spotted Warbler.* - - - -	Cabinet.
78	Sylvicola pardalina,	*Spotted Canada Warbler* (m. & f.).	Cabinet.
79	Sylvicola cærulea,	*Blue-grey Warbler.* - - -	Cabinet.
80	Sylvicola blackburnia,	*Blackburnian Warbler.* - -	———
81	Sylvicola castanea,	*Bay-breasted Warbler* (f.). -	Cabinet.
82	Sylvicola striata,	*Blackpoll Warbler.* - - -	Cabinet.
83	Sylvicola discolor,	*Prairie Warbler.* - - -	Cabinet.
84	Sylvicola americana;	*Blue Yellow-backed Warbler* (f.).	Cabinet.
85	Sylvicola canadensis,	*Black-throated Blue Warbler.*	Cabinet.
86	Sylvicola æstiva,	*Summer Yellowbird* (m. & f.).	Cabinet.
87	Sylvicola virens,	*Black-throated Green Warbler* (m. & f.).	Cabinet.
88	Sylvicola pinus,	*Pine Warbler* (m. & f.). -	Cabinet.
89	Sylvicola icterocephala,	*Chesnut-sided Warbler.* - -	Cabinet.
90	Sylvicola parus,	*Hemlock Warbler.* - - -	———
91	Sylvicola maritima,	*Cape-May Warbler.* - - -	Cabinet.
92	Sylvicola formosa,	*Kentucky Warbler.* - - -	Cabinet.
93	Wilsonia mitrata,	*Hooded Warbler* (m. & f.). -	Cabinet.
94	Wilsonia pusilla,	*Green Black-capped Warbler* (m. & f.).	Cabinet.

FAMILY MUSCICAPIDÆ.

	Latin Names.	English Names.	
95	Culicivora cærulea,	*Blue-grey Gnatcatcher.* - -	Cabinet.
96	Muscicapa ruticilla,	*American Redstart* (m. & f.).	Cabinet.
97	Muscicapa acadica,	*Small Green-crested Flycatcher* (f.).	Cabinet.
98	Muscicapa flaviventris,	*Yellow-bellied Flycatcher.* -	———
99	Muscicapa virens,	*Wood Pewee* (f.). - - - -	Cabinet.
100	Muscicapa fusca,	*Phœbebird.* - - - - - -	Cabinet.
101	Tyrannus intrepidus,	*Kingbird* (m. & f.). - - -	Cabinet.
102	Tyrannus cooperi,	*Olive-sided Kingbird* (f.). -	Cabinet.
103	Tyrannus crinitus,	*Great-crested Kingbird.* -	Cabinet.

FAMILY VIREONIDÆ.

104	Vireo flavifrons,	*Yellow-throated Greenlet* (three).	Cabinet.
105	Vireo solitarius,	*Solitary Greenlet.* - - -	Cabinet.
106	Vireo noveboracensis,	*White-eyed Greenlet* (m. & f.).	Cabinet.
107	Vireo gilvus,	*Warbling Greenlet.* - - -	Cabinet.
108	Vireo olivaceus,	*Red-eyed Greenlet* (m. & f.).	Cabinet.
109	Icteria viridis,	*Yellow-breasted Chat* (m. & f.).	Cabinet.

FAMILY LANIDÆ.

110	Lanius septentrionalis,	*Northern Butcherbird* (m. & f.).	Cabinet.

FAMILY CORVIDÆ.

111	Garrulus cristatus,	*Blue Jay* (m. & f.). - - -	Cabinet.
112	Garrulus canadensis,	*Canada Jay.* - - - - - -	———
113	Pica caudata,	*Magpie.* - - - - - - -	Cabinet.
114	Corvus americanus,	*Common Crow* (m. & f.). -	Cabinet.
115	Corvus corax,	*Raven.* - - - - - - - -	Cabinet.
116	Corvus ossifragus,	*Fish Crow.* - - - - - -	Cabinet.

FAMILY QUISCALIDÆ.

117	Quiscalus versicolor,	*Common Crow Blackbird* (m. & f.).	Cabinet.
118	Quiscalus ferrugineus,	*Rusty Crow Blackbird* (m. & f.).	Cabinet,
119	Sturnella ludovicianus,	*Meadow Lark* (m. & f.). -	Cabinet.
120	Icterus baltimore,	*Golden Oriole* (m. & f.)). -	Cabinet.
121	Icterus spurius,	*Orchard Oriole* (m. & f.). -	Cabinet.

	Latin Names.	English Names.	
122	Icterus phœniceus,	*Red-winged Oriole* (m. & f.).	Cabinet.
123	Molothrus pecoris,	*Cow Bunting* (m. & f.). - -	Cabinet.
124	Dolichonyx oryzivorus,	*Boblink* (m. & f.). - - -	Cabinet.

FAMILY FRINGILLIDÆ.

125	Coccoborus cæruleus,	*Blue Grosbeak.* - - - - -	———
126	Coccoborus ludovicianus,	*Rose-breasted Grosbeak* (m. & f.).	Cabinet.
127	Struthus hyemalis,	*Snowbird.* - - - - - - -	Cabinet.
128	Fringilla iliaca,	*Fox-colored Sparrow* (m. & f.).	Cabinet.
129	Fringilla melodia,	*Song Sparrow.* - - - - -	Cabinet.
130	Fringilla graminea,	*Bay-winged Sparrow* (m. & f.).	Cabinet.
131	Fringilla pennsylvanica,	*White-throated Sparrow* (m. & f.).	Cab.
132	Fringilla leucophrys,	*White-crowned Sparrow.* -	Cabinet.
133	Emberiza americana,	*Black-throated Bunting* (m. & f.).	Cab.
134	Emberiza passerina,	*Yellow-winged Bunting* (m. & f.).	Cab.
135	Emberiza henslowi,	*Varied Bunting.* - - - -	Cabinet.
136	Emberiza pusilla,	*Field Bunting* (m. & f.). -	Cabinet.
137	Emberiza socialis,	*Chipbird.* - - - - - - -	Cabinet.
138	Emberiza canadensis,	*Tree Bunting* (m. & f.). -	Cabinet.
139	Emberiza savana,	*Savannah Bunting* (m. & f.).	Cabinet.
140	Emberiza lincolni,	*Blue-striped Bunting.*	
141	Ammodramus maritimus,	*Seaside Finch.* - - - -	Cabinet.
142	Ammodramus caudacutus,	*Quailhead* (m. & f.). - - -	Cabinet.
143	Ammodramus palustris,	*Swamp Finch* (m. & f.). - -	Cabinet.
144	Carduelis tristis,	*Yellowbird*, or *American Goldfinch* (three).	Cabinet.
145	Carduelis pinus,	*Pine Finch* (m. & f.). - -	Cabinet.
146	Linaria minor,	*Lesser Redpoll* (m. & f.). -	Cabinet.
147	Linaria borealis,	*Mealy Redpoll.*	
148	Erythrospiza purpurea,	*Crested Purple Finch* (f.). -	Cabinet.
149	Pitylus cardinalis,	*Cardinal Grosbeak* (m. & f.).	Cabinet.
150	Pipilo erythrophthalmus,	*Chewink*, or *Ground Robin* (two).	Cab.
151	Spiza cyanea,	*Indigobird* (m. & f.). - -	Cabinet.
152	Pyranga æstiva,	*Redbird.* - - - - - - -	Cabinet.

	Latin Names.	English Names.	
153	Pyranga rubra,	*Black-winged Redbird* (m. & f.).	Cabinet.
154	Plectrophanes lapponicus,	*Lapland Snowbird* (m. & f.).	Cabinet.
155	Plectrophanes nivalis,	*White Snowbird.* - - - -	Cabinet.
156	Alauda cornuta,	*Horned Lark* (m. & f.). - -	Cabinet.
157	Corythus enucleator,	*Pine Bulfinch* (three). - -	Cabinet.
158	Loxia americana,	*American Crossbill* (m. & f.).	Cabinet.
159	Loxia leucoptera,	*White-winged Crossbill* (m. & f.).	Cabinet.

FAMILY PICIDÆ.

160	Picus pileatus,	*Crested Woodpecker* (m. & f.).	Cabinet.
161	Picus erythrocephalus,	*Red-headed Woodpecker* (m. & f.).	Cabinet.
162	Picus villosus,	*Hairy Woodpecker.* - - -	Cabinet.
163	Picus pubescens,	*Downy Woodpecker.* - - -	Cabinet.
164	Picus varius,	*Yellow-bellied Woodpecker* (m. & f.).	Cabinet.
165	Picus carolinus,	*Red-bellied Woodpecker.* -	Cabinet.
166	Picus arcticus,	*Arctic Woodpecker.* - - -	Cabinet.
167	Picus hirsutus,	*Banded Woodpecker.*	
168	Picus auratus,	*Golden-winged Woodpecker*, or *Clape* (two).	Cabinet.

FAMILY CUCULIDÆ.

169	Coccyzus americanus,	*Yellow-bellied Cuckoo.* - -	Cabinet.
170	Coccyzus erythrophthalmus,	*Black-billed Cuckoo* (m. & f.).	Cab.

FAMILY COLUMBIDÆ.

171	Ectopistes migratoria,	*Wild Pigeon* (m. & f.). - -	Cabinet.
172	Ectopistes carolinensis,	*Carolina Turtle Dove.* - -	———

ORDER III. GALLINÆ.

FAMILY PHASIANIDÆ.

173	Meleagris gallopavo,	*Wild Turkey.* - - - - -	Cabinet.

FAMILY TETRAONIDÆ.

174	Ortyx virginiana,	*Quail* (m. & f., and a circle of five).	Cabinet.
175	Tetrao umbellus,	*Ruffed Grouse* (m. f. & y.). -	Cabinet.
176	Tetrao cupido,	*Pinnated Grouse* (m. & f.). -	Cabinet.
177	Tetrao canadensis,	*Spotted Grouse* (m. & f.). -	Cabinet.

ORDER IV. GRALLÆ.

FAMILY CHARADRIDÆ.

	Latin Names.	English Names.
178	Charadrius semipalmatus,	*American Ring Plover* (m. & f.). Cab.
179	Charadrius melodus,	*Piping Plover.* - - - - Cabinet.
180	Charadrius wilsonius,	*Wilson's Plover.* - - - - Cabinet.
181	Charadrius vociferus,	*Kildeer Plover* (m. & f.). - Cabinet.
182	Charadrius virginiacus,	*Golden Plover* (m. & f.). - Cabinet.
183	Squatarola helvetica,	*Whistling Plover.* - - - Cabinet.
184	Strepsilas interpres,	*Turnstone* (m. & f.). - - - Cabinet.
185	Hæmatopus palliatus,	*American Oystercatcher* (m. & f.). Cab.

FAMILY GRUIDÆ.

186	Grus americana,	*American Crane.*
187	Ardea herodias,	*Great Blue Heron* (m. & f.). Cabinet.
188	Ardea leuce,	*Great White Heron.*
189	Ardea candidissima,	*White-crested Heron* (m. & f.). Cabinet.
190	Ardea cærulea,	*Blue Heron* (m. & f.). - - Cabinet.
191	Ardea ludoviciana,	*Louisiana Heron.* - - - ———
192	Ardea virescens,	*Green Heron.* - - - - - Cabinet.
193	Ardea exilis,	*Small Bittern.* - - - - Cabinet.
194	Ardea minor,	*American Bittern.* - - - Cabinet.
195	Ardea discors,	*Black-crowned Night Heron* (m. & f.). Cabinet.
196	Ardea violacea,	*Yellow-crowned Night Heron* (m. & f.). Cabinet.

FAMILY TANTALIDÆ.

197	Ibis alba,	*White Ibis.*
198	Ibis mexicanus,	*Glossy Ibis* (m. & f.). - - Cabinet.

FAMILY SCOLOPACIDÆ.

199	Numenius longirostris,	*Long-billed Curlew.* - - - Cabinet.
200	Numenius hudsonicus,	*Jack Curlew* (m. & f.). - - Cabinet.
201	Numenius borealis,	*Small Esquimaux Curlew.* - Cabinet.
202	Hemipalma himantopus,	*Long-legged Sandpiper.* - Cabinet.
203	Heteropoda semipalmata,	*Semipalmated Sandpiper.* - Cabinet.

	Latin Names.	English Names.	
204	Tringa maritima,	*Purple Sandpiper* (f.). - -	Cabinet.
205	Tringa rufescens,	*Buff-breasted Sandpiper.* -	Cabinet.
206	Tringa subarquata,	*Curlew Sandpiper* (m. & f.).	Cabinet.
207	Tringa cinclus,	*Black-breasted Sandpiper.* -	———
208	Tringa schinzi,	*Schinz's Sandpiper* (m. & f.).	Cabinet
209	Tringa pectoralis,	*Pectoral Sandpiper.* - - -	Cabinet.
210	Tringa canutus,	*Red-breasted Sandpiper* (m. & f.).	Cab.
211	Tringa pusilla,	*Wilson's Sandpiper* (m. & f.).	Cabinet.
212	Caledris arenaria,	*Sanderling* (m. & f.). - -	Cabinet.
213	Totanus macularius,	*Spotted Sandlark* (m. & f.).	Cabinet.
214	Totanus bartramius,	*Grey Plover.* - - - - - -	Cabinet.
215	Totanus flavipes,	*Yellowlegs.* - - - - - -	Cabinet.
216	Totanus chloropygius,	*Solitary Tatler* (f.). - - -	Cabinet.
217	Totanus melanoleucus,	*Varied Tatler* (m. & f.). - -	Cabinet.
218	Totanus semipalmatus,	*Willet.* - - - - - - - -	Cabinet.
219	Limosa fedoa,	*Marlin* (m. & f.). - - - -	Cabinet.
220	Limosa hudsonica,	*Ring-tailed Marlin* (m. & f.).	Cabinet.
221	Scolopax noveboracensis,	*Dowitchee.* - - - - - - -	Cabinet.
222	Scolopax wilsoni,	*Common American Snipe* (m. & f.).	Cabinet.
223	Rusticola minor,	*American Woodcock.* - - -	Cabinet.

FAMILY RALLIDÆ.

224	Rallus crepitans,	*Saltwater Meadow-hen* (three).	Cabinet
225	Rallus elegans,	*Freshwater Meadow-hen.* -	Cabinet.
226	Rallus virginianus,	*Mudhen.* - - - - - - -	Cabinet.
227	Ortygometra carolina,	*Sora Rail.* - - - - - - -	Cabinet.
228	Ortygometra noveboracensis,	*New-York Rail.* - - -	Cabinet.
229	Gallinula galeata,	*Florida Gallinule* (m. & f.).	Cabinet.

FAMILY RECURVIROSTRIDÆ.

230	Himantopus nigricollis,	*Lawyer.* - - - - - - -	Cabinet
231	Recurvirostra americana,	*American Avoset.* - - - -	Cabinet.

FAMILY PHALAROPODIDÆ.

	Latin Names.	English Names.	
232	Phalaropus fulicarius,	*Red Phalarope.*	
233	Lobipes hyperboreus,	*Hyperborean Lobefoot* (m. & f.).	Cabinet.
234	Holopodius wilsoni,	*Wilson's Holopode.*	

ORDER V. LOBIPEDES.

FAMILY PODICIPIDÆ.

235	Fulica americana,	*American Coot* (m. & f.). -	Cabinet.
236	Podiceps cornutus,	*Horned Grebe.* - - - - - -	Cabinet.
237	Podiceps cristatus,	*Crested Grebe.* - - - - -	Cabinet.
238	Podiceps rubricollis,	*Red-necked Grebe.* - - -	———
239	Hydroka carolinensis,	*Dipper* (three). - - - -	Cabinet.

ORDER VI. NATATORES.

FAMILY ALCIDÆ.

240	Uria grylle,	*Black Guillemot.* - - - -	Cabinet.
241	Uria troile,	*Foolish Guillemot.* - - -	Cabinet.
242	Mergulus alle,	*Sea Dove.* - - - - - - -	Cabinet.
243	Mormon arcticus,	*Arctic Puffin.* - - - - -	Cabinet.
244	Alca torda,	*Razorbill* (three). - - - -	Cabinet.

FAMILY COLYMBIDÆ.

245	Colymbus glacialis,	*Great Loon,* or *Diver.* - -	Cabinet.
246	Colymbus septentrionalis,	*Red-throated Loon* (m. & f.).	Cabinet.

FAMILY PROCELLARIDÆ.

247	Puffinus cinereus,	*Large Shearwater.* - - -	Cabinet.
248	Puffinus obscurus,	*Little Shearwater.* - - -	Cabinet.
249	Thalassidroma wilsoni,	*Wilson's Petrel.* - - - -	Cabinet.
250	Thalassidroma leachi,	*Fork-tailed Petrel.* - - -	Cabinet.

FAMILY PELECANIDÆ.

251	Phalacracorax carbo,	*Cormorant.* - - - - - -	———
252	Phalacracorax dilophus,	*Double-crested Cormorant* (two).	Cab.
253	Pelecanus fuscus,	*Brown Pelican.* - - - -	Cabinet.
254	Sula americana,	*American Gannet.* - - -	Cabinet.

FAMILY LARIDÆ.

	Latin Names.	English Names.	
255	Rhynchops nigra,	*Black Skimmer* (m. & f.). -	Cabinet.
256	Sterna hirundo,	*Common Tern.* - - - -	Cabinet.
257	Sterna cayaña,	*Cayenne Tern.* - - - -	Cabinet.
258	Sterna nigra,	*Black Tern* (m. & f.). - -	Cabinet.
259	Sterna anglica,	*Marsh Tern* (m. & f.). - -	Cabinet.
260	Sterna arctica,	*Arctic Tern.*	
261	Sterna cantiaca,	*Sandwich Tern.*	
262	Sterna dougalli,	*Roseate Tern.*	
263	Sterna argentea,	*Silvery Tern* (m. & f.). - -	Cabinet.
264	Larus argentatus,	*Winter Gull* (1 & y.) - -	Cabinet.
265	Larus marinus,	*Great Black-backed Gull.* -	Cabinet.
266	Larus zonorrhynchus,	*Common American Gull* (2 old and 3 young).	Cabinet.
267	Larus atricilla,	*Laughing Gull* (three). - -	Cabinet.
268	Larus bonapartii,	*Bonaparte's Gull* (m. & f.).	Cabinet.
269	Larus sabini,	*Fork-tailed Gull.* - - -	———
270	Larus tridactylus,	*Kittiwake*, or *Three-toed Gull.*	
271	Lestris buffoni,	*Arctic Hawk Gull.* - - -	———
272	Lestris richardsonii,	*Richardson's Hawk Gull* (three).	Cabinet.
273	Lestris pomarinus,	*Pomarine Hawk Gull* (three).	Cabinet.

FAMILY ANATIDÆ.

274	Mergus merganser,	*Buff-breasted Sheldrake* (m. & f.).	Cabinet.
275	Mergus serrator,	*Red-breasted Sheldrake* (m. & f.).	Cabinet.
276	Mergus cucullatus,	*Hooded Sheldrake* (m. & f.).	Cabinet.
277	Fuligula valisneria,	*Canvasback* (m. & f.). - -	Cabinet.
278	Fuligula erythrocephala,	*Redhead.* - - - - - - -	Cabinet.
279	Fuligula marila,	*Broadbill.* - - - - - - -	Cabinet.
280	Fuligula minor,	*Creek Broadbill.* - - - -	Cabinet.
281	Fuligula rufitorques,	*Bastard Broadbill.* - - -	Cabinet.
282	Fuligula labradora,	*Pied Duck* (f.). - - - -	Cabinet.
283	Fuligula rubida,	*Ruddy Duck* (m. & f.). - -	Cabinet.

	Latin Names.	English Names.	
284	Fuligula glacialis,	*Oldwife*, or *Squaw Duck* (four).	Cabinet.
285	Fuligula albeola,	*Buffle-headed Duck.* - - -	Cabinet.
286	Fuligula clangula,	*Whistler.* - - - - - - -	Cabinet.
287	Fuligula histrionica,	*Harlequin Duck.* - - - -	Cabinet.
288	Fuligula mollissima,	*Eider Duck* (m. & f.). - -	Cabinet.
289	Fuligula spectabilis,	*King Duck.* - - - - -	Cabinet.
290	Fuligula perspicillata,	*Surf Duck* or *Coot.* - - -	Cabinet.
291	Fuligula americana,	*Broad-billed Coot.* - - -	Cabinet.
292	Fuligula fusca,	*White-winged Coot.* - - -	Cabinet.
293	Anas sponsa,	*Wood Duck* (m. & f.). - -	Cabinet.
294	Anas discors,	*Blue-winged Teal* (m. & f.).	Cabinet.
295	Anas carolinensis,	*Green-winged Teal* (three). -	Cabinet.
296	Anas acuta,	*Pintail Duck* (m. & f.). - -	Cabinet.
297	Anas clypeata,	*Shoveller*, or *Spoonbill* (m. & f.).	Cabinet.
298	Anas strepera,	*Grey Duck*, or *Gadwall.* -	Cabinet.
299	Anas obscura,	*Black Duck.* - - - - - -	Cabinet.
300	Anas americana,	*American Widgeon*, or *Baldpate.*	Cab.
301	Anas penelope,	*European Widgeon.*	
302	Anas boschas,	*Mallard* (m. & f.). - - -	Cabinet.
303	Anser canadensis,	*Wild Goose.* - - - - - -	Cabinet.
304	Anser albifrons,	*White-fronted Goose.* - -	———
305	Anser hyperboreus,	*Snow Goose.* - - - - - -	Cabinet.
306	Anser bernicla,	*Brant.* - - - - - - - -	Cabinet.
307	Anser hutchinsi,	*Hutchins's Goose.*	
308	Cygnus americanus,	*American Swan.* - - - - -	Cabinet.
309	Gallinula martinica,	*Purple Gallinule**. - - -	Cabinet.

* This specimen was obtained by Mr. J. G. Bell, of New-York, within this State, and furnished by him to the Collection. It is considered *extra-limital* by Dr. De Kay (See his Birds of New-York, p. 264)

ZOOLOGY OF NEW-YORK,

OR THE

New-York Fauna.

BY JAMES E. DE KAY.

PARTS III & IV. REPTILES AND AMPHIBIA.

ZOOLOGY.

CLASS III. REPTILES.

ORDER I. TESTUDINATA.

FAMILY CHELONIDÆ.

	Latin Name.	English Name.	In the
1	Chelonia mydas,	*Green Turtle.*	
2	Sphargis coriacea,	*Leather Turtle.*	
3	Trionyx ferox,	*Soft-shelled Turtle.*	
4	Chelonura serpentina,	*Snapping Turtle* (m. f. & eggs).	Cabinet.
5	Emys palustris,	*Saltwater Terrapin.*	
6	Emys terrapin,	*Smooth Terrapin* (2 shells). -	Cabinet.
7	Emys picta,	*Painted Tortoise* (m. & f.). -	Cabinet.
8	Emys guttata,	*Spotted Tortoise* (m. & f.). -	Cabinet.
9	Emys insculpta,	*Wood Terrapin* (m. & f.). -	Cabinet.
10	Emys rubriventris,	*Red-bellied Terrapin.*	
11	Emys muhlenbergii,	*Muhlenberg's Tortoise.*	
12	Emys geographica,	*Geographic Tortoise.*	
13	Emys pseudogeographica,	*Pseudogeographic Tortoise.*	
14	Kinostemon pennsylvanicum,	*Mud Tortoise.*	
15	Sternothærus odoratus,	*Musk Tortoise* (in alcohol). -	Cabinet.
16	Cistuda carolina,	*Common Box Tortoise* (m. & f.).	Cabinet.
17	Cistuda blandingii,	*Blanding's Box Tortoise.*	

ORDER II. SAURIA.

FAMILY SCINCIDÆ.

	Latin Names.	English Names.	
18	SCINCUS FASCIATUS,	*Blue-tailed Skink.*	

FAMILY AGAMIDÆ.

19	TROPIDOLEPIS UNDULATUS,	*Brown Swift* (in alcohol). -	Cabinet.

ORDER III. OPHIDIA.

FAMILY COLUBERIDÆ.

20	COLUBER CONSTRICTOR,	*Black Snake* (2 in alcohol). -	Cabinet.
21	COLUBER ALLEGHANIENSIS,	*Pilot Blacksnake* (in alcohol).	Cabinet.
22	COLUBER GETULUS,	*Chain Snake* (in alcohol). -	Cabinet.
23	COLUBER EXIMIUS,	*Milk Snake* (4 in alcohol). -	Cabinet.
24	COLUBER PUNCTATUS,	*Ring Snake* (in alcohol). - -	Cabinet.
25	COLUBER VERNALIS,	*Grass Snake* (one, and 1 in alcohol).	Cabinet.
26	TROPIDONOTUS SIPEDON,	*Water Snake* (in alcohol). -	Cabinet.
27	TROPIDONOTUS TÆNIA,	*Striped Snake* (one, and 1 in alc.).	Cab.
28	TROPIDONOTUS LEBERIS,	*Yellow-bellied Snake* (in alcohol).	Cabinet.
29	TROPIDONOTUS DEKAYI,	*Small Brown Snake* (one, & 1 in alc.).	Cab.
30	LEPTOPHIS SAURITA,	*Ribbon Snake* (one, & 1 in alc.).	Cabinet.
31	CALAMARIA AMŒNA,	*Red Snake.*	
32	HETERODON PLATYRRHINOS,	*Hog-nosed Snake.* - - - -	Cabinet.

FAMILY CROTALIDÆ.

33	TRIGONOCEPHALUS CONTORTRIX,	*Copperhead.*	
34	CROTALUS DURISSUS,	*Northern Rattlesnake* (m. & f., and 2 in alcohol and 4 young).	Cabinet.

35 CROTALOPHORUS TERGEMINUS (Say). *Triple-spotted Rattlesnake.* Cab.
(See Annual Report of 1858.)

ZOOLOGY.

CLASS IV. AMPHIBIA.

FAMILY RANIDÆ.

	Latin Name.	English Name.	In the
1	Rana pipiens,	*Bulfrog* (2 in alcohol). - -	Cabinet.
2	Rana horiconensis,	*Large Northern Bulfrog* (two, and 2 in alcohol).	Cabinet.
3	Rana fontinalis,	*Spring Frog* (in alcohol). -	Cabinet.
4	Rana palustris,	*Marsh Frog* (in alcohol). - -	Cabinet.
5	Rana halecina,	*Shad Frog* (two, and 1 in alc.).	Cabinet.
6	Rana sylvatica,	*Wood Frog* (one, and 2 in alc.).	Cabinet.
7	Scaphiopus solitarius,	*Hermit Spadefoot.*	
8	Bufo americanus,	*Common American Toad* (one, and 2 in alcohol).	Cabinet.
9	Hylodes pickeringi,	*Pickering's Hylodes.*	
10	Hylodes gryllus,	*Cricket Hylodes.*	
11	Hyla versicolor,	*Northern Tree-toad* (one, and 2 in alc.).	Cabinet.
12	Hyla squirella,	*Squirrel Tree-toad* (two). -	Cabinet.

FAMILY SALAMANDRIDÆ.

	Latin Name.	English Name.	In the
13	Salamandra symmetrica,	*Yellow-bellied Salamander* (m. & f.).	Cab.
14	Salamandra subviolacea,	*Violet-colored Salamander* (one, and 1 in alcohol).	Cabinet.
15	Salamandra erythronota,	*Red-backed Salamander* (m. & f.).	Cab.
16	Salamandra picta,	*Painted Salamander* (in alcohol).	Cab.
17	Salamandra salmonea,	*Salmon-colored Salamander.*	

	Latin Names.	English Names.	
18	Salamandra fasciata,	*Blotched Salamander.* - -	———
19	Salamandra longicauda,	*Long-tailed Salamander.*	
20	Salamandra granulata,	*Granulated Salamander.*	
21	Salamandra bilineata,	*Striped-backed Salamander.* -	———
22	Salamandra rubra,	*Red Salamander* (m. & f.). -	Cabinet.
23	Salamandra coccinea,	*Scarlet Salamander.*	
24	Salamandra glutinosa,	*Blue-spotted Salamander.* -	———
25	Triton tigrinus,	*Tiger Triton.*	
26	Triton millepunctatus,	*Crimson-spotted Triton* (m. & f.).	Cab.
27	Triton niger,	*Dusky Triton.*	
28	Triton porphyriticus,	*Grey-spotted Triton* (m. & f.).	Cabinet.

FAMILY SIRENIDÆ.

29	Menobranchus lateralis,	*Banded Proteus.*	

FAMILY AMPHIUMIDÆ.

30	Menopoma alleghaniensis,	*Allegany Hellbender.*	

31 Plethodon cinereus (Baird). - - - - - - - Cabinet.

32 Hemidactylum scutatum (Baird). - - - - - - Cabinet.

ZOOLOGY OF NEW-YORK,

OR THE

New-York Fauna.

BY JAMES E. DE KAY.

PART V. FISHES.

BOTANY OF NEW-YORK,

OR THE

New-York Flora.

BY JOHN TORREY.

DIVISION I. PHÆNOGAMOUS PLANTS.

BOTANY.

DIVISION I. PHÆNOGAMOUS PLANTS.

CLASS I. EXOGENOUS PLANTS.

Vol. 1.] ORDER I. RANUNCULACEÆ.

	Latin Name.	English Name.	In the
1	Clematis ochroleuca,	*Silky Virgin's-bower* (3 specimens).	Cabinet.
2	Clematis virginiana,	*Virginian Virgin's-bower*(3).	Cabinet.
3	Clematis verticillaris,	*Whorl-leaved Virgin's-bower*(3).	Cabinet.
4	Anemone nemorosa,	*Wood Anemone*(6). - - -	Cabinet.
5	Anemone cylindrica,	*Cylindrical-headed Windflower*(4).	Cabinet.
6	Anemone virginiana,	*Thimbleweed*(3). - - -	Cabinet.
7	Anemone multifida,	*Cut-leaved Windflower.*	
8	Anemone pennsylvanica,	*Pennsylvanian Windflower*(2).	Cabinet.
9	Hepatica triloba,	*Common Liverleaf*(6). - -	Cabinet.
10	Ranunculus aquatilis,	*Water Crowfoot*(3). - -	Cabinet.
11	Ranunculus flammula,	*Spearwort*(2). - - - -	Cabinet.
12	Ranunculus reptans,	*Least Spearwort*(7). - -	Cabinet.
13	Ranunculus pusillus,	*Small-flowered Crowfoot*(3).	Cabinet.
14	Ranunculus cymbalaria,	*Sea Crowfoot*(5). - - -	Cabinet.
15	Ranunculus abortivus,	*Kidney-leaved Crowfoot*(2).	Cabinet.
16	Ranunculus sceleratus,	*Celery-leaved Crowfoot*(2).	Cabinet.
17	Ranunculus purshii,	*Pursh's Crowfoot*(2). - -	Cabinet.
18	Ranunculus acris,	*Tall Crowfoot*(2). - - -	Cabinet.

	Latin Names.	English Names.	
19	Ranunculus repens,	*Creeping Crowfoot*(5). -	Cabinet.
20	Ranunculus fascicularis,	*Bunch-rooted Crowfoot*(3).	Cabinet.
21	Ranunculus pennsylvanicus,	*Pennsylvanian Crowfoot*(2).	Cabinet.
22	Ranunculus recurvatus,	*Sanicle-leaved Crowfoot*(2).	Cabinet.
23	Ranunculus bulbosus,	*Buttercups*(1). - - - -	Cabinet.
24	Caltha palustris,	*Common Marsh-marigold*(3).	Cabinet.
25	Trollius laxus,	*American Globeflower*(3). -	Cabinet.
26	Coptis trifolia,	*Common Goldthread*(4). -	Cabinet.
27	Helleborus viridis,	*Green Hellebore*(2). - -	Cabinet.
28	Aquilegia canadensis,	*Canadian Columbine*(2). -	Cabinet.
29	Delphinium consolida,	*Common Larkspur*(1). - -	Cabinet.
30	Aconitum uncinatum,	*American Monkshood*(1). -	Cabinet.
31	Actæa rubra,	*Red Cohosh*(4). - - - -	Cabinet.
32	Actæa alba,	*White Cohosh*(3). - - -	Cabinet.
33	Cimicifuga racemosa,	*Blacksnakeroot*, or *Rattleweed*(4).	Cabinet.
34	Thalictrum dioicum,	*Early Meadowrue*(3). - -	Cabinet.
35	Thalictrum cornuti,	*Common Meadowrue*(5). -	Cabinet.
36	Thalictrum anemonoides,	*Rue Anemone*(8). - - -	Cabinet.
37	Zanthorrhiza apiifolia,	*Pearly-leaved Yellowroot*(1).	Cabinet.
38	Hydrastis canadensis,	*Canadian Yellowroot*(3). -	Cabinet.

Vol. 2.]

ORDER II. MAGNOLIACEÆ.

39	Magnolia glauca,	*Common Magnolia*, or *Sweet Bay*(3).	Cabinet.
40	Magnolia acuminata,	*Cucumber-tree*(2). - - -	Cabinet.
41	Liriodendron tulipifera,	*Tulip Poplar*(2). - - -	Cabinet.

ORDER III. ANONACEÆ.

42	Uvaria triloba,	*Papaw*(2). - - - - -	Cabinet.

ORDER IV. MENISPERMACEÆ.

43	Menispermum canadense,	*Canadian Moonseed*(3). -	Cabinet.

ORDER V. BERBERIDACEÆ.

44	Berberis vulgaris,	*Barberry*(3). - - - - -	Cabinet.
45	Leontice thalictroides,	*Blue Cohosh*, or *Pappoose-root*(4).	Cabinet.

	Latin Names.	English Names.	
46	JEFFERSONIA DIPHYLLA,	*Rheumatism-root*(3). - -	Cabinet.
47	PODOPHYLLUM PELTATUM,	*Mayapple*, or *Mandrake*(1). -	Cabinet.

ORDER VI. CABOMBACEÆ.

48	BRASENIA PELTATA,	*Watershield*(2). - - - -	Cabinet.

ORDER VII. NELUMBIACEÆ.

49	NELUMBIUM LUTEUM,	*Great Yellow Waterlily.*	

ORDER VIII. NYMPHÆACEÆ.

50	NYMPHÆA ODORATA,	*Great White Waterlily*(3). -	Cabinet.
51	NUPHAR LUTEA,	*Small-flowered Yellow Pondlily*(4).	Cabinet.
52	NUPHAR ADVENA,	*Common Yellow Pondlily*(3).	Cabinet.

ORDER IX. SARRACENIACEÆ.

53	SARRACENIA PURPUREA,	*Common Sidesaddleflower*(3).	Cabinet.

ORDER X. PAPAVERACEÆ.

54	SANGUINARIA CANADENSIS,	*Bloodroot*(5). - - - - -	Cabinet.
55	CHELIDONIUM MAJUS,	*Common Celandine*(2). - -	Cabinet.

ORDER XI. FUMARIACEÆ.

56	DICENTRA CUCULLARIA,	*Dutchman's-breeches*(2). - -	Cabinet.
57	DICENTRA CANADENSIS,	*Squirrel-corn*(4). - - - -	Cabinet.
58	DICENTRA EXIMIA,	*Choice Dicentra*(2). - - -	Cabinet.
59	ADLUMIA CIRRHOSA,	*Climbing Fumitory*(1). - -	Cabinet.
60	CORYDALIS AUREA,	*Golden Corydalis*(3). - - -	Cabinet.
61	CORYDALIS GLAUCA,	*Glaucous Corydalis*(3). - -	Cabinet.
62	FUMARIA OFFICINALIS,	*Common Fumitory*(2). - -	Cabinet.

Vol. 3.] ORDER XII. CRUCIFERÆ.

63	NASTURTIUM PALUSTRE,	*Marsh Cress*(4). - - - -	Cabinet.
64	NASTURTIUM HISPIDUM,	*Hispid Cress*(3). - - - -	Cabinet.
65	NASTURTIUM NATANS,	*Floating Cress*(2). - - -	Cabinet.
66	BARBAREA VULGARIS,	*Scurvygrass*(3). - - - -	Cabinet.
67	TURRITIS STRICTA,	*Straight Tower-mustard.*	
68	ARABIS HIRSUTA,	*Hairy Wallcress.*	
69	ARABIS DENTATA,	*Toothed Wallcress*(1). - -	Cabinet.

	Latin Names.	English Names.	
70	Arabis lyrata,	*Lyre-leaved Wallcress*(2). -	Cabinet.
71	Arabis lævigata,	*Smooth Wallcress*(2). - - -	Cabinet.
72	Arabis canadensis,	*Sicklepod*(5). - - - - -	Cabinet.
73	Cardamine rhomboidea,	*Spring Cress*(8). - - - -	Cabinet.
74	Cardamine pratensis,	*Bittercress*, or *Cuckooflower*(3).	Cabinet.
75	Cardamine hirsuta,	*Watercress*(6). - - - - -	Cabinet.
76	Dentaria laciniata,	*Common Toothwort*(4). - -	Cabinet.
77	Dentaria diphylla,	*Pepper-root*(4). - - - - -	Cabinet.
78	Dentaria maxima,	*Large Toothwort.*	
79	Sisymbrium officinale,	*Common Hedge-mustard*(2). -	Cabinet.
80	Sisymbrium thalianum,	*Mousear Cress*(3). - - - -	Cabinet.
81	Erysimum cheiranthoides,	*Treacle Mustard*(3). - - -	Cabinet.
82	Sinapis nigra,	*Black Mustard.*	
83	Sinapis arvensis,	*Wild Mustard*, or *Charlock*(2).	Cabinet.
84	Draba arabisans,	*Arabis-like Whitlowgrass*(5).	Cabinet.
85	Draba caroliniana,	*Carolina Whitlowgrass*(2). -	Cabinet.
86	Draba verna,	*Common Whitlowgrass*(3). -	Cabinet.
87	Camelina sativa,	*Common Gold-of-pleasure.*	
88	Thlaspi arvense,	*Mithridate Mustard.*	
89	Lepidium campestre,	*Mithridate Pepperwort*(3). -	Cabinet.
90	Lepidium virginicum,	*Wild Peppergrass*(3). - -	Cabinet.
91	Capsella bursa-pastoris,	*Common Shepherdspurse*(1). -	Cabinet.
92	Cakile maritima,	*Sea Rocket*(2). - - - - -	Cabinet.
93	Raphanus raphanistrum,	*Wild Radish*(2). - - - -	Cabinet.

Vol. 4.] ORDER XIII. CAPPARIDACEÆ.

94	Polanisia graveolens,	*Heavy-scented Polanisia*(2). -	Cabinet.

ORDER XIV. VIOLACEÆ.

95	Viola pedata,	*Pedate Violet*(4). - - - -	Cabinet.
96	Viola palmata,	*Palmate Violet*(3). - - -	Cabinet.
97	Viola cucullata,	*Hood-leaved Violet*(2). - -	Cabinet.
98	Viola selkirkii,	*Selkirk's Violet.*	
99	Viola sagittata,	*Arrow-leaved Violet*(7). - -	Cabinet.

	Latin Names.	English Names.	
100	VIOLA ROTUNDIFOLIA,	*Round-leaved Violet*(5). - -	Cabinet.
101	VIOLA BLANDA,	*Sweetscented White Violet*(5).	Cabinet.
102	VIOLA PRIMULÆFOLIA,	*Primrose-leaved Violet.*	
103	VIOLA LANCEOLATA,	*Lance-leaved Violet*(6). - -	Cabinet.
104	VIOLA STRIATA,	*Striated Violet*(1). - - - -	Cabinet.
105	VIOLA MUHLENBERGII,	*Muhlenberg's Violet*(6). - -	Cabinet.
106	VIOLA ROSTRATA,	*Long-spurred Violet*(4). - -	Cabinet.
107	VIOLA PUBESCENS,	*Yellow Violet*(3). - - - -	Cabinet.
108	VIOLA CANADENSIS,	*Canadian Violet*(2). - - -	Cabinet.
109	VIOLA TRICOLOR,	*Pansey*, or *Heartsease*(3). -	Cabinet.
110	SOLEA CONCOLOR,	*Green-flowered Solea*(1). - -	Cabinet.

ORDER XV. CISTACEÆ.

111	HELIANTHEMUM CANADENSE,	*Frostweed*(9). - - - - - -	Cabinet.
112	LECHEA MAJOR,	*Larger Lechea*(4). - - - -	Cabinet.
113	LECHEA THYMIFOLIA,	*Thyme-leaved Lechea*(2). - -	Cabinet.
114	LECHEA MINOR,	*Pinweed*(7). - - - - - - -	Cabinet.
115	HUDSONIA ERICOIDES,	*Heath-like Hudsonia*(1). - -	Cabinet.
116	HUDSONIA TOMENTOSA,	*Woolly Hudsonia*(4). - - -	Cabinet.

ORDER XVI. DROSERACEÆ.

117	DROSERA ROTUNDIFOLIA,	*Round-leaved Sundew*(4). -	Cabinet.
118	DROSERA LONGIFOLIA,	*Long-leaved Sundew*(4). - -	Cabinet.
119	DROSERA FILIFORMIS,	*Thread-leaved Sundew*(3). -	Cabinet.
120	PARNASSIA CAROLINIANA,	*Carolina Grass-of-Parnassus*(3).	Cabinet.

ORDER XVII. HYPERICACEÆ.

121	ASCYRUM STANS,	*Upright St. Peter's-wort*(1).	Cabinet.
122	HYPERICUM PYRAMIDICUM,	*Giant St. John's-wort*	
123	HYPERICUM KALMIANUM,	*Kalm's St. John's-wort*(2). -	Cabinet.
124	HYPERICUM PERFORATUM,	*Common St. John's-wort*(2). -	Cabinet.
125	HYPERICUM CORYMBOSUM,	*Corymbed St. John's-wort*(3).	Cabinet.
126	HYPERICUM ELLIPTICUM,	*Elliptical-leaved St. John's-wort*(4).	Cab.
127	HYPERICUM MUTILUM,	*Small-flowered St. John's-wort*(2).	Cabinet.

	Latin Names.	English Names.	
128	Hypericum canadense,	*Canadian St. John's-wort*(4).	Cabinet.
129	Hypericum sarothra,	*Groundpine*, or *Nitweed*(5). -	Cabinet.
130	Elodea virginica,	*Virginian Elodea*(3). - - -	Cabinet.

ORDER XVIII. ELATINACEÆ.

131	Elatine americana,	*American Waterwort*(4). - -	Cabinet.

Vol. 5.]

ORDER XIX. CARYOPHYLLACEÆ.

132	Honckenya peploides,	*Common Sea Chickweed*(3). -	Cabinet.
133	Sagina procumbens,	*Procumbent Pearlwort*(7). -	Cabinet.
134	Sagina apetala,	*Apetalous Pearlwort*(10). -	Cabinet.
135	Arenaria serpyllifolia,	*Thyme-leaved Sandwort*(5). -	Cabinet
136	Arenaria squarrosa,	*Squarrose Sandwort*(5). - -	Cabinet.
137	Arenaria stricta,	*Upright Sandwort*(5). - -	Cabinet.
138	Arenaria grœnlandica,	*Greenland Sandwort*(3). - -	Cabinet.
139	Mœhringia lateriflora,	*Lateral-flowered Mœhringia*(5).	Cabinet.
140	Stellaria media,	*Common Chickweed*(2). - -	Cabinet.
141	Stellaria longifolia,	*Long-leaved Stitchwort*(2). -	Cabinet.
142	Stellaria borealis,	*Northern Stitchwort*(5). - -	Cabinet.
143	Cerastium vulgatum,	*Common Mousear Chickweed*(1).	Cabinet.
144	Cerastium viscosum,	*Viscous Mousear Chickweed*(3).	Cabinet.
145	Cerastium arvense,	*Field Chickweed*(3). - - -	Cabinet.
146	Cerastium oblongifolium,	*Oblong-leaved Chickweed.*	
147	Cerastium nutans,	*Nodding Chickweed*(3). - -	Cabinet.
148	Silene stellata,	*Four-leaved Campion*(4). - -	Cabinet.
149	Silene antirrhina,	*Snapdragon Catchfly*(2). - -	Cabinet.
150	Silene noctiflora,	*Night-flowering Catchfly*(1).	Cabinet.
151	Silene pennsylvanica,	*Wild Pink*(3). - - - - -	Cabinet.
152	Silene virginica,	*Virginian Catchfly*(1). - -	Cabinet.
153	Lychnis githago,	*Rose Campion*, or *Corncockle*(2).	Cabinet.
154	Saponaria officinalis,	*Common Soapwort*, or *Bouncing-Bet*(2).	Cab.
155	Saponaria vaccaria,	*Perfoliate Soapwort.*	
156	Mollugo verticillata,	*Carpetweed*(3). - - - - -	Cabinet.

ORDER XX. ILLECEBRACEÆ.

	Latin Names.	English Names.	
157	Anychia dichotoma,	*Common Forked Chickweed*(4).	Cabinet.
158	Spergula arvensis,	*Corn Spurry*, or *Tare*(3). -	Cabinet.
159	Spergula rubra,	*Red-flowered Spurry*(6). - -	Cabinet.
160	Scleranthus annuus,	*Common Knawel*(2). - - -	Cabinet.

Vol. 6.]

ORDER XXI. PORTULACACEÆ.

161	Portulaca oleracea,	*Common Purselane*(1). - -	Cabinet.
162	Claytonia virginica,	*Narrow-leaved Spring-beauty*(6).	Cab.
163	Claytonia caroliniana,	*Broad-leaved Spring-beauty*(6).	Cabinet.

ORDER XXII. MALVACEÆ.

164	Malva rotundifolia,	*Dwarf* or *Running Mallow*(1).	Cabinet.
165	Malva sylvestris,	*High Mallow.*	
166	Althæa officinalis,	*Common Marshmallow.*	
167	Abutilon avicennæ,	*Velvetleaf*(1). - - - - -	Cabinet.
168	Sida spinosa,	*Prickly Sida*(1). - - - -	Cabinet.
169	Hibiscus virginicus,	*Sweating-weed*(1). - - - -	Cabinet.
170	Hibiscus moscheutos,	*Mallowrose*(1). - - - - -	Cabinet.
171	Hibiscus trionum,	*Venetian Mallow*(1). - - -	Cabinet.

ORDER XXIII. TILIACEÆ.

172	Tilia americana,	*Basswood*(2). - - - - -	Cabinet.

ORDER XXIV. LINACEÆ.

173	Linum virginianum,	*Wild Flax*(5). - - - - -	Cabinet.
174	Linum usitatissimum,	*Common Flax.*	

ORDER XXV. GERANIACEÆ.

175	Geranium maculatum,	*Spotted Cranesbill*(2). - -	Cabinet.
176	Geranium carolinianum,	*Carolinian Cranesbill*(4). - -	Cabinet.
177	Geranium pusillum,	*Small-flowered Cranesbill*(5).	Cabinet.
178	Geranium robertianum,	*Herb-robert*(1). - - - - -	Cabinet.
179	Erodium cicutarium,	*Hemlock Heronsbill*(2). - -	Cabinet.

ORDER XXVI. OXALIDACEÆ.

	Latin Names.	English Names.	
180	Oxalis acetosella,	*Common Woodsorrel*(5). - -	Cabinet.
181	Oxalis violacea,	*Violet Woodsorrel*(6). - - -	Cabinet.
182	Oxalis stricta,	*Yellow Woodsorrel*(4). - -	Cabinet.

ORDER XXVII. BALSAMINACEÆ.

183	Impatiens pallida,	*Touch-me-not*, or *Snapweed*(1).	Cabinet.
184	Impatiens fulva,	*Balsam-weed*, or *Jewel-weed*(2).	Cabinet.

ORDER XXVIII. LIMNANTHACEÆ.

185	Flœrkea proserpinacoides,	*False Mermaid*(3). - - -	Cabinet.

ORDER XXIX. ANACARDIACEÆ.

186	Rhus typhina,	*Stagshorn Sumach*(2). - -	Cabinet.
187	Rhus glabra,	*Smooth Sumach*(1). - - -	Cabinet.
188	Rhus copallina,	*Mountain Sumach*(4). - - -	Cabinet.
189	Rhus venenata,	*Poison Sumach*(3). - - - -	Cabinet.
190	Rhus toxicodendron,	*Poisonvine*, or *Mercury*(4). -	Cabinet.
191	Rhus aromatica,	*Sweet-scented Sumach*(2). -	Cabinet.

ORDER XXX. XANTHOXYLACEÆ.

192	Zanthoxylum americanum,	*Common Prickly-ash*(4). -	Cabinet.
193	Ptelea trifoliata,	*Swamp Dogwood*(2). - - -	Cabinet.

Vol. 7.]

ORDER XXXI. ACERACEÆ.

194	Acer pennsylvanicum,	*Striped Maple*(6). - - - -	Cabinet.
195	Acer spicatum,	*Mountain Maple*(1). - - -	Cabinet.
196	Acer saccharinum,	*Sugar Maple*(3). - - - -	Cabinet.
197	Acer dasycarpum,	*White Maple*(2). - - - -	Cabinet.
198	Acer rubrum,	*Red Maple*(9). - - - - -	Cabinet.

ORDER XXXII. HIPPOCASTANACEÆ.

199	Æsculus hippocastanum,	*Common Horse-chesnut*(1). -	Cabinet.

ORDER XXXIII. CELASTRACEÆ.

200	Staphylea trifolia,	*American Bladdernut*(4). -	Cabinet.
201	Celastrus scandens,	*Bittersweet*(3). - - - - -	Cabinet.
202	Euonymus atropurpureus,	*Burning-bush*(2). - - - -	Cabinet.
203	Euonymus americanus,	*Strawberry-tree*(2). - - -	Cabinet.

ORDER XXXIV. RHAMNACEÆ.

Latin Names.	English Names.	
204 RHAMNUS CATHARTICUS,	*Common Buckthorn.*	
205 RHAMNUS ALNIFOLIUS,	*Alder-leaved Buckthorn*(3). -	Cabinet.
206 CEANOTHUS AMERICANUS,	*New-Jersey Tea*, or *Redroot*(3).	Cabinet.
207 CEANOTHUS OVALIS,	*Narrow-leaved Ceanothus.*	

ORDER XXXV. VITACEÆ.

208 VITIS LABRUSCA,	*Fox Grape*(4). - - - - -	Cabinet.
209 VITIS ÆSTIVALIS,	*Summer Grape*(1). - - -	Cabinet.
210 VITIS CORDIFOLIA,	*Frost Grape*(3). - - - -	Cabinet.
211 VITIS RIPARIA,	*Winter Grape*(1). - - - -	Cabinet.
212 AMPELOPSIS QUINQUEFOLIA,	*Virginian Creeper*(3), - -	Cabinet.

ORDER XXXVI. POLYGALACEÆ.

213 POLYGALA SANGUINEA,	*Purple Milkwort*(3). - - -	Cabinet.
214 POLYGALA CRUCIATA,	*Cross-leaved Milkwort*(3). -	Cabinet.
215 POLYGALA VERTICILLATA,	*Whorl-leaved Milkwort*(3). -	Cabinet.
216 POLYGALA AMBIGUA,	*Ambiguous Milkwort*(4). - -	Cabinet.
217 POLYGALA SENEGA,	*Seneca Snakeroot*(1). - - -	Cabinet.
218 POLYGALA POLYGAMA,	*Polygamous Milkwort*(3).	Cabinet.
219 POLYGALA PAUCIFOLIA,	*Fringed Milkwort*(3). - -	Cabinet.

Vol. 8.]

ORDER XXXVII. LEGUMINOSÆ.

220 VICIA AMERICANA,	*American Vetch*(1). - - -	Cabinet.
221 VICIA CRACCA,	*Tufted Vetch*(1), - - - -	Cabinet.
222 VICIA TETRASPERMA,	*Slender Vetch*(2). - - - -	Cabinet.
223 VICIA SATIVA,	*Common Vetch*(3). - - - -	Cabinet.
224 ERVUM HIRSUTUM,	*Hairy Tare*(2). - - - - -	Cabinet.
225 LATHYRUS MARITIMUS,	*Seaside Vetchling*(3). - - -	Cabinet.
226 LATHYRUS OCHROLEUCUS,	*Cream-colored Vetchling*(1). -	Cabinet.
227 LATHYRUS MYRTIFOLIUS,	*Myrtle-leaved Vetchling*(3). -	Cabinet.
228 LATHYRUS PALUSTRIS,	*Marsh Vetchling*(2). - - -	Cabinet.
229 PHASEOLUS PERENNIS,	*Perennial Kidneybean*(2). -	Cabinet.
230 PHASEOLUS DIVERSIFOLIUS,	*Various-leaved Kidneybean*(2).	Cabinet.

	Latin Names.	English Names.	
231	PHASEOLUS HELVOLUS,	*Long-stalked Kidneybean*(2).	Cabinet.
232	APIOS TUBEROSA,	*Groundnut*(5). - - - - -	Cabinet.
233	GALACTIA GLABELLA,	*Smooth Milkvine.*	
234	CLITORIA MARIANA,	*Maryland Clitoria*(3). - -	Cabinet.
235	AMPHICARPÆA MONOICA,	*Common Hognut*(4). - - -	Cabinet.
236	ROBINIA PSEUDACACIA,	*Common Locust-tree*(1). - -	Cabinet.
237	TEPHROSIA VIRGINIANA,	*Goat's-rue*, or *Catgut*(2). - -	Cabinet.
238	TRIFOLIUM ARVENSE,	*Stone Clover*(6). - - - -	Cabinet.
239	TRIFOLIUM PRATENSE,	*Red Clover*(3). - - - - -	Cabinet.
240	TRIFOLIUM REFLEXUM,	*Buffalo Clover*(1). - - - -	Cabinet.
241	TRIFOLIUM REPENS,	*White Clover*(2). - - - -	Cabinet.
242	TRIFOLIUM AGRARIUM,	*Yellow Clover*(1). - - - -	Cabinet.
243	MELILOTUS OFFICINALIS,	*Yellow Melilot*(1). - - - -	Cabinet.
244	MELILOTUS LEUCANTHA,	*White Melilot*(3). - - - -	Cabinet.
245	MEDICAGO SATIVA,	*Spanish Trefoil*, or *Lucern.*	
246	MEDICAGO LUPULINA,	*Black Medick*, or *Nonesuch*(3).	Cabinet.
247	ASTRAGALUS CANADENSIS,	*Canadian Milkvetch*(3). - -	Cabinet.
248	PHACA NEGLECTA,	*Bastard Vetch*(3). - - - -	Cabinet.
249	STYLOSANTHES ELATIOR,	*Pencilflower*(4). - - - -	Cabinet.
Vol. 9.]			
250	DESMODIUM NUDIFLORUM,	*Naked-flowered Desmodium*(3).	Cabinet.
251	DESMODIUM ACUMINATUM,	*Pointed-leaved Desmodium*(2).	Cabinet.
252	DESMODIUM CANADENSE,	*Canadian Desmodium*(4). -	Cabinet.
253	DESMODIUM CANESCENS,	*Hoary Desmodium*(2). - -	Cabinet.
254	DESMODIUM DILLENII,	*Dillenius's Desmodium*(3). -	Cabinet.
255	DESMODIUM CUSPIDATUM,	*Large-bracted Desmodium*(3).	Cabinet.
256	DESMODIUM VIRIDIFLORUM,	*Velvet-leaved Desmodium*(3).	Cabinet.
257	DESMODIUM MARILANDICUM,	*Smooth Small-leaved Desm.*(2).	Cabinet.
258	DESMODIUM CILIARE,	*Hairy Small-leaved Desm.*(1).	Cabinet.
259	DESMODIUM RIGIDUM,	*Rigid Desmodium*(1). - - -	Cabinet.
260	DESMODIUM PANICULATUM,	*Panicled Desmodium*(2). - -	Cabinet.
261	DESMODIUM ROTUNDIFOLIUM,	*Round-leaved Desmodium*(1).	Cabinet.

	Latin Names.	English Names.	
262	Lespedeza procumbens,	*Trailing Lespedeza*(2). - -	Cabinet.
263	Lespedeza repens,	*Slender Lespedeza*(2). - - -	Cabinet.
264	Lespedeza violacea,	*Bush Clover*(7). - - - -	Cabinet.
265	Lespedeza hirta,	*Hairy Lespedeza*(3). - - -	Cabinet.
266	Lespedeza capitata,	*Round-headed Lespedeza*(5). -	Cabinet.
267	Genista tinctoria,	*Dyer's Greenweed.*	
268	Crotalaria sagittalis,	*Small Annual Rattlebox*(4). -	Cabinet.
269	Lupinus perennis,	*Common Wild Lupine*(1). -	Cabinet.
270	Baptisia tinctoria,	*Common Wild Indigo*(3). -	Cabinet.
271	Baptisia australis,	*Blue-flowered False Indigo.*	
272	Cercis canadensis,	*American Judas-tree*(1). - -	Cabinet.
273	Cassia marilandica,	*American Senna*(2). - - -	Cabinet.
274	Cassia chamæcrista,	*Sensitive Pea*(1). - - - -	Cabinet.
275	Cassia nictitans,	*Sensitive-plant*(2). - - - -	Cabinet.
276	Gymnocladus canadensis,	*Coffee-tree*(1). - - - - -	Cabinet.
277	Gleditschia triacanthos,	*Honey Locust*(4). - - - -	Cabinet.

Vol. 10.] ORDER XXXVIII. ROSACEÆ.

278	Prunus americana,	*Red* or *Yellow Plum*(2). - -	Cabinet.
279	Prunus maritima,	*Beach* or *Sand Plum*(6). - -	Cabinet.
280	Cerasus pumila,	*Sand Cherry*(2). - - - -	Cabinet.
281	Cerasus pennsylvanica,	*Bird Cherry*(2). - - - -	Cabinet.
282	Cerasus virginiana,	*Chokecherry*(3). - - - -	Cabinet.
283	Cerasus serotina,	*Wild Cherry*(2)- - - - -	Cabinet.
284	Spiræa opulifolia,	*Ninebark*(2). - - - - -	Cabinet.
285	Spiræa salicifolia,	*Queen-of-the-meadow*(2). - -	Cabinet.
286	Spiræa tomentosa,	*Hardhack*, or *Steeplebush*(2).	Cabinet.
287	Spiræa aruncus,	*Goatsbeard.*	
288	Gillenia trifoliata,	*Indian-physic*, or *Bowman's-root*(2).	Cabinet.
289	Gillenia stipulacea,	*American Ipecacuanha*(1). -	Cabinet.
290	Geum virginianum,	*Virginian Avens*(2). - - -	Cabinet.
291	Geum strictum,	*Small-flowered Yellow Avens*(1).	Cabinet.
292	Geum rivale,	*Water Avens*(2). - - - -	Cabinet.

	Latin Names.	English Names.	
293	GEUM TRIFLORUM,	*Three-flowered Purple Avens*(2).	Cabinet.
294	WALDSTEINIA FRAGARIOIDES,	*Strawberry-like Waldsteinia*(2).	Cab.
295	SANGUISORBA CANADENSIS,	*American Great Burnet*(3). -	Cabinet.
296	AGRIMONIA EUPATORIA,	*Common Agrimony*(2). - -	Cabinet.
297	POTENTILLA NORVEGICA,	*Norwegian Cinquefoil*(2). -	Cabinet.
298	POTENTILLA TRIDENTATA,	*Three-toothed Cinquefoil*(4). -	Cabinet.
299	POTENTILLA CANADENSIS,	*Common Cinquefoil*, or *Fivefinger*(2).	Cab.
300	POTENTILLA ARGENTEA,	*Silver-leaved Cinquefoil*(1). -	Cabinet.
301	POTENTILLA ARGUTA,	*Close-flowered Cinquefoil*)1). -	Cabinet.
302	POTENTILLA FRUTICOSA,	*Shrubby Cinquefoil*(3). - -	Cabinet.
303	POTENTILLA ANSERINA,	*Wild Tansey*, or *Silverweed*(5).	Cabinet.
304	COMARUM PALUSTRE,	*Common* or *Marsh Cinquefoil*(1).	Cabinet.
305	FRAGARIA VIRGINIANA,	*Wild Strawberry*(1). - - -	Cabinet.
306	FRAGARIA VESCA,	*Wild Strawberry*(3). - - -	Cabinet.
307	DALIBARDA REPENS,	*Creeping Dalibarda*(4). - -	Cabinet.
308	RUBUS ODORATUS,	*Flowering Raspberry*(1). - -	Cabinet.
309	RUBUS TRIFLORUS,	*Dwarf Raspberry*(4). - - -	Cabinet.
310	RUBUS STRIGOSUS,	*Red Wild Raspberry*(2). - -	Cabinet.
311	RUBUS OCCIDENTALIS,	*Black Raspberry*, or *Thimbleberry*(3).	Cabinet.
312	RUBUS VILLOSUS,	*Common Blackberry*(4). - -	Cabinet.
313	RUBUS CANADENSIS,	*Low Blackberry*, or *Dewberry*(1).	Cabinet.
314	RUBUS HISPIDUS,	*Running Swamp Blackberry*(7).	Cabinet.
315	RUBUS CUNEIFOLIUS,	*Sand Blackberry*(3). - - -	Cabinet.
316	ROSA CAROLINA,	*Swamp Rose*(1). - - - -	Cabinet.
317	ROSA LUCIDA,	*Dwarf Wild Rose*(6). - - -	Cabinet.
318	ROSA BLANDA,	*Early Wild Rose*(2). - - -	Cabinet.
319	ROSA RUBIGINOSA,	*Sweetbriar*, or *Eglantine*(2).	Cabinet.
320	CRATÆGUS OXYCANTHA,	*Hawthorn*, or *English Thorn*(4).	Cabinet.
321	CRATÆGUS CRUS-GALLI,	*Cockspur Thorn*(3). - - -	Cabinet.
322	CRATÆGUS COCCINEA,	*White Thorn*(4). - - - -	Cabinet.
323	CRATÆGUS TOMENTOSA,	*Black Thorn*(2). - - - -	Cabinet.
324	CRATÆGUS PUNCTATA,	*Common Thorn*(2). - - -	Cabinet.

Latin Names.	English Names.	
325 PYRUS CORONARIA,	*Crabapple*(3). - - - - - -	Cabinet.
326 PYRUS ARBUTIFOLIA,	*Chokeberry*(6). - - - - -	Cabinet.
327 PYRUS AMERICANA,	*Mountain Ash*(1). - - - -	Cabinet.
328 AMELANCHIER CANADENSIS,	*Common Juneberry*(6). - -	Cabinet.

Vol. 11.] ORDER XXXIX. MELASTOMACEÆ.

329 RHEXIA VIRGINICA,	*Meadow-beauty*, or *Deergrass*(3).	Cabinet.

ORDER XL. LYTHRACEÆ.

330 AMMANNIA HUMILIS,	*Dwarf Ammannia.*	
331 LYTHRUM HYSSOPIFOLIA,	*Common Purple Loosestrife.*	
332 DECODON VERTICILLATUM,	*Swamp Willowherb*(2). - -	Cabinet.
333 CUPHEA VISCOSISSIMA,	*Viscid Cuphea.*	

ORDER XLI. ONAGRACEÆ.

334 EPILOBIUM ANGUSTIFOLIUM,	*Rosebay Willowherb*(2). - -	Cabinet.
335 EPILOBIUM ALPINUM,	*Alpine Willowherb*(2). - -	Cabinet.
336 EPILOBIUM COLORATUM,	*Purple-leaved Willowherb*(2).	Cabinet.
337 EPILOBIUM MOLLE,	*Soft Willowherb.*	
338 EPILOBIUM PALUSTRE,	*Narrow-leaved Willowherb*(2).	Cabinet.
339 ŒNOTHERA BIENNIS,	*Common Evening Primrose*(2).	Cabinet.
340 ŒNOTHERA FRUTICOSA,	*Sundrops*(2). - - - - - -	Cabinet.
341 ŒNOTHERA LINEARIS,	*Narrow-leaved Evening Primrose.*	
342 ŒNOTHERA CHRYSANTHA,	*Golden-flowered Evening Primrose.*	
343 ŒNOTHERA PUMILA,	*Dwarf Evening Primrose*(1).	Cabinet.
344 GAURA BIENNIS,	*Biennial Gaura*(3). - - -	Cabinet.
345 LUDWIGIA ALTERNIFOLIA,	*Seedbox*(3). - - - - - - -	Cabinet.
346 LUDWIGIA SPHÆROCARPA,	*Round-fruited Ludwigia*(1).	Cabinet.
347 LUDWIGIA PALUSTRIS,	*Water Purselane*(2). - - -	Cabinet.
348 CIRCÆA LUTETIANA,	*Common Enchanter's Nightshade*(2).	Cabinet.
349 CIRCÆA ALPINA,	*Alpine Enchanter's Nightshade.*	
350 PROSERPINACA PALUSTRIS,	*Marsh Mermaid-weed*(4). -	Cabinet.
351 PROSERPINACA PECTINACEA,	*Cut-leaved Mermaid-weed*(3).	Cabinet.
352 MYRIOPHYLLUM SPICATUM,	*Spiked Water-milfoil.*	

	Latin Names.	English Names.	
353	Myriophyllum verticillatum,	*Whorled Water-milfoil*(1).	Cabinet.
354	Myriophyllum heterophyllum,	*Various-leaved Water-milf.*(2).	Cab.
355	Myriophyllum ambiguum,	*Polymorphous Water-milfoil*(1).	Cabinet.
356	Myriophyllum tenellum,	*Leafless Water-milfoil*(5). -	Cabinet.
357	Hippuris vulgaris,	*Common Marestail*(2). - -	Cabinet.

ORDER XLII. CACTACEÆ.

358 Opuntia vulgaris, *Common Indian-fig*, or *Prickly-pear*(7). Cabinet.

ORDER XLIII. GROSSULACEÆ.

359	Ribes cynosbati,	*Prickly Gooseberry*(6). - -	Cabinet.
360	Ribes rotundifolium,	*Round-leaved Gooseberry*(2).	Cabinet.
361	Ribes lacustre,	*Swamp Gooseberry*(2). - -	Cabinet.
362	Ribes floridum,	*Wild Black Currant*(2). - -	Cabinet.
363	Ribes prostratum,	*Fetid Currant*(2). - - - -	Cabinet.

ORDER XLIV. CUCURBITACEÆ.

364	Sicyos angulatus,	*Common Single-seeded Cucumber*(1).	Cabinet.
365	Echinocystis lobata,	*Wild Balsamapple*(2). - -	Cabinet.

ORDER XLV. CRASSULACEÆ.

366	Tillæa simplex,	*Pigmyweed.*	
367	Sedum telephioides,	*American Orpine.*	
368	Sedum telephium,	*Liveforever*(2). - - - - -	Cabinet.
369	Penthorum sedoides,	*Virginian Stonecrop*(1). - -	Cabinet.

ORDER XLVI. SAXIFRAGACEÆ.

370	Saxifraga virginiensis,	*Virginian Saxifrage*(1). - -	Cabinet.
371	Saxifraga pennsylvanica,	*Pennsylvanian Saxifrage*(4).	Cabinet.
372	Heuchera americana,	*Common Alumroot.*	
373	Mitella diphylla,	*Common Bishopscap*(3). - -	Cabinet.
374	Mitella nuda,	*Stoloniferous Bishopscap*(4).	Cabinet.
375	Tiarella cordifolia,	*Heart-leaved Mitrewort*(1). -	Cabinet.
376	Chrysosplenium americanum,	*Golden Saxifrage*(8). - -	Cabinet.

ORDER XLVII. HAMAMELACEÆ.

377	Hamamelis virginica,	*Witch Hazel*(2). - - - -	Cabinet.

Vol. 12.] ORDER XLVIII. UMBELLIFERÆ.

	Latin Names.	English Names.	
378	Hydrocotyle americana,	*American Marsh-pennywort*(4).	Cabinet.
379	Hydrocotyle umbellata,	*Many-flowered Marsh-pennywort*(4).	Cab.
380	Crantzia lineata,	*Narrow-leaved Crantzia.*	
381	Sanicula marilandica,	*Long-styled Sanicle*(4). - -	Cabinet.
382	Sanicula canadensis,	*Canadian Sanicle*(3). - - -	Cabinet.
383	Discopleura capillacea,	*Few-rayed Discopleura*(2). -	Cabinet.
384	Bupleurum rotundifolium,	*Thoroughwax*, or *Modesty*(1).	Cabinet.
385	Cicuta maculata,	*Water-hemlock*, or *Spotted Cowbane*(3).	Cabinet.
386	Cicuta bulbifera,	*Bulbiferous Water-hemlock*(4).	Cabinet.
387	Sium latifolium,	*Broad-leaved Water-parsnep*(4).	Cabinet.
388	Sium lineare,	*Narrow-leaved Water-parsnep*(4).	Cabinet.
389	Cryptotænia canadensis,	*Common Honewort*(2). - -	Cabinet.
390	Zizia cordata,	*Heart-leaved Alexanders*(4). -	Cabinet.
391	Zizia aurea,	*Golden Meadow-parsnep*(1). -	Cabinet.
392	Zizia integerrima,	*Entire-leaved Zizia*(2). - -	Cabinet.
393	Thaspium atropurpureum,	*Purple Alexanders*(1). - -	Cabinet.
394	Thaspium aureum,	*Golden Thaspium*(3). - - -	Cabinet.
395	Thaspium barbinode,	*Hairy-jointed Thaspium*(3). -	Cabinet.
396	Æthusa cynapium,	*Common Fool's Parsley*(2). -	Cabinet.
397	Conioselinum canadense,	*Canadian Conioselinum*(4). -	Cabinet.
398	Archangelica atropurpurea,	*Common Angelica*(7). -	Cabinet.
399	Archangelica hirsuta,	*Downy Angelica*(3). - - -	Cabinet.
400	Archemora rigida,	*Rigid-leaved Archemora*(5). -	Cabinet.
401	Pastinaca sativa,	*Common* or *Wild Parsnep*(3).	Cabinet.
402	Heracleum lanatum,	*American Cow Parsnep*(5). -	Cabinet.
403	Daucus carota,	*Common* or *Wild Carrot*(2).	Cabinet.
404	Osmorhiza longistylis,	*True Sweet Cicely*(2). - - -	Cabinet.
405	Osmorhiza brevistylis,	*Spurious Sweet Cicely*(4). -	Cabinet.
406	Conium maculatum,	*Common Poison Hemlock*(4).	Cabinet.
407	Erigenia bulbosa,	*Bulbous-rooted Erigenia*(4). -	Cabinet.

Vol. 13.] ORDER XLIX. ARALIACEÆ.

	Latin Names.	English Names.	
408	Aralia racemosa,	*Spikenard*(1). - - - - - -	Cabinet.
409	Aralia nudicaulis,	*Wild Sarsaparilla*(1). - -	Cabinet.
410	Aralia hispida,	*Wild Elder*(1). - - - - -	Cabinet.
411	Panax quinquefolium,	*Common Ginseng*(4). - - -	Cabinet.
412	Panax trifolium,	*Dwarf Ginseng*(4). - - -	Cabinet.

ORDER L. CORNACEÆ.

413	Cornus alternifolia,	*Alternate-leaved Dogwood*(2).	Cabinet.
414	Cornus circinata,	*Round-leaved Dogwood*(2). -	Cabinet.
415	Cornus stolonifera,	*White-berried Dogwood*(2). -	Cabinet.
416	Cornus paniculata,	*Panicled Dogwood*(3). - -	Cabinet.
417	Cornus sericea,	*Swamp Dogwood*(3). - - -	Cabinet.
418	Cornus florida,	*Common Dogwood*(4). - - -	Cabinet.
419	Cornus canadensis,	*Dwarf Dogwood*(3). - - -	Cabinet.

ORDER LI. CAPRIFOLIACEÆ.

420	Linnæa borealis,	*Two-flowered Linnæa*(4). - -	Cabinet.
421	Symphoricarpus racemosa,	*Common Snowberry*(2). - -	Cabinet.
422	Symphoricarpus vulgaris,	*Indian Currant*(2). - - -	Cabinet.
423	Lonicera sempervirens,	*Trumpet Honeysuckle*(4). -	Cabinet.
424	Lonicera grata,	*Wild Honeysuckle.*	
425	Lonicera flava,	*Yellow Honeysuckle.*	
426	Lonicera hirsuta,	*Hairy Honeysuckle*(4). - -	Cabinet.
427	Lonicera parviflora,	*Small-flowered Honeysuckle*(5).	Cabinet.
428	Lonicera ciliata,	*Fly Honeysuckle*(4). - - -	Cabinet.
429	Lonicera cærulea,	*Hairy Fly Honeysuckle*(1). -	Cabinet.
430	Lonicera oblongifolia,	*Long-stalked Honeysuckle*(1).	Cabinet.
431	Diervilla trifida,	*Common Bush Honeysuckle*(1).	Cabinet.
432	Triosteum perfoliatum,	*Feverwort*, or *Horse Gentian*(1).	Cabinet.
433	Sambucus pubens,	*Red-berried Elder*(2). - - -	Cabinet.
434	Sambucus canadensis,	*Common Elder*(2). - - - -	Cabinet.
435	Viburnum nudum,	*Swamp Viburnum*(7). - - -	Cabinet.

Latin Names.	English Names.	
436 Viburnum prunifolium,	*Black Haw*, or *Sloe*(1). - -	Cabinet.
437 Viburnum lentago,	*Sweet Viburnum*(2). - - -	Cabinet.
438 Viburnum dentatum,	*Arrow-wood*(3). - - - - -	Cabinet.
439 Viburnum pubescens,	*Pubescent Viburnum*(4). - -	Cabinet.
440 Viburnum acerifolium,	*Maple-leaved Arrow-wood*(3).	Cabinet.
441 Viburnum pauciflorum,	*Mountain Bush Cranberry*(1).	Cabinet.
442 Viburnum opulus,	*High Cranberry*(2). - - -	Cabinet.
443 Viburnum lantanoides,	*Hobblebush*(3). - - - - -	Cabinet.

Vol. 14.] ORDER LII. RUBIACEÆ.

444 Galium aparine,	*Common Cleavers*, or *Goosegrass*(1).	Cabinet.
445 Galium trifidum,	*Small Bedstraw*(9). - - -	Cabinet.
446 Galium asprellum,	*Rough Bedstraw*(2). - - -	Cabinet.
447 Galium triflorum,	*Sweetscented Bedstraw*(1). -	Cabinet.
448 Galium pilosum,	*Hairy Bedstraw*(3). - - -	Cabinet.
449 Galium circæzans,	*Wild Liquorice*(5). - - -	Cabinet.
450 Galium boreale,	*Northern Bedstraw*(2). - -	Cabinet.
451 Cephalanthus occidentalis,	*Butterbush*, *Pond Dogwood*(2).	Cab.
452 Mitchella repens,	*Partridgeberry*(3). - - -	Cabinet.
453 Hedyotis cærulea,	*Common Bluets*, or *Dwarf Risk*(5).	Cabinet.
454 Hedyotis ciliolata,	*Fringed-leaved Bluets*(4). -	Cabinet.
455 Hedyotis longifolia,	*Long-leaved Bluets*(6). - -	Cabinet.
456 Hedyotis glomerata,	*Cluster-flowered Bluets.*	

ORDER LIII. VALERIANACEÆ.

457 Valeriana sylvatica,	*Tall Swamp Valerian*(2). -	Cabinet.
458 Fedia fagopyrum,	*Buckwheat Cornsalad*(3). -	Cabinet.

ORDER LIV. DIPSACEÆ.

459 Dipsacus sylvestris,	*Wild Teasel*(2). - - - -	Cabinet.

Vol. 15.] ORDER LV. COMPOSITÆ.

460 Vernonia noveboracensis,	*Common Ironweed*(3). - - -	Cabinet.
461 Liatris cylindracea,	*Small Buttonsnakeroot*(1). -	Cabinet.
462 Liatris spicata,	*Tall Buttonsnakeroot*(1). - -	Cabinet.

	Latin Names.	English Names.	
463	Liatris scariosa,	*Large-flowered Buttonsnakeroot*(4).	Cabinet.
464	Eupatorium purpureum,	*Joe-Pye-weed*(6). - - - -	Cabinet.
465	Eupatorium leucolepis,	*White-scaled Hempweed.*	
466	Eupatorium teucrifolium,	*Germander-leaved Hempweed*(2).	Cabinet.
467	Eupatorium rotundifolium,	*Round-leaved Hempweed.*	
468	Eupatorium sessilifolium,	*Upland Boneset*(1). - - -	Cabinet.
469	Eupatorium perfoliatum,	*Boneset*, or *Thoroughwort*(1).	Cabinet.
470	Eupatorium ageratoides,	*White Snakeroot*(1). - - -	Cabinet.
471	Eupatorium aromaticum,	*Sweetscented Hempweed*(2). -	Cabinet.
472	Mikania scandens,	*Common Climbing Hempweed*(3).	Cabinet.
473	Nardosmia palmata,	*Sweet Coltsfoot.*	
474	Tussilago farfara,	*Common Coltsfoot*(5). - - -	Cabinet.
475	Sericocarpus conyzoides,	*Broad-leaved Sericocarpus*(2).	Cabinet.
476	Sericocarpus solidagineus,	*Narrow-leaved Sericocarpus*(2).	Cabinet.

Vol. 16.]

477	Aster corymbosus,	*Corymbed Aster*(2). - - -	Cabinet.
478	Aster macrophyllus,	*Large-leaved Aster*(1). - -	Cabinet.
479	Aster radula,	*Rasp-leaved Aster.*	
480	Aster spectabilis,	*Showy Aster.*	
481	Aster patens,	*Spreading Aster*(2). - - -	Cabinet.
482	Aster lævis,	*Smooth Blue Aster*(1). - -	Cabinet.
483	Aster undulatus,	*Various-leaved Aster*(3). - -	Cabinet.
484	Aster cordifolius,	*Heart-leaved Aster*(1). - -	Cabinet.
485	Aster sagittifolius,	*Arrow-leaved Aster.*	
486	Aster ericoides,	*Heath-like Aster.*	
487	Aster multiflorus,	*Many-flowered Aster*(2). - -	Cabinet.
488	Aster dumosus,	*Bushy Aster*(1). - - - -	Cabinet.
489	Aster tradescanti,	*Tradescant's Aster*(2). - -	Cabinet.
490	Aster miser,	*Starved Aster.*	
491	Aster simplex,	*Willow-leaved Aster*(4). - -	Cabinet.
492	Aster tenuifolius,	*Slender-leaved Aster.*	
493	Aster greenii,	*Green's Aster.*	

	Latin Names.	English Names.	
494	ASTER LAXUS,	*Loosely-branched Aster.*	
495	ASTER ELODES,	*Blue Smooth Marsh Aster*(1).	Cabinet.
496	ASTER PUNICEUS,	*Hispid Tall Aster*(5). - -	Cabinet.
497	ASTER PRENANTHOIDES,	*Prenanthes-like Aster*(1). -	Cabinet.
498	ASTER NOVÆ-ANGLIÆ,	*New-England Aster*(2). - -	Cabinet.
499	ASTER ACUMINATUS,	*Acuminate Aster*(2). - - -	Cabinet.
500	ASTER PTARMICOIDES,	*Ptarmicoid Aster*(2). - - -	Cabinet.
501	ASTER FLEXUOSUS,	*Perennial Salt-marsh Aster*(1).	Cabinet.
502	ASTER LINIFOLIUS,	*Annual Salt-marsh Aster*(3).	Cabinet.
503	DIPLOPAPPUS LINARIIFOLIUS,	*Narrow-leaved Diplopappus*(6).	Cabinet.
504	DIPLOPAPPUS CORNIFOLIUS,	*Cornel-leaved Diplopappus*(4).	Cabinet.
505	DIPLOPAPPUS UMBELLATUS,	*Umbelled Diplopappus.*	
506	ERIGERON CANADENSE,	*Horseweed*, or *Butterweed*(1).	Cabinet.
507	ERIGERON BELLIDIFOLIUM,	*Poor Robert's Plantain*(2). -	Cabinet.
508	ERIGERON PHILADELPHICUM,	*Philadelphia Fleabane*(2). -	Cabinet.
509	ERIGERON ANNUUM,	*Sweet Scabious, Daisy, &c.*(1).	Cabinet.
510	ERIGERON STRIGOSUM,	*Fleabane*(1). - - - - - -	Cabinet.

Vol. 17.]

511	SOLIDAGO SQUARROSA,	*Squarrose Goldenrod*(1). - -	Cabinet.
512	SOLIDAGO BICOLOR,	*White Goldenrod*(4). - - -	Cabinet.
513	SOLIDAGO LATIFOLIA,	*Broad-leaved Goldenrod*(4). -	Cabinet.
514	SOLIDAGO CÆSIA,	*Blue-stemmed Goldenrod*(3).	Cabinet.
515	SOLIDAGO STRICTA,	*Willow-leaved Goldenrod*(4).	Cabinet.
516	SOLIDAGO VIRGA-AUREA,	*European Goldenrod*(3). - -	Cabinet.
517	SOLIDAGO RIGIDA,	*Rigid-leaved Goldenrod*(2). -	Cabinet.
518	SOLIDAGO OHIOENSIS,	*Ohio Goldenrod*(2). - - -	Cabinet.
519	SOLIDAGO SEMPERVIRENS,	*Salt-marsh Goldenrod*(2). -	Cabinet.
520	SOLIDAGO NEGLECTA,	*Neglected Goldenrod*(1). - -	Cabinet.
521	SOLIDAGO PATULA,	*Spreading Goldenrod*(3). - -	Cabinet.
522	SOLIDAGO ARGUTA,	*Sharp-toothed Goldenrod*(1).	Cabinet.
523	SOLIDAGO MUHLENBERGII,	*Muhlenberg's Goldenrod*(2). -	Cabinet.
524	SOLIDAGO ALTISSIMA,	*Tall Hairy Goldenrod*(1). -	Cabinet.

	Latin Names.	English Names.	
525	Solidago ulmifolia,	*Elm-leaved Goldenrod.*	
526	Solidago odora,	*Sweetscented Goldenrod*(2). -	Cabinet.
527	Solidago nemoralis,	*Gray Goldenrod*(3). - - -	Cabinet.
528	Solidago canadensis,	*Canadian Goldenrod*(1). - -	Cabinet.
529	Solidago serotina,	*Late-flowering Goldenrod*(2).	Cabinet.
530	Solidago gigantea,	*Tall Smooth Goldenrod*(1). -	Cabinet.
531	Solidago lanceolata,	*Bushy Goldenrod*(1). - - -	Cabinet.
532	Solidago tenuifolia,	*Slender-leaved Goldenrod*(2).	Cabinet.
533	Chrysopsis falcata,	*Sickle-leaved Chrysopsis*(2). -	Cabinet.
534	Chrysopsis mariana,	*Maryland Chrysopsis*(3). - -	Cabinet.
535	Baccharis halimifolia,	*Groundselbush*(1). - - - -	Cabinet.
536	Pluchea camphorata,	*Seaside Marsh-fleabane*(2). -	Cabinet.
537	Inula helenium,	*Common Elecampane*(1). - -	Cabinet.

Vol. 18.]

538	Polymnia canadensis,	*Small-flowered Leafcup*(3). -	Cabinet.
539	Polymnia uvedalia,	*Large-flowered Leafcup*(2). -	Cabinet.
540	Silphium trifoliatum,	*Ternate Silphium.*	
541	Iva frutescens,	*Highwater-shrub*(2). - - -	Cabinet.
542	Ambrosia trifida,	*Three-lobed Ragweed*(2). - -	Cabinet.
543	Ambrosia artemisiæfolia,	*Hogweed*, or *Bitterweed*(1). -	Cabinet.
544	Xanthium strumarium,	*Common Cocklebur*(1). - -	Cabinet.
545	Xanthium echinatum,	*Sea Cocklebur*(2). - - - -	Cabinet.
546	Xanthium spinosum,	*Thorny Cocklebur*(1). - - -	Cabinet.
547	Heliopsis lævis,	*Oxeye*(1). - - - - - - -	Cabinet.
548	Rudbeckia hirta,	*Large Hairy Rudbeckia*(2). -	Cabinet.
549	Rudbeckia laciniata,	*Tall Smooth Rudbeckia*(2). -	Cabinet.
550	Lepachys pinnata,	*Tall Lepachys*(2). - - - -	Cabinet.
551	Helianthus giganteus,	*Tall Wild Sunflower*(4). -	Cabinet.
552	Helianthus strumosus,	*Wild Sunflower*(2). - - -	Cabinet.
553	Helianthus decapetalus,	*Wild Sunflower*(1). - - -	Cabinet.
554	Helianthus divaricatus,	*Small Rough-leaved Sunflower*(3).	Cabinet.
555	Helianthus tuberosus,	*Jerusalem Artichoke*(1). - -	Cabinet.

	Latin Names.	English Names.	
556	ACTINOMERIS SQUARROSA,	*Squarrose Actinomeris*(1). -	Cabinet.
557	COREOPSIS TRICHOSPERMA,	*Tickseed Sunflower*(1). - -	Cabinet.
558	COREOPSIS ROSEA,	*Small Rose-colored Coreopsis*(1).	Cabinet.
559	BIDENS FRONDOSA,	*Common Bur-marigold*, or *Sticktight*(2).	Cabinet.
560	BIDENS CONNATA,	*Swamp Beggarticks*(2). - -	Cabinet.
561	BIDENS CERNUA,	*Swamp Beggarticks.*	
562	BIDENS CHRYSANTHEMOIDES,	*Large-flowered Bur-marigold*(1).	Cab.
563	BIDENS BECKII,	*Water Marigold*(2). - - -	Cabinet.
564	BIDENS BIPINNATA,	*Spanish-needles*(2). - - -	Cabinet.
565	HELENIUM AUTUMNALE,	*Sneezeweed*(2). - - - - -	Cabinet.

Vol. 19.]

566	MARUTA COTULA,	*Fetid Chamomile*, or *Mayweed*(1).	Cabinet.
567	ANTHEMIS ARVENSIS,	*Wild Chamomile*(1). - - -	Cabinet.
568	ACHILLEA MILLEFOLIUM,	*Common Yarrow*(1). - - -	Cabinet.
569	LEUCANTHEMUM VULGARE,	*Whiteweed*, or *Daisy*(2). - -	Cabinet.
570	TANACETUM VULGARE,	*Common Tansey*(1). - - -	Cabinet.
571	ARTEMISIA CANADENSIS,	*Wild Wormwood*(1). - - -	Cabinet.
572	ARTEMISIA CAUDATA,	*Tall Biennial Wormwood*(2).	Cabinet.
573	ARTEMISIA VULGARIS,	*Mugwort.*	
574	GNAPHALIUM DECURRENS,	*Decurrent Cudweed*(1). - -	Cabinet.
575	GNAPHALIUM POLYCEPHALUM,	*Life-everlasting*(2). - - -	Cabinet.
576	GNAPHALIUM ULIGINOSUM,	*Marsh Cudweed*(2). - - -	Cabinet.
577	GNAPHALIUM PURPUREUM,	*Purple Cudweed*(4). - - -	Cabinet.
578	ANTENNARIA MARGARITACEA,	*Pearly Everlasting*(2). -	Cabinet.
579	ANTENNARIA PLANTAGINIFOLIA,	*Plantain-leaved Cudweed*(3).	Cabinet.
580	FILAGO GERMANICA,	*Herba Impia*(2). - - - -	Cabinet.
581	ERECHTITES HIERACIFOLIUS,	*Common Fireweed*(1). - - -	Cabinet.
582	CACALIA SUAVEOLENS,	*Sweetscented Indian Plantain.*	
583	CACALIA ATRIPLICIFOLIA,	*Indian Plantain*(1). - - -	Cabinet.
584	SENECIO VULGARIS,	*Common Groundsel*(1). - -	Cabinet.
585	SENECIO AUREUS,	*Life-root*, or *Squaw-weed*(7).	Cabinet.
586	ARNICA MOLLIS,	*Soft Arnica*(2). - - - -	Cabinet.

	Latin Names.	English Names.	
587	Centaurea cyanus,	*Bluebottle*, or *French Pink*(1).	Cabinet.
588	Carduus benedictus,	*Common Blessed-thistle.*	
589	Cirsium lanceolatum,	*Common Thistle*(1). - - -	Cabinet.
590	Cirsium discolor,	*Two-colored Thistle*(2). - -	Cabinet.
591	Cirsium muticum,	*Awnless Swamp Thistle*(2). -	Cabinet.
592	Cirsium pumilum,	*Pasture Thistle*(2). - - -	Cabinet.
593	Cirsium horridulum,	*Yellow Thistle*(1). - - - -	Cabinet.
594	Cirsium arvense,	*Canada Thistle*(2). - - -	Cabinet.
595	Lappa major,	*Common Burdock*(1). - - -	Cabinet.
Vol. 20.]			
596	Krigia virginica,	*Common Dwarf Dandelion*(4).	Cabinet.
597	Cynthia virginica,	*Virginian Cynthia*(3). - -	Cabinet.
598	Cichorium intybus,	*Wild Succory*, or *Chicory*(2).	Cabinet.
599	Hieracium canadense,	*Sharp-toothed Hawkweed*(2).	Cabinet.
600	Hieracium scabrum,	*Rough Hawkweed*(1). - - -	Cabinet.
601	Hieracium gronovii,	*Gronovius's Hawkweed*(2). -	Cabinet.
602	Hieracium venosum,	*Rattlesnakeweed*(1). - - -	Cabinet.
603	Hieracium paniculatum,	*Panicled Hawkweed*(2). - -	Cabinet.
604	Nabalus albus,	*Lionsfoot*, or *White Lettuce*(5).	Cabinet.
605	Nabalus altissimus,	*Tall Nabalus*(1). - - - -	Cabinet.
606	Nabalus fraseri,	*Gall-of-the-earth.*	
607	Nabalus nanus,	*Dwarf Nabalus*(1). - - -	Cabinet.
608	Nabalus boottii,	*Boott's Nabalus.*	
609	Taraxacum dens-leonis,	*Common Dandelion*(1). - -	Cabinet.
610	Lactuca elongata,	*Wild Lettuce*, or *Fireweed*(4).	Cabinet.
611	Mulgedium acuminatum,	*Sharp-leaved Mulgedium*(2).	Cabinet.
612	Mulgedium leucophæum,	*Tall Mulgedium*(4). - - -	Cabinet.
613	Sonchus oleraceus,	*Common Sowthistle*(1). - -	Cabinet.
614	Sonchus asper,	*Spiny-leaved Sowthistle.*	
615	Sonchus arvensis,	*Large-flowered Sowthistle*(1).	Cabinet.

Vol. 21.] ORDER LVI. LOBELIACEÆ.

	Latin Names.	English Names.	
616	LOBELIA KALMII,	*Kalm's Lobelia*(8). - - - -	Cabinet.
617	LOBELIA NUTTALLII,	*Nuttall's Lobelia*(3). - - -	Cabinet.
618	LOBELIA SPICATA,	*Pale-spiked Lobelia*(3). - -	Cabinet.
619	LOBELIA DORTMANNA,	*Water Gladiole*(3). - - -	Cabinet.
620	LOBELIA SYPHILITICA,	*Blue Cardinalflower*(2). - -	Cabinet.
621	LOBELIA INFLATA,	*Indian Tobacco*(3). - - - -	Cabinet.
622	LOBELIA CARDINALIS,	*Cardinalflower*(3). - - - -	Cabinet.

ORDER LVII. CAMPANULACEÆ.

623	CAMPANULA ROTUNDIFOLIA,	*Harebell*(3). - - - - - -	Cabinet.
624	CAMPANULA APARINOIDES,	*Slender Swamp Bellflower*(3).	Cabinet.
625	CAMPANULA AMERICANA,	*American Bellflower*(2). - -	Cabinet.
626	SPECULARIA PERFOLIATA,	*Clasping Specularia*(5). - -	Cabinet.

ORDER LVIII. ERICACEÆ.

627	ARCTOSTAPHYLOS UVA-URSI,	*Bearberry*(3). - - - - -	Cabinet.
628	CLETHRA ALNIFOLIA,	*Common Sweet Pepperbush*(3).	Cabinet.
629	EPIGÆA REPENS,	*Ground Laurel*(4). - - - -	Cabinet.
630	GAUTIERA PROCUMBENS,	*Partridgeberry*, or *Teaberry*(6).	Cabinet.
631	ANDROMEDA POLYFOLIA,	*Wild Rosemary*(2). - - -	Cabinet.
632	ANDROMEDA CALYCULATA,	*Leatherleaf*(3). - - - - -	Cabinet.
633	ANDROMEDA MARIANA,	*Kill-lamb*, or *Staggerbush*(3).	Cabinet.
634	ANDROMEDA RACEMOSA,	*Racemed Andromeda*(2). - -	Cabinet.
635	ANDROMEDA LIGUSTRINA,	*Privet Andromeda*(2). - -	Cabinet.
636	RHODODENDRON MAXIMUM,	*Great Laurel*(2). - - - -	Cabinet.
637	RHODODENDRON LAPPONICUM,	*Procumbent Alpine Rosebay*(5).	Cabinet.
638	RHODODENDRON NUDIFLORUM,	*Upright Wild Honeysuckle*(4).	Cabinet.
639	RHODODENDRON VISCOSUM,	*White Wild Honeysuckle*(3).	Cabinet.
640	RHODODENDRON HISPIDUM,	*Hispid Azalea.*	
641	RHODODENDRON RHODORA,	*Rhodora*(2). - - - - - -	Cabinet.
642	KALMIA LATIFOLIA,	*Calicobush*(3). - - - - -	Cabinet.
643	KALMIA ANGUSTIFOLIA,	*Dwarf* or *Sheep Laurel*(2). -	Cabinet.

	Latin Names.	English Names.	
644	Kalmia glauca,	*Swamp Laurel*(4). - - - -	Cabinet.
645	Ledum palustre,	*Labrador-tea*(3). - - - -	Cabinet.
646	Vaccinium uliginosum,	*Alpine Bilberry*(1). - - -	Cabinet.
647	Vaccinium vacillans,	*Low Blue Huckleberry*(1). -	Cabinet.
648	Vaccinium pennsylvanicum,	*Dwarf Blue Huckleberry*(3).	Cabinet.
649	Vaccinium corymbosum,	*Tall Swamp Huckleberry*(5).	Cabinet.
650	Vaccinium canadense,	*Black Bilberry*(1). - - -	Cabinet.
651	Vaccinium stamineum,	*Deerberry*, or *Squaw Huckleberry*(3).	Cabinet.
652	Vaccinium oxycoccus,	*Small Cranberry*(2). - - -	Cabinet.
653	Vaccinium macrocarpon,	*Common Cranberry*(5). - -	Cabinet.
654	Gaylussacia hirtella,	*Dwarf Swamp Huckleberry.*	
655	Gaylussacia frondosa,	*Bluetangle*, or *Dangleberry*(1).	Cabinet.
656	Gaylussacia resinosa,	*Black Huckleberry*(2). - -	Cabinet.
657	Chiogenes hispidula,	*Creeping Snowberry*(2). - -	Cabinet.
658	Pyrola rotundifolia,	*Round-leaved Wintergreen*(3).	Cabinet.
659	Pyrola elliptica,	*Shinleaf*(3). - - - - - - -	Cabinet.
660	Pyrola chlorantha,	*Greenish-flowered Wintergreen*(2).	Cabinet.
661	Pyrola uliginosa,	*Swamp Wintergreen.*	
662	Pyrola secunda,	*Onesided Wintergreen*(4). -	Cabinet.
663	Pyrola uniflora,	*One-flowered Wintergreen*(6).	Cabinet.
664	Chimaphila umbellata,	*Pipsissewa*, or *Prince's-pine*(4).	Cabinet.
665	Chimaphila maculata,	*Spotted Wintergreen*(4). - -	Cabinet.
666	Monotropa uniflora,	*Indian-pipe*(6). - - - - -	Cabinet.
667	Monotropa lanuginosa,	*Pinesap*, or *False Beechdrops*(7).	Cabinet.
668	Pterospora andromedea,	*Giant Birdsnest*(2). - - -	Cabinet.

Vol. 22.] ORDER LIX. AQUIFOLIACEÆ.

669	Ilex opaca,	*American Holly*(3). - - -	Cabinet.
670	Ilex ambiguus,	*Ambiguous Ilex*(2). - - -	Cabinet.
671	Prinos verticillatus,	*Common Winterberry*(3). -	Cabinet.
672	Prinos lævigatus,	*Smooth Winterberry*(2). - -	Cabinet.
673	Prinos glaber,	*Evergreen Winterberry*, or *Inkberry*(2).	Cabinet.
674	Nemopanthes canadensis,	*Mountain Holly*(2). - - -	Cabinet.

ORDER LX. EBENACEÆ.

	Latin Names.	English Names.	
675	Diospyros virginiana,	*Persimmon*(3). - - - - -	Cabinet.

ORDER LXI. PRIMULACEÆ.

676	Primula mistassinica,	*Dwarf Canadian Primrose*(6).	Cabinet.
677	Lysimachia stricta,	*Racemed Loosestrife*(2). - -	Cabinet.
678	Lysimachia quadrifolia,	*Whorled Loosestrife*(3). - -	Cabinet.
679	Lysimachia ciliata,	*Fringed Loosestrife*(2). - -	Cabinet.
680	Lysimachia hybrida,	*Hybrid Loosestrife*(1). - -	Cabinet.
681	Lysimachia longifolia,	*Revolute Loosestrife*(1). - -	Cabinet.
682	Lysimachia thyrsiflora,	*Tufted Loosestrife*(3). - - -	Cabinet.
683	Trientalis americana,	*Chickweed Wintergreen*(4). -	Cabinet.
684	Anagallis arvensis,	*Scarlet Pimpernel*(4). - -	Cabinet.
685	Hottonia inflata,	*American Waterfeather*(1). -	Cabinet.
686	Samolus valerandi,	*Common Water Pimpernel*(3).	Cabinet.

ORDER LXII. PLANTAGINACEÆ.

687	Plantago major,	*Broad-leaved Plantain*(1). -	Cabinet.
688	Plantago cordata,	*Heart-leaved Plantain*(2). -	Cabinet.
689	Plantago lanceolata,	*Ribgrass*(2). - - - - -	Cabinet.
690	Plantago virginica,	*White Plantain*(4). - - -	Cabinet.
691	Plantago maritima,	*Sea Plantain*(4). - - - -	Cabinet.
692	Plantago pusilla,	*Dwarf Plantain*(10). - - -	Cabinet.

ORDER LXIII. PLUMBAGINACEÆ.

693	Statice limonium,	*Common Marsh Rosemary*(1).	Cabinet.

ORDER LXIV. LENTIBULACEÆ.

694	Pinguicula vulgaris,	*Common Butterwort*(3). - -	Cabinet.
695	Utricularia inflata,	*Spongy-leaved Bladderwort*(2).	Cabinet.
696	Utricularia purpurea,	*Purple Bladderwort.*	
697	Utricularia vulgaris,	*Common Bladderwort*(3). -	Cabinet.
698	Utricularia cornuta,	*Sharp-horned Bladderwort*(5).	Cabinet.
699	Utricularia striata,	*Striated Bladderwort.*	
700	Utricularia intermedia,	*Intermediate Bladderwort.*	
701	Utricularia minor,	*Lesser Bladderwort.*	

ORDER LXV. OROBANCHACEÆ.

	Latin Names.	English Names.	
702	Orobanche americana,	*Squawroot*(2). - - - - - -	Cabinet.
703	Orobanche uniflora,	*Long-stalked Broomrape*(4).	Cabinet.
704	Epiphegus americana,	*Beechdrops*, or *Cancer-root*(3).	Cabinet.

Vol. 23.]

ORDER LXVI. BIGNONIACEÆ.

705 Catalpa syringæfolia, *Indian Bean.*

ORDER LXVII. PEDALIACEÆ.

706 Martynia proboscidea, *Unicorn-plant*(2). - - - - Cabinet.

ORDER LXVIII. ACANTHACEÆ.

707 Dianthera americana, *Water Willow*(2. - - - - Cabinet.

ORDER LXIX. SCROPHULARIACEÆ.

708	Verbascum thapsus,	*Common Mullein*(2). - - -	Cabinet.
709	Verbascum blattaria,	*Moth Mullein*(2). - - - -	Cabinet.
710	Verbascum lychnitis,	*White Mullein*(4). - - - -	Cabinet.
711	Scrophularia marilandica,	*Figwort*(2). - - - - - -	Cabinet.
712	Linaria elatine,	*Hairy Toadflax.*	
713	Linaria vulgaris,	*Common Toadflax*(3). - - -	Cabinet.
714	Linaria canadensis,	*Canadian Toadflax*(4). - -	Cabinet.
715	Collinsia verna,	*May-beauty*(5). - - - - -	Cabinet.
716	Chelone glabra,	*Shellflower*, or *Snakehead*(2).	Cabinet.
717	Pentstemon pubescens,	*Pubescent Pentstemon*(1). -	Cabinet.
718	Mimulus ringens,	*Common Monkeyflower*(2). -	Cabinet.
719	Mimulus alatus,	*Wing-stemmed Monkeyflower*(2).	Cabinet.
720	Gratiola virginica,	*Common Hedgehyssop*(3). -	Cabinet.
721	Gratiola aurea,	*Golden Hedgehyssop*(4). - -	Cabinet.
722	Lindernia dilatata,	*Long-stalked Lindernia*(3). -	Cabinet.
723	Lindernia attenuata,	*Short-stalked Lindernia*(3). -	Cabinet.
724	Buchnera americana,	*Bluehearts*(4). - - - - -	Cabinet.
725	Limosella aquatica,	*Common Mudwort*(5). - - -	Cabinet.
726	Veronica serpyllifolia,	*Paul's Betony*(7). - - - -	Cabinet.
727	Veronica officinalis,	*Common Speedwell.*	

Latin Names.	English Names.	
728 VERONICA BECCABUNGA,	*American Brooklime*(2). - -	Cabinet.
729 VERONICA ANAGALLIS,	*Water Speedwell*(1). - - -	Cabinet.
730 VERONICA SCUTELLATA,	*Marsh Speedwell*(3). - - -	Cabinet.
731 VERONICA PEREGRINA,	*Neckweed.*	
732 VERONICA ARVENSIS,	*Corn Speedwell*(5). - - -	Cabinet.
733 VERONICA AGRESTIS,	*Field Speedwell*(1). - - -	Cabinet.
734 VERONICA HEDERIFOLIA,	*Ivy-leaved Speedwell*(8). - -	Cabinet.
735 PÆDEROTA VIRGINICA,	*Culver's-physic*(5). - - - -	Cabinet.
736 GERARDIA TENUIFOLIA,	*Slender-stalked Gerardia*(4).	Cabinet.
737 GERARDIA PURPUREA,	*Rough-leaved Gerardia*(2). -	Cabinet.
738 GERARDIA MARITIMA,	*Saltmarsh Gerardia*(2). - -	Cabinet.
739 GERARDIA PEDICULARIA,	*Bushy Gerardia*(3). - - -	Cabinet.
740 GERARDIA FLAVA,	*Pubescent False-foxglove*(3).	Cabinet.
741 GERARDIA QUERCIFOLIA,	*Glaucous False-foxglove*(3). -	Cabinet.
742 CASTILLEJA COCCINEA,	*Scarlet Paintedcup*, or *Redrobin*(3).	Cabinet.
743 PEDICULARIS CANADENSIS,	*Common Lousewort*(4). - -	Cabinet.
744 PEDICULARIS LANCEOLATA,	*Tall Lousewort*(2). - - -	Cabinet.
745 MELAMPYRUM AMERICANUM,	*American Cow-wheat*(3). - -	Cabinet.

Vol. 24.] ORDER LXX. VERBENACEÆ.

746 VERBENA HASTATA,	*Tall Blue Vervain*(3). - -	Cabinet.
747 VERBENA URTICIFOLIA,	*Common Vervain*(3). - - -	Cabinet.
748 VERBENA SPURIA,	*Procumbent Vervain.*	
749 VERBENA ANGUSTIFOLIA,	*Narrow-leaved Vervain*(2). -	Cabinet.
750 PHRYMA LEPTOSTACHYA,	*Lopseed*(2). - - - - - - -	Cabinet.

ORDER LXXI. LABIATÆ.

751 ISANTHUS CÆRULEUS,	*False Pennyroyal*(1). - - -	Cabinet.
752 MENTHA VIRIDIS,	*Spearmint*(1). - - - - - -	Cabinet.
753 MENTHA PIPERITA,	*Peppermint*(2). - - - -	Cabinet.
754 MENTHA CANADENSIS,	*Canadian Mint*(2). - - -	Cabinet.
755 LYCOPUS SINUATUS,	*Common Water Horehound*(2).	Cabinet.
756 LYCOPUS VIRGINICUS,	*Bugleweed*(1). - - - - -	Cabinet.
757 MONARDA DIDYMA,	*Oswego-tea*(2). - - - - -	Cabinet.

	Latin Names.	English Names.	
758	MONARDA FISTULOSA,	*Wild Bergamot*(1). - - -	Cabinet.
759	MONARDA PUNCTATA,	*Horsemint.*	
760	BLEPHILIA HIRSUTA,	*Hairy Blephilia*(2). - - -	Cabinet.
761	PYCNANTHEMUM INCANUM,	*Common Mountain-mint*(2). -	Cabinet.
762	PYCNANTHEMUM CLINOPODIOIDES,	*Basil-leaved Mountain-mint*(1).	Cab.
763	PYCNANTHEMUM TORREI,	*Torrey's Mountain-mint*(2). -	Cabinet.
764	PYCNANTHEMUM MUTICUM,	*Broad-leaved Mountain-mint*(2).	Cabinet.
765	PYCNANTHEMUM LANCEOLATUM,	*Virginian Thyme*(2). -	Cabinet.
766	PYCNANTHEMUM LINIFOLIUM,	*Narrow-leaved Thyme*(1). -	Cabinet.
767	ORIGANUM VULGARE,	*Wild Marjoram*(2). - - -	Cabinet.
768	COLLINSONIA CANADENSIS,	*Common Horsebalm*(2). - -	Cabinet.
769	CUNILA MARIANA,	*Common Dittany*(3). - - -	Cabinet.
770	HEDEOMA PULEGIOIDES,	*Pennyroyal*(3). - - - - -	Cabinet.
771	MICROMERIA GLABELLA,	*Niagara Thyme*(5). - - -	Cabinet.
772	MELISSA CLINOPODIUM,	*Wild Basil*(3). - - - - -	Cabinet.
773	MELISSA OFFICINALIS,	*Common Balm*(1). - - - -	Cabinet.
774	PRUNELLA VULGARIS,	*Common Selfheal*, or *Healall*(3).	Cabinet.
775	SCUTELLARIA PILOSA,	*Hairy Scullcap*(2). - - -	Cabinet.
776	SCUTELLARIA INTEGRIFOLIA,	*Entire-leaved Scullcap*(2). -	Cabinet.
777	SCUTELLARIA PARVULA,	*Small Scullcap*(4). - - -	Cabinet.
778	SCUTELLARIA NERVOSA,	*Nerved Scullcap.*	
779	SCUTELLARIA GALERICULATA,	*Common Scullcap*(2). - -	Cabinet.
780	SCUTELLARIA LATERIFLORA,	*Mad-dog Scullcap*(1). - - -	Cabinet.
781	LOPHANTHUS NEPETOIDES,	*Yellow Giant-hyssop*(1). - -	Cabinet.
782	LOPHANTHUS SCROPHULARIÆFOLIUS,	*Purple Giant-hyssop*(2).	Cabinet.
783	NEPETA CATARIA,	*Common Catnep*(2). - - -	Cabinet.
784	NEPETA GLECHOMA,	*Groundivy*, or *Gill*(2). - -	Cabinet.
785	DRACOCEPHALUM PARVIFLORUM,	*Small-flowered Dragonshead*(2).	Cab.
786	PHYSOSTEGIA VIRGINIANA,	*Virginian Dragonshead*(3). -	Cabinet.
787	LAMIUM AMPLEXICAULE,	*Common Deadnettle*, or *Henbit*(2).	Cabinet.
788	LEONURA CARDIACA,	*Common Motherwort*(2). - -	Cabinet.
789	MARRUBIUM VULGARE,	*Common Horehound*(2). - -	Cabinet.

	Latin Names.	English Names.	
790	Galeopsis tetrahit,	*Common Hempnettle*(2). - -	Cabinet.
791	Stachys aspera,	*Rough Hedgenettle*(1). - -	Cabinet.
792	Stachys palustris,	*Marsh Hedgenettle*(1). - -	Cabinet.
793	Stachys hyssopifolia,	*Narrow-leaved Hedgenettle*(2).	Cabinet.
794	Trichostema dichotoma,	*Bluecurls*, or *False Pennyroyal*(2).	Cabinet.
795	Teucrium canadense,	*Woodsage*, or *Germander*(2).	Cabinet.

Vol. 25.] ORDER LXXII. BORAGINACEÆ.

796	Onosmodium hispidum,	*False Gromwell*(2). - - -	Cabinet.
797	Echium vulgare,	*Viper's Bugloss*(2). - - -	Cabinet.
798	Pulmonaria virginica,	*Virginian Lungwort*(2). - -	Cabinet.
799	Lithospermum arvense,	*Corn Gromwell*, or *Stoneweed*(2).	Cabinet.
800	Lithospermum officinale,	*Common Gromwell.*	
801	Batschia canescens,	*Common Puccoon*(2(. - - -	Cabinet.
802	Lycopsis arvensis,	*Small Bugloss*(1). - - - -	Cabinet.
803	Myosotis palustris,	*American Forget-me-not*(5). -	Cabinet.
804	Myosotis arvensis,	*Field Scorpion-grass*(5). - -	Cabinet.
805	Symphitum officinale,	*Common Comfrey*(1). - - -	Cabinet.
806	Cynoglossum officinale,	*Common Houndstongue*(2). -	Cabinet.
807	Cynoglossum virginicum,	*Wild Comfrey*(2). - - - -	Cabinet.
808	Echinospermum lappula,	*Narrow-leaved Stickseed*(2). -	Cabinet.
809	Echinospermum virginicum,	*Broad-leaved Stickseed*(2). -	Cabinet.

ORDER LXXIII. HYDROPHYLLACEÆ.

810	Hydrophyllum virginicum,	*Virginian Waterleaf*(3). -	Cabinet.
811	Hydrophyllum canadense,	*Canadian Waterleaf*(2). -	Cabinet.
812	Hydrophyllum appendiculatum,	*Hairy Waterleaf*(1). -	Cabinet.

ORDER LXXIV. POLEMONIACEÆ.

813	Phlox divaricata,	*Divaricate Phlox*(1). - - -	Cabinet.
814	Phlox subulata,	*Mountain Pink*(1). - - -	Cabinet.
815	Polemonium reptans,	*Jacob's-ladder*(1). - - - -	Cabinet.

ORDER LXXV. DIAPENSIACEÆ.

816	Diapensia lapponica,	*Lapland Diapensia*(7). - -	Cabinet.

Vol. 26.] ORDER LXXVI. CONVOLVULACEÆ.

	Latin Names.	English Names.	
817	Convolvulus arvensis,	*Common Bindweed*(2). - -	Cabinet.
818	Convolvulus panduratus,	*Man-of-the-earth*(4). - - -	Cabinet.
819	Calystegia sepium,	*Great Bindweed*(6). - - -	Cabinet.
820	Calystegia spithamæa,	*Upright Bindweed*(3). - -	Cabinet.
821	Cuscuta gronovii,	*Common Dodder*(4). - - -	Cabinet.
822	Cuscuta umbrosa,	*Smooth-flowered Dodder.*	
823	Cuscuta epilinum,	*Flax Dodder*(1). - - - -	Cabinet.

ORDER LXXVII. SOLANACEÆ.

824	Nicotiana rustica,	*Wild Tobacco*(2). - - - -	Cabinet.
825	Datura stramonium,	*Jamestown-weed*, or *Stinkweed*(1).	Cabinet.
826	Hyoscyamus niger,	*Common Henbane*(2). - - -	Cabinet.
827	Nicandra physaloides,	*Apple-of-Peru*(2). - - - -	Cabinet.
828	Physalis viscosa,	*Groundcherry*(3). - - - -	Cabinet.
829	Solanum dulcamara,	*Bittersweet*(2). - - - - -	Cabinet.
830	Solanum nigrum,	*Common Nightshade*)2). - -	Cabinet.
831	Solanum carolinianum,	*Horsenettle.*	

ORDER LXXVIII. GENTIANACEÆ.

832	Gentiana saponaria,	*Soap Gentian*(2). - - - -	Cabinet.
833	Gentiana andrewsii,	*Andrews's Gentian*(7). - -	Cabinet.
834	Gentiana ochroleuca,	*Ochroleucous Gentian.*	
835	Gentiana quinqueflora,	*Five-flowered Gentian*(1). -	Cabinet.
836	Gentiana detonsa,	*Smaller-fringed Gentian*(2).	Cabinet.
837	Gentiana crinita,	*Large-fringed Gentian*(3). -	Cabinet.
838	Frasera carolinensis,	*American Columbo*(3). - -	Cabinet.
839	Halenia deflexa,	*Deflexed Halenia*(1). - - -	Cabinet.
840	Erythræa centaurium,	*Common Centaury*(1). - - -	Cabinet.
841	Erythræa muhlenbergii,	*Muhlenberg's Centaury*(1). -	Cabinet.
842	Bartonia tenella,	*Late-flowered Bartonia*(5). -	Cabinet.
843	Sabbatia stellaris,	*Saltmarsh Centaury*(7). - -	Cabinet.
844	Sabbatia angularis,	*American Centaury*(3). - -	Cabinet.

	Latin Names.	English Names.	
845	Sabbatia chloroides,	*Large-flowered Sabbatia*(5). -	Cabinet.
846	Menyanthes trifoliata,	*Buckbean*(2). - - - - - -	Cabinet.
847	Limnanthemum lacunosum,	*Floatingheart*(2). - - -	Cabinet.

Vol. 27.] ORDER LXXIX. APOCYNACEÆ.

848	Apocynum androsæmifolium,	*Dogsbane*(5). - - - -	Cabinet.
849	Apocynum cannabinum,	*Indian Hemp*(2). - - - -	Cabinet.

ORDER LXXX. ASCLEPIADACEÆ

850	Asclepias cornuti,	*Silkweed*, or *Milkweed*(2). -	Cabinet.
851	Asclepias purpurascens,	*Purple Silkweed*(5). - - -	Cabinet.
852	Asclepias phytolaccoides,	*Poke-leaved Milkweed*(3). -	Cabinet.
853	Asclepias obtusifolia,	*Waved-leaved Milkweed*(2). -	Cabinet.
854	Asclepias variegata,	*Variegated Silkweed*(2). - -	Cabinet.
855	Asclepias quadrifolia,	*Four-leaved Silkweed*(2). -	Cabinet.
856	Asclepias incarnata,	*Swamp Silkweed*(2). - - -	Cabinet.
857	Asclepias tuberosa,	*Pleurisy-root*, or *Butterfly-weed*(2).	Cabinet.
858	Asclepias verticillata,	*Whorled Silkweed*(3). - - -	Cabinet.
859	Acerates viridiflora,	*Green-flowered Silkweed*(3). -	Cabinet.

ORDER LXXXI. OLEACEÆ.

860	Fraxinus americana,	*White Ash*(5). - - - - - -	Cabinet.
861	Fraxinus sambucifolia,	*Black Ash*, or *Water Ash*(1).	Cabinet.
862	Fraxinus pubescens,	*Gray Ash*(1). - - - - - -	Cabinet.
863	Ligustrum vulgare,	*Common Privet*(2). - - -	Cabinet.

Vol. 28.] ORDER LXXXII. ARISTOLOCHIACEÆ.

864	Aristolochia serpentaria,	*Virginia Snakeroot*(2). - -	Cabinet.
865	Asarum canadense,	*Wild Ginger*, or *Coltsfoot*(2).	Cabinet.

ORDER LXXXIII. CHENOPODIACEÆ.

866	Chenopodium album,	*Goosefoot*, or *Lamb's-quarters*(2).	Cabinet.
867	Chenopodium hybridum,	*Maple-leaved Goosefoot*(3). -	Cabinet.
868	Ambrina botrys,	*Jerusalem-oak*(2). - - - -	Cabinet.
869	Ambrina anthelmintica,	*Wormseed*(1). - - - - - -	Cabinet.

	Latin Names.	English Names.	
870	AMBRINA AMBROSIOIDES,	*Mexican Tea*(1). - - - -	Cabinet.
871	BLITUM MARITIMUM,	*Saltmarsh Blite.*	
872	BLITUM CAPITATUM,	*Strawberry Blite*(1). - - -	Cabinet.
873	BLITUM BONUS-HENRICUS,	*Good-King-Henry*(2). - - -	Cabinet.
874	ATRIPLEX PATULA,	*Halbert-leaved Orach*(3). - -	Cabinet.
875	OBIONE ARENARIA,	*Seabeach Orach*(1). - - -	Cabinet.
876	ACNIDA CANNABINA,	*Common Waterhemp*(1). - -	Cabinet.
877	ACNIDA RUSOCARPA,	*Rough-fruited Waterhemp*(1).	Cabinet.
878	SALICORNIA HERBACEA,	*Common Saltwort*, or *Samphire*(2).	Cabinet.
879	SALICORNIA MUCRONATA,	*Dwarf Saltwort*(6). - - -	Cabinet.
880	SALICORNIA AMBIGUA,	*Perennial Saltwort*(1). - -	Cabinet.
881	SUEDA MARITIMA,	*Smooth Glasswort*(1). - - -	Cabinet.
882	SALSOLA KALI,	*Common Glasswort*(1). - -	Cabinet.

ORDER LXXXIV. AMARANTHACEÆ.

883	AMARANTHUS HYBRIDUS,	*Hybrid Amaranth*(1). - -	Cabinet.
884	AMARANTHUS GRÆCIZANS,	*Bushy Amaranth*(1). - - -	Cabinet.
885	AMARANTHUS PUMILUS,	*Dwarf Amaranth*(1). - - -	Cabinet.
886	AMARANTHUS DEFLEXUS,	*Prostrate Amaranth*(1). - -	Cabinet.

Vol. 29.]

ORDER LXXXV. POLYGONACEÆ.

887	POLYGONUM ORIENTALE,	*Princesfeather*(1). - - - -	Cabinet.
888	POLYGONUM FAGOPYRUM,	*Buckwheat*(2). - - - - -	Cabinet.
889	POLYGONUM CONVOLVULUS,	*Black Bindweed*(1). - - -	Cabinet.
890	POLYGONUM CILINODE,	*Fringe-jointed Polygonum*(1).	Cabinet.
891	POLYGONUM DUMETORUM,	*Climbing Buckwheat*(1). - -	Cabinet.
892	POLYGONUM SAGITTATUM,	*Arrow-leaved Tearthumb*(2).	Cabinet.
893	POLYGONUM ARIFOLIUM,	*Halbert-leaved Tearthumb*(2).	Cabinet.
894	POLYGONUM AMPHIBIUM,	*Water Persicaria*(2). - - -	Cabinet.
895	POLYGONUM PERSICARIA,	*Ladysthumb*(3). - - - -	Cabinet.
896	POLYGONUM PENNSYLVANICUM,	*Hairy-stalked Persicaria*(2).	Cabinet.
897	POLYGONUM MITE,	*Bearded Persicaria*(3). - -	Cabinet.
898	POLYGONUM HYDROPIPER,	*Water Pepper*, or *Smartweed*(3).	Cabinet.
899	POLYGONUM VIRGINIANUM,	*Virgate Persicaria*(1). - -	Cabinet.

	Latin Names.	English Names.	
900	POLYGONUM AVICULARE,	*Knotgrass*, or *Doorweed*(3). -	Cabinet.
901	POLYGONUM MARITIMUM,	*Seaside Knotgrass*(2). - - -	Cabinet.
902	POLYGONUM TENUE,	*Slender Knotgrass*(4). - -	Cabinet.
903	POLYGONUM ARTICULATUM,	*Jointweed*(5). - - - - - -	Cabinet.
904	RUMEX CRISPUS,	*Curled Dock*(1). - - - -	Cabinet.
905	RUMEX OBTUSIFOLIUS,	*Broad-leaved Dock*(2). - -	Cabinet.
906	RUMEX VERTICILLATUS,	*Long-stalked Waterdock*(1). -	Cabinet.
907	RUMEX BRITANNICA,	*Yellow-rooted Waterdock*(2).	Cabinet.
908	RUMEX ACETOSELLA,	*Sheepsorrel*(3). - - - - - -	Cabinet.

ORDER LXXXVI. PHYTOLACCACEÆ.

909	PHYTOLACCA DECANDRA,	*Common Pokeweed*(3). - -	Cabinet.

ORDER LXXXVII. LAURACEÆ.

910	SASSAFRAS OFFICINALE,	*Sassafras*(4). - - - - - -	Cabinet.
911	BENZOIN ODORIFERUM,	*Wild Alspice*, or *Spicebush*(4).	Cabinet.

ORDER LXXXVIII. SANTALACEÆ.

912	COMANDRA UMBELLATA,	*Bastard Toadflax*(3). - - -	Cabinet.
913	NYSSA MULTIFLORA,	*Blackgum*(6). - - - - - -	Cabinet.

ORDER LXXXIX. THYMELACEÆ.

914	DIRCA PALUSTRIS,	*Leatherwood*(4). - - - -	Cabinet.

ORDER XC. ELEAGNACEÆ.

915	SHEPHERDIA CANADENSIS,	*Canadian Shepherdia*(2). -	Cabinet.

ORDER XCI. ULMACEÆ.

916	ULMUS AMERICANA,	*American* or *White Elm*(4). -	Cabinet.
917	ULMUS FULVA,	*Slippery* or *Red Elm*(4). - -	Cabinet.
918	ULMUS RACEMOSA,	*Thomas's Elm*(3). - - - -	Cabinet.
919	CELTIS OCCIDENTALIS,	*Nettletree*, or *Sugarberry*(3).	Cabinet.

Vol. 30.] ORDER XCII. SAURURACEÆ.

920	SAURURUS CERNUUS,	*Lizardstail*(1). - - - - -	Cabinet.

ORDER XCIII. CERATOPHYLLACEÆ.

921	CERATOPHYLLUM ECHINATUM,	*Rough-fruited Hornwort*(3).	Cabinet.

ORDER XCIV. CALLITRICHACEÆ.

Latin Names. English Names.

922 Callitriche verna, *Common Water Chickweed*(7). Cabinet.

ORDER XCV. PODOSTEMACEÆ.

923 Podostemum ceratophyllum, *Riverweed*(6). - - - - Cabinet.

ORDER XCVI. EUPHORBIACEÆ.

924 Acalypha virginica, *Common Three-seeded Mercury*(5). Cabinet.

925 Euphorbia helioscopia, *Waterwort Spurge*(3). - - Cabinet.

926 Euphorbia platyphylla, *Broad-leaved Spurge*.

927 Euphorbia corollata, *Flowering Spurge*(2). - - Cabinet.

928 Euphorbia hypericifolia, *Upright Spotted Spurge*(3). Cabinet.

929 Euphorbia maculata, *Small Spurge*(2). - - - - Cabinet.

930 Euphorbia ipecacuanha, *Wild Ipecac*(2). - - - - Cabinet.

931 Euphorbia polygonifolia, *Seaside Spurge*(2). - - - Cabinet.

ORDER XCVII. EMPETRACEÆ.

932 Empetrum nigrum, *Common Crowberry*(2). - - Cabinet.

ORDER XCVIII. JUGLANDACEÆ.

933 Juglans nigra, *Black Walnut*(1). - - - - Cabinet.

934 Juglans cinerea, *Butternut*(1). - - - - - Cabinet.

935 Carya alba, *Shellbark Hickory*.

936 Carya tomentosa, *White-heart Hickory*(2). - - Cabinet.

937 Carya glabra, *Broom Hickory*, or *Pignut*(2). Cabinet.

938 Carya amara, *Swamp Hickory*, or *Bitternut*(1). Cabinet.

Vol. 31.]

ORDER XCIX. CUPULIFERÆ.

939 Ostrya virginica, *Hop Hornbeam*, or *Ironwood*(5). Cabinet.

940 Carpinus americana, *Water Beech*, or *Hornbeam*(3). Cabinet.

941 Corylus americana, *American Hazlenut*(2). - - Cabinet.

942 Corylus rostrata, *Beaked Hazlenut*(1). - - - Cabinet.

943 Quercus phellos, *Peach-leaved* or *Willow Oak*(2). Cabinet.

944 Quercus nigra, *Black-jack Oak*(5). - - - Cabinet.

945 Quercus tinctoria, *Black Oak*, or *Quercitron*(1). Cabinet.

	Latin Names.	English Names.	
946	QUERCUS COCCINEA,	*Scarlet Oak*(4). - - - -	Cabinet.
947	QUERCUS RUBRA,	*Red Oak*(2). - - - - - -	Cabinet.
948	QUERCUS PALUSTRIS,	*Pin Oak*, or *Water Spanish Oak*(2).	Cabinet.
949	QUERCUS ILICIFOLIA,	*Barren Scrub Oak*(3). - -	Cabinet.
950	QUERCUS OBTUSILOBA,	*Post Oak*, or *Box White Oak*(3).	Cabinet.
951	QUERCUS MACROCARPA,	*Overcup White Oak*(3). - -	Cabinet.
952	QUERCUS OLIVÆFORMIS,	*Mossycup Oak.*	
953	QUERCUS ALBA,	*White Oak*(2). - - - - -	Cabinet.
954	QUERCUS BICOLOR,	*Swamp White Oak*(1). - -	Cabinet.
955	QUERCUS MONTANA,	*Rock Chesnut Oak*(1). - -	Cabinet.
956	QUERCUS CASTANEA,	*Yellow* or *Chesnut Oak*(1). -	Cabinet.
957	QUERCUS PRINOIDES,	*Chinquapin Oak*(2). - - -	Cabinet.
958	FAGUS FERRUGINEA,	*Beech*(5). - - - - - -	Cabinet.
959	CASTANEA VESCA,	*American Chestnut*(1). - -	Cabinet.
960	CASTANEA PUMILA,	*Chinquapin.*	

ORDER C. MYRICACEÆ.

961	MYRICA GALE,	*Dutch Myrtle*, or *Sweet Gale*(3)	Cabinet.
962	MYRICA CERIFERA,	*Wax Myrtle*, or *Bayberry*(6).	Cabinet.
963	COMPTONIA ASPLENIFOLIA,	*Sweet Fern*(4). - - - - -	Cabinet.

ORDER CI. BETULACEÆ.

964	BETULA POPULIFOLIA,	*White Birch*(2). - - - -	Cabinet.
965	BETULA PAPYRACEA,	*Paper* or *Canoe Birch.*	
966	BETULA LENTA,	*Black* or *Sweet Birch*(3). -	Cabinet.
967	BETULA EXCELSA,	*Yellow Birch*(2). - - - -	Cabinet.
968	BETULA NIGRA,	*Red Birch*(1). - - - - -	Cabinet.
969	BETULA NANA,	*Dwarf Birch*(1). - - - -	Cabinet.
970	ALNUS SERRULATA,	*Common Alder*(2). - - - -	Cabinet.
971	ALNUS INCANA,	*Black Alder*(1). - - - -	Cabinet.
972	ALNUS VIRIDIS,	*Mountain Alder*(2). - - -	Cabinet.

ORDER CII. SALICACEÆ.

973	SALIX CANDIDA,	*White-leaved Willow*(8). - -	Cabinet.

	Latin Names.	English Names.	
974	Salix muhlenbergiana,	*Muhlenberg's Willow*(5). -	Cabinet.
975	Salix tristis,	*Dwarf Downy Willow*(4). -	Cabinet.
976	Salix discolor,	*Glaucous Willow*(13). - -	Cabinet.
977	Salix petiolaris,	*Dark Long-leaved Willow*(7).	Cabinet.
978	Salix myricoides,	*Gale-leaved Willow.*	
979	Salix viminalis,	*Basket Osier*(2). - - - -	Cabinet.
980	Salix lucida,	*Glossy Broad-leaved Willow*(9).	Cabinet.
981	Salix nigra,	*Black Willow*(9). - - - -	Cabinet.

Vol. 33.]

982	Salix longifolia,	*Long-leaved Sand Willow*(1).	Cabinet.
983	Salix vitellina,	*Yellow Willow*(1). - - - -	Cabinet.
984	Salix rostrata,	*Ochre-flowered Willow*(17).	Cabinet.
985	Salix cordata,	*Heart-leaved Willow*(9). - -	Cabinet.
986	Salix rigida,	*Rigid Heart-leaved Willow*(4).	Cabinet.
987	Salix pedicellaris,	*Long-stalked Willow*(2). - -	Cabinet.
988	Salix cutleri,	*Cutler's Willow*, or *Bearberry*(3).	Cabinet.
989	Populus tremuloides,	*American Aspen*(2). - - -	Cabinet.
990	Populus grandidentata,	*Large Aspen*(4). - - - -	Cabinet.
991	Populus monilifera,	*Virginian Poplar*(8). - - -	Cabinet.
992	Populus heterophylla,	*Cotton-tree*(2). - - - - -	Cabinet.
993	Populus nigra,	*Birch-leaved Poplar.*	
994	Populus balsamifera,	*Balsam Poplar*, or *Tacamahac*(1).	Cabinet.
995	Populus candicans,	*Balm-of-Gilead Poplar*(2). -	Cabinet.

Vol. 34.] ORDER CIII. BALSAMIFLUÆ.

996	Liquidambar styraciflua,	*Common Sweetgum*(3). - -	Cabinet.

ORDER CIV. PLATANACEÆ.

997	Platanus occidentalis,	*Buttonwood*, or *Sycamore*(2).	Cabinet.

ORDER CV. URTICACEÆ.

998	Morus rubra,	*Red Mulberry*(1). - - - -	Cabinet.
999	Morus alba,	*White Mulberry*(2). - - -	Cabinet.
1000	Urtica dioica,	*Common Stinging Nettle.*	

	Latin Names.	English Names.	
1001	Urtica urens,	*Small Stinging Nettle*(2). -	Cabinet.
1002	Urtica canadensis,	*Canadian Nettle*(2). - - -	Cabinet.
1003	Adike pumila,	*Richweed*, or *Clearweed*(8). -	Cabinet.
1004	Bœhmeria cylindrica,	*False Nettle*(2). - - - -	Cabinet.
1005	Parietaria pennsylvanicum,	*Pennsylvanian Pellitory*(4).	Cabinet.
1006	Cannabis sativa,	*Common Hemp*(2). - - - -	Cabinet.
1007	Humulus lupulus,	*Hop*(1). - - - - - - - -	Cabinet.

CLASS II. GYMNOSPERMOUS PLANTS.

Vol. 35.] ORDER CV. CONIFERÆ.

1008	Pinus resinosa,	*Red Pine.*	
1009	Pinus rigida,	*Pitch Pine*(2). - - - - -	Cabinet.
1010	Pinus strobus,	*White Pine*(1). - - - - -	Cabinet.
1011	Pinus mitis,	*Yellow Pine.*	
1012	Pinus balsamea,	*Balsam Fir*, or *Balm-of-Gilead Fir.*	
1013	Pinus canadensis,	*Hemlock Spruce*(2). - - -	Cabinet.
1014	Pinus nigra,	*Black* or *Double Spruce.*	
1015	Pinus alba,	*White* or *Single Spruce.*	
1016	Pinus pendula,	*American Larch*, or *Tamarack*(2).	Cabinet.
1017	Cupressus thuyoides,	*White Cedar*(3). - - - -	Cabinet.
1018	Thuya occidentalis,	*Common Arbor-vitæ*(3). - -	Cabinet.
1019	Juniperus communis,	*Common Juniper*(3). - - -	Cabinet.
1020	Juniperus virginiana,	*Red Cedar*(4). - - - - -	Cabinet.
1021	Taxus canadensis,	*American Yew*(1). - - - -	Cabinet.

CLASS III. ENDOGENOUS PLANTS.

Vol. 36.] ORDER CVI. ARACEÆ.

1022	Arisæma triphylla,	*Indian Turnip*(2). - - - -	Cabinet.
1023	Arisæma dracontium,	*Greendragon*(1). - - - -	Cabinet.
1024	Peltandra virginica,	*Arrow-leaved Arum*(2). - -	Cabinet.
1025	Calla palustris,	*Water Arum*(1). - - - -	Cabinet.

	Latin Names.	English Names.	
1026	Symplocarpus fœtidus,	*Common Skunk-cabbage*(4). -	Cabinet.
1027	Orontium aquaticum,	*Goldenclub*(4). - - - - -	Cabinet.
1028	Acorus calamus,	*Common Calamus*, or *Sweetflag*(2).	Cabinet.

ORDER CVII. LEMNACEÆ.

1029	Lemna minor,	*Lesser Duckweed*(3). - - -	Cabinet.
1030	Lemna perpusilla,	*Smallest Duckweed*(1). - -	Cabinet.
1031	Lemna trisulca,	*Star Duckweed*(2). - - -	Cabinet.
1032	Lemna gibba,	*Gibbous Duckweed.*	
1033	Lemna polyrrhiza,	*Greater Duckweed*(2). - -	Cabinet.

ORDER CVIII. TYPHACEÆ.

1034	Typha latifolia,	*Broad-leaved Cattail*(2). - -	Cabinet.
1035	Typha angustifolia,	*Narrow-leaved Cattail*(1). -	Cabinet.
1036	Sparganium ramosum,	*Branching Bur-reed*(2). - -	Cabinet.
1037	Sparganium simplex,	*Smaller Bur-reed*(4). - - -	Cabinet.

ORDER CIX. NAJADACEÆ.

1038	Najas canadensis,	*Canadian Waternymph*(3). -	Cabinet.
1039	Zostera marina,	*Common Grasswrack*(2). - -	Cabinet.
1040	Ruppia maritima,	*Ditchgrass*(1). - - - - -	Cabinet.
1041	Zannichellia palustris,	*Horned Pondweed*(2). - - -	Cabinet.
1042	Potamogeton natans,	*Broad-leaved Floating Pondweed*(5).	Cab.
1043	Potamogeton heterophyllus,	*Various-leaved Pondweed*(1).	Cab.
1044	Potamogeton hybridus,	*Small Floating Pondweed*(3).	Cabinet.
1045	Potamogeton lucens,	*Shining Pondweed*(3). - -	Cabinet.
1046	Potamogeton perfoliatus,	*Perfoliate Pondweed*(1). -	Cabinet.
1047	Potamogeton zosterifolius,	*Grass-leaved Pondweed*(6).	Cabinet.
1048	Potamogeton pusillus,	*Small Pondweed*(3). - - -	Cabinet.
1049	Potamogeton pauciflorus,	*Few-flowered Pondweed*(4).	Cabinet.
1050	Potamogeton pectinatus,	*Fennel-leaved Pondweed*(1). -	Cabinet.

ORDER CX. ALISMACEÆ.

1051	Alisma plantago,	*Common Water Plantain*(2).	Cabinet.
1052	Sagittaria sagittifolia,	*Common Arrowhead*(14). - -	Cabinet.

	Latin Names.	English Names.	
1053	Sagittaria pusilla,	*Least Arrowhead.*	
1054	Triglochin palustre,	*Marsh Arrowgrass*(3). - -	Cabinet.
1055	Triglochin maritimum,	*Seaside Arrowgrass*(4). - -	Cabinet.
1056	Triglochin elatum,	*Tall Arrowgrass*(1). - - -	Cabinet.
1057	Scheuchzeria palustris,	*Marsh Scheuchzeria*(3). - -	Cabinet.

ORDER CXI. HYDROCHARIDACEÆ.

1058	Hydrocharis cordifolia,	*Heart-leaved Frogsbit.*	
1059	Udora canadensis,	*Little Watersnakeweed*(4). -	Cabinet.
1060	Valisneria spiralis,	*Tapegrass*, or *Eelgrass.*	

Vol. 37.] ORDER CXII. ORCHIDACEÆ.

1061	Microstylis monophyllos,	*Short-stalked Addersmouth*(2).	Cabinet.
1062	Microstylis ophioglossoides,	*Long-stalked Addersmouth*(2).	Cab.
1063	Corallorrhiza innata,	*Vernal Coralroot*(3). - - -	Cabinet.
1064	Corallorrhiza odontorrhiza,	*Small Late Coralroot*(4).	Cabinet.
1065	Corallorrhiza multiflora,	*Large Coralroot*(5). - -	Cabinet.
1066	Aplectrum hyemale,	*Puttyroot*, or *Adam-and-Eve*(2).	Cabinet.
1067	Liparis liliifolia,	*Common Twayblade*(2). - -	Cabinet.
1068	Liparis lœselii,	*Smaller Twayblade*(2). - -	Cabinet.
1069	Tipularia discolor,	*Cranefly Orchis*(2). - - -	Cabinet.
1070	Orchis spectabilis,	*Showy Orchis*(2). - - - -	Cabinet.
1071	Gymnadenia tridentata,	*Three-toothed Gymnadenia*(2).	Cabinet.
1072	Platanthera obtusata,	*Obtuse-leaved Platanthera*(1).	Cabinet.
1073	Platanthera orbiculata,	*Large-leaved Orchis*(1). - -	Cabinet.
1074	Platanthera hookeri,	*Hooker's Orchis*(1). - - -	Cabinet.
1075	Platanthera flava,	*Small Pale-yellow Orchis*(4).	Cabinet.
1076	Platanthera hyperborea,	*Northern Orchis*(1). - -	Cabinet.
1077	Platanthera dilatata,	*Small White-flowered Orchis*(4).	Cabinet.
1078	Platanthera blephariglottis,	*Fringed White Orchis*(3).	Cabinet.
1079	Platanthera ciliaris,	*Fringed Yellow Orchis*(2). -	Cabinet.
1080	Platanthera psycodes,	*Purple Swamp Orchis*(4). -	Cabinet.
1081	Platanthera lacera,	*Ragged Orchis*(2). - - - -	Cabinet.

Latin Names. English Names.

1082 PLATANTHERA BRACTEATA, *Green-flowered Orchis.*

1083 ARETHUSA BULBOSA, *Arethusa*(3). - - - - - - Cabinet.

1084 POGONIA OPHIOGLOSSOIDES, *Single leaved Pogonia*(4). - Cabinet.

1085 POGONIA VERTICILLATA, *Verticillate Pogonia*(2). - - Cabinet.

1086 POGONIA PENDULA, *Nodding Pogonia*(3). - - - Cabinet.

1087 CALOPOGON PULCHELLUS, *Calapogon*(4). - - - - - - Cabinet.

1088 SPIRANTHES GRACILIS, *Slender Lady's-tresses*(7). - Cabinet.

1089 SPIRANTHES CERNUA, *Nodding Lady's-tresses*(4). - Cabihet.

1090 SPIRANTHES PLANTAGINEA, *Common Lady's-tresses*(4). - Cabinet.

1091 GOODYERA PUBESCENS, *Larger Rattlesnake Plantain*(3). Cabinet.

1092 GOODYERA REPENS, *Smaller Rattlesnake Plantain*(3). Cabinet.

1093 LISTERA CORDATA, *Heart-leaved Twayblade*(4). - Cabinet.

1094 CYPRIPEDIUM PUBESCENS, *Large Yellow Ladyslipper*(1). Cabinet.

1095 CYPRIPEDIUM PARVIFLORUM, *Smaller Yellow Ladyslipper*(1). Cabinet.

1096 CYPRIPEDIUM SPECTABILE, *Showy Ladyslipper*(2). - - Cabinet.

1097 CYPRIPEDIUM ACAULE, *Purple Ladyslipper*, or *Noah's-ark*(2). Cab.

1098 CYPRIPEDIUM ARIETINUM, *Ramshead*(1). - - - - - - Cabinet.

Vol. 38.]

ORDER CXIII. HYPOXIDACEÆ.

1099 HYPOXIS ERECTA, *Common Stargrass*(3). - - Cabinet.

ORDER CXIV. IRIDACEÆ.

1100 IRIS VERSICOLOR, *Blue Flag*(2). - - - - - - Cabinet.

1101 IRIS VIRGINICA, *Slender Blue-flag*(3). - - - Cabinet.

1102 SISYRINCHIUM BERMUDIANA, *Common Blueyed-grass*(3). - Cabinet.

ORDER CXV. DIOSCOREACEÆ.

1103 DIOSCOREA VILLOSA, *Wild Yamroot*(4). - - - - Cabinet.

ORDER CXVI. SMILACEÆ.

1104 MEDEOLA VIRGINICA, *Cucumber-root*(3). - - - - Cabinet.

1105 TRILLIUM ERYTHROCARPUM, *Red-berried 3-leaved Nightshade*(2). Cab.

1106 TRILLIUM CERNUUM, *Nodding 3-leaved Nightshade*(1). Cabinet.

1107 TRILLIUM ERECTUM, *False Wakerobin*(5). - - - Cabinet.

1108 TRILLIUM GRANDIFLORUM, *Large-flowered Trillium*(2). - Cabinet.

	Latin Names.	English Names.	
1109	SMILACINA STELLATA,	*Star-flowered Solomon's-seal*(2).	Cabinet.
1110	SMILACINA TRIFOLIA,	*Three-leaved Smilacina*(4). -	Cabinet.
1111	SMILACINA RACEMOSA,	*Wild Spikenard*(1). - - -	Cabinet.
1112	SMILACINA BIFOLIA,	*Two-leaved Solomon's-seal*(7).	Cabinet.
1113	POLYGONATUM MULTIFLORUM,	*Common Solomon's-seal*(4).	Cabinet.
1114	CLINTONIA BOREALIS,	*Large-flowered Clintonia*(3).	Cabinet.
1115	CLINTONIA UMBELLATA,	*Small-flowered Clintonia.*	
1116	SMILAX ROTUNDIFOLIA,	*Common Greenbrier*(5). - -	Cabinet.
1117	SMILAX HISPIDA,	*Hispid Greenbrier.*	
1118	SMILAX SPINULOSA,	*Spinulose Greenbrier*(2). - -	Cabinet.
1119	SMILAX HERBACEA,	*Carrionflower*(1). - - - -	Cabinet.

ORDER CXVII. LILIACEÆ.

1120	LILIUM PHILADELPHICUM,	*Red Lily*(4). - - - - -	Cabinet.
1121	LILIUM CANADENSE,	*Wild Yellow Lily*(2). - - -	Cabinet.
1122	LILIUM SUPERBUM,	*Superb Lily*, or *Turk's-cap*(2).	Cabinet.
1123	ERYTHRONIUM AMERICANUM,	*American Dogstooth Violet*(3).	Cabinet.
1124	ERYTHRONIUM ALBIDUM,	*White Dogstooth Violet*(2). -	Cabinet.
1125	ORNITHOGALUM UMBELLATUM,	*Common Star-of-Bethlehem*(3).	Cab.
1126	ALLIUM CANADENSE,	*Meadow Garlic.*	
1127	ALLIUM VINEALE,	*Wild Garlic*(1). - - - -	Cabinet.
1128	ALLIUM TRICOCCUM,	*Wild Leek*(1). - - - - -	Cabinet.
1129	ALLIUM CERNUUM,	*Wild Onion*(2). - - - -	Cabinet.
1130	ASPARAGUS OFFICINALIS,	*Common Asparagus*(2). - -	Cabinet.
1131	ALETRIS FARINOSA,	*Colicroot*(1). - - - - - -	Cabinet.

Vol. 39.]

ORDER CXVIII. PONTEDERIACEÆ.

1132	PONTEDERIA CORDATA,	*Common Pickerelweed*(2). -	Cabinet.
1133	HETERANTHERA RENIFORMIS,	*Mud Plantain*(2). - - -	Cabinet.
1134	HETERANTHERA GRAMINEA,	*Water Stargrass*(2). - -	Cabinet.

ORDER CXIX. MELANTHACEÆ.

1135	ZYGADENUS GLAUCUS,	*Glaucous-leaved Zygadenus*(2).	Cabinet.
1136	MELANTHIUM VIRGINICUM,	*Virginian Melanthium*(2). -	Cabinet.

	Latin Names.	English Names.	
1137	Veratrum viride,	*White Hellebore*, or *Indian Poke*(2).	Cabinet.
1138	Helonias dioica,	*Devilsbit*, or *Unicorn-plant*(2).	Cabinet.
1139	Uvularia perfoliata,	*Perfoliate Bellwort*(4). - -	Cabinet.
1140	Uvularia grandiflora,	*Large-flowered Bellwort*(1). -	Cabinet.
1141	Uvularia sessilifolia,	*Sessile-leaved Bellwort*(2). -	Cabinet.
1142	Prosartes lanuginosa,	*Pale-flowered Prosartes*(2). -	Cabinet.
1143	Streptopus amplexifolius,	*Smooth Twistedstalk*(1). -	Cabinet.
1144	Streptopus roseus,	*Rose Twistedstalk*(1). - - -	Cabinet.

ORDER CXX. JUNCACEÆ.

1145	Luzula campestris,	*Common Woodrush*(4). - -	Cabinet.
1146	Luzula pilosa,	*Broad-leaved Hairy Woodrush*(4).	Cabinet.
1147	Luzula parviflora,	*Small-flowered Woodrush*(2).	Cabinet.
1148	Juncus effusus,	*Soft Rush*(2). - - - - - -	Cabinet.
1149	Juncus filiformis,	*Slender Rush*(4). - - - -	Cabinet.
1150	Juncus balticus,	*Baltic Rush*(4). - - - -	Cabinet.
1151	Juncus nodosus,	*Smaller Roundheaded Rush*(9).	Cabinet.
1152	Juncus polycephalus,	*Many-headed Rush*(6). - -	Cabinet.
1153	Juncus acuminatus,	*Sharp-fruited Rush*(3). - -	Cabinet.
1154	Juncus pelocarpus,	*Brownish-fruited Rush.*	
1155	Juncus conradi,	*Conrad's Rush*(6). - - - -	Cabinet.
1156	Juncus bufonius,	*Toad Rush*(2). - - - - -	Cabinet.
1157	Juncus tenuis,	*Slender Rush*(6). - - - -	Cabinet.
1158	Juncus greenei,	*Greene's Rush.*	
1159	Juncus gerardi,	*Blackgrass*(3). - - - - -	Cabinet.
1160	Juncus marginatus,	*Grass-leaved Rush*(4). - -	Cabinet.
1161	Juncus stygius,	*Large-fruited Rush*(6). - -	Cabinet.
1162	Juncus trifidus,	*Slender-fringed Rush*(6). -	Cabinet.

ORDER CXXI. COMMELYNACEÆ.

1163	Commelyna angustifolia,	*Narrow-leaved Dayflower.*	
1164	Tradescantia virginica,	*Virginian Spiderwort*(1). -	Cabinet.

ORDER CXXII. XYRIDACEÆ.

1165	Xyris caroliniana,	*Common Yelloweyed-grass*(3).	Cabinet.

ORDER CXXIII. ERIOCAULONACEÆ.

	Latin Names.	English Names.	
1166	Eriocaulon septangulare,	*Pellucid Pipewort*(4). - -	Cabinet.

Vol. 40.]

ORDER CXXIV. CYPERACEÆ.

1167	Dulichium spathaceum,	*Dulichium*(3). - - - - - -	Cabinet.
1168	Cyperus flavescens,	*Yellowish Dwarf Galingale*(4).	Cabinet.
1169	Cyperus diandrus,	*Diandrous Galingale*(15). -	Cabinet.
1170	Cyperus nuttallii,	*Nuttall's Galingale*(3). - -	Cabinet.
1171	Cyperus michauxianus,	*Michaux's Galingale*(1). - -	Cabinet.
1172	Cyperus strigosus,	*Tall Galingale*(6). - - -	Cabinet.
1173	Cyperus repens,	*Creeping Galingale*(1). - -	Cabinet.
1174	Cyperus filiculmis,	*Slender-stalked Galingale*(4).	Cabinet.
1175	Cyperus grayi,	*Gray's Galingale*(2). - - -	Cabinet.
1176	Cyperus dentatus,	*Toothed Galingale*(3). - -	Cabinet.
1177	Cyperus inflexus,	*Dwarf Odorous Galingale*(7).	Cabinet.
1178	Cyperus schweinitzii,	*Schweinitz's Galingale*(2). -	Cabinet.
1179	Cyperus ovularis,	*Oval-headed Galingale*(2). -	Cabinet.
1180	Cyperus retrofractus,	*Bent-flowered Galingale.*	
1181	Fuirena squarrosa,	*Squarrose Fuirena*(7). - -	Cabinet.
1182	Eleocharis palustris,	*Common Spikerush*(7). - -	Cabinet.
1183	Eleocharis olivacea,	*Olive-fruited Spikerush*(2). -	Cabinet.
1184	Eleocharis rostellata,	*Beaked Spikerush*(2). - - -	Cabinet.
1185	Eleocharis intermedia,	*Intermediate Spikerush*(3). -	Cabinet.
1186	Eleocharis obtusa,	*Obtuse-headed Spikerush*(4).	Cabinet.
1187	Eleocharis tuberculosa,	*Large-tubercled Spikerush*(2).	Cabinet.
1188	Eleocharis acicularis,	*Capillary Spikerush*(6). - -	Cabinet.
1189	Eleocharis tenuis,	*Slender Spikerush*(1). - -	Cabinet.
1190	Eleocharis pygmæa,	*Dwarf Spikerush*(8). - - -	Cabinet.
1191	Scirpus planifolius,	*Small Flat-leaved Clubrush*(2).	Cabinet.
1192	Scirpus subterminalis,	*Floating Clubrush*(2). - -	Cabinet.
1193	Scirpus cæspitosus,	*Scaly-stalked Clubrush*(3). -	Cabinet.
1194	Scirpus debilis,	*Weak-stalked Clubrush*(4). -	Cabinet.
1195	Scirpus triqueter,	*Chairmaker's Rush*(7). - -	Cabinet.

	Latin Names.	English Names.	
1196	Scirpus mucronatus,	*Longheaded Triangular Rush*(1).	Cabinet.
1197	Scirpus lacustris,	*Bulrush*(3). - - - - - - -	Cabinet.
1198	Scirpus maritimus,	*Sea Clubrush*(3). - - - -	Cabinet.
1199	Scirpus atrovirens,	*Dark-green Clubrush*(2). - -	Cabinet.
1200	Scirpus brunneus,	*Brown-headed Clubrush*(1). -	Cabinet.
1201	Scirpus eriophorus,	*Brown Woolgrass*(3). - - -	Cabinet.
1202	Scirpus lineatus,	*Loose-flowered Woolgrass*(2).	Cabinet.
1203	Eriophorum alpinum,	*Alpine Cottongrass*(3). - -	Cabinet.
1204	Eriophorum vaginatum,	*Harestail*(3). - - - - - -	Cabinet.
1205	Eriophorum virginicum,	*Rusty Cottongrass*(3). - -	Cabinet.
1206	Eriophorum polystachyum,	*Broad-leaved Cottongrass*(3).	Cabinet.
1207	Eriophorum angustifolium,	*Narrow-leaved Cottongrass*(5).	Cab.
1208	Fimbristylis spadicea,	*Tall Brown-spiked Fimbristylis*(2).	Cab.
1209	Isolepis capillaris,	*Hair-like Isolepis*(2). - - -	Cabinet.
1210	Trichelostylis mucronulata,	*Common Trichelostylis*(6).	Cabinet.
1211	Hemicarpha subsquarrosa,	*Dwarf Hemicarpha*(6). -	Cabinet.
1212	Rhynchospora alba,	*White Beakrush*(2). - - -	Cabinet.
1213	Rhynchospora capillacea,	*Small Capillary Beakrush*(3).	Cabinet.
1214	Rhynchospora fusca,	*Brown Beakrush*(5). - - -	Cabinet.
1215	Rhynchospora gracilenta,	*Tall Slender Beakrush*(1).	Cabinet.
1216	Rhynchospora glomerata,	*Common Beakrush*(3). - -	Cabinet.
1217	Rhynchospora cephalantha,	*Roundheaded Beakrush*(2).	Cabinet.
1218	Cladium mariscoides,	*Smooth Twigrush*(4). - - -	Cabinet.
1219	Scleria reticularis,	*Sessile-spiked Nutrush*(2)- -	Cabinet.
1220	Scleria laxa,	*Loose-flowered Nutrush*(4). -	Cabinet.
1221	Scleria triglomerata,	*Three-clustered Nutrush*(4). -	Cabinet.
1222	Scleria pauciflora,	*Few-flowered Nutrush*(2). -	Cabinet.
1223	Scleria verticillata,	*Dwarf Verticillate Nutrush*(2).	Cabinet.

Vol. 41.]

1224	Carex dioica,	*Diœcious Sedge*(1). - - -	Cabinet.
1225	Carex exilis,	*Slender Sedge*(5). - - - -	Cabinet.
1226	Carex pauciflora,	*Few-flowered Sedge*(6). - -	Cabinet.

	Latin Names.	English Names.	
1227	Carex polytrichoides,	*Bristle-stalked Sedge*(3). - -	Cabinet.
1228	Carex willdenovii,	*Willdenow's Sedge*(5). - -	Cabinet.
1229	Carex backii,	*Back's Sedge*(2). - - - -	Cabinet.
1230	Carex disperma,	*Two-seeded Sedge*(2). - - -	Cabinet.
1231	Carex chordorrhiza,	*Long-rooted Sedge*(6). - -	Cabinet.
1232	Carex cephalophora,	*Oval-headed Sedge*(5). - -	Cabinet.
1233	Carex muhlenbergii,	*Muhlenberg's Sedge*(3). - -	Cabinet.
1234	Carex siccata,	*Dry-spiked Sedge*(3). - - -	Cabinet.
1235	Carex rosea,	*Rose Sedge*(4). - - - - -	Cabinet.
1236	Carex retroflexa,	*Retroflexed Sedge*(2). - - -	Cabinet.
1237	Carex sparganioides,	*Bur-reed Sedge*(6). - - -	Cabinet.
1238	Carex stipata,	*Awl-fruited Sedge*(3). - -	Cabinet.
1239	Carex vulpinoidea,	*Fox Sedge*(8). - - - - -	Cabinet.
1240	Carex setacea,	*Bristly-spiked Sedge.*	
1241	Carex bromoides,	*Bromus-like Sedge*(9). - -	Cabinet.
1242	Carex alopecoidea,	*Foxtail Sedge.*	
1243	Carex sartwellii,	*Sartwell's Sedge*(3). - - -	Cabinet.
1244	Carex teretiuscula,	*Lesser-panicled Sedge*(5). -	Cabinet.
1245	Carex decomposita,	*Large-panicled Sedge*(3). -	Cabinet.
1246	Carex trisperma,	*Three-seeded Sedge*(2). - -	Cabinet.
1247	Carex deweyana,	*Dewey's Sedge*(3). - - - -	Cabinet.
1248	Carex canescens,	*White Sedge*(6). - - - -	Cabinet.
1249	Carex stellulata,	*Little Prickly Sedge*(2). - -	Cabinet.
1250	Carex tenuiflora,	*Slender Cluster-spiked Sedge*(2).	Cabinet.
1251	Carex scoparia,	*Broom-like Sedge*(10). - -	Cabinet.
1252	Carex straminea,	*Straw-colored Sedge*(19). -	Cabinet.
1253	Carex pedunculata,	*Long-stalked Sedge*(4). - -	Cabinet.
1254	Carex squarrosa,	*Squarrose-headed Sedge*(4). -	Cabinet.
1255	Carex buxbaumii,	*Buxbaum's Sedge*(4). - - -	Cabinet.
1256	Carex triceps,	*Three-headed Pubescent Sedge*(5).	Cabinet.
1257	Carex virescens,	*Green-spiked Pubescent Sedge*(4).	Cabinet.
1258	Carex gracillima,	*Slender Nodding Sedge*(3). -	Cabinet.

	Latin Names.	English Names.	
1259	Carex formosa,	*Showy Sedge*(3). - - - -	Cabinet.
1260	Carex davisii,	*Davis's Sedge*(3). - - - -	Cabinet.
1261	Carex rigida,	*Rigid Sedge*(4). - - - -	Cabinet.
1262	Carex angustata,	*Large Bog Sedge*(3). - - -	Cabinet.
1263	Carex cæspitosa,	*Smaller Bog Sedge.*	
1264	Carex aquatilis,	*Water Sedge*(2). - - - -	Cabinet.
1265	Carex aurea,	*Golden-fruited Sedge*(6). -	Cabinet.
Vol. 42.]			
1266	Carex crinita,	*Fringed Sedge*(4). - - - -	Cabinet.
1267	Carex oligosperma,	*Few-fruited Sedge*(3). - -	Cabinet.
1268	Carex inflata,	*Inflated Sedge.*	
1269	Carex cylindrica,	*Cylindrical-spiked Sedge.*	
1270	Carex utriculata,	*Bladder-fruited Sedge*(9). -	Cabinet.
1271	Carex subulata,	*Awl-fruited Sedge*(4). - -	Cabinet.
1272	Carex folliculata,	*Tall Yellow Sedge*(7). - -	Cabinet.
1273	Carex intumescens,	*Swollen-fruited Sedge*(4). -	Cabinet.
1274	Carex lupulina,	*Hop Sedge*(4). - - - - -	Cabinet.
1275	Carex scabrata,	*Rough-fruited Sedge*(3). - -	Cabinet.
1276	Carex schweinitzii,	*Schweinitz's Sedge*(2). - -	Cabinet.
1277	Carex retrorsa,	*Backward-fruited Sedge*(2). -	Cabinet.
1278	Carex tentaculata,	*Long-pointed Sedge*(3). - -	Cabinet.
1279	Carex hystricina,	*Porcupine Sedge*(5). - - -	Cabinet.
1280	Carex pseudo-cyperus,	*Cypress-like Sedge.*	
1281	Carex longirostris,	*Long-beaked Sedge*(3). - -	Cabinet.
1282	Carex trichocarpa,	*Hairy-fruited Sedge.*	
1283	Carex aristata,	*Awned Sedge*(3). - - - -	Cabinet.
1284	Carex umbellata,	*Umbel-spiked Sedge*(8). - -	Cabinet.
1285	Carex pennsylvanica,	*Pennsylvanian Sedge*(7). - -	Cabinet.
1286	Carex novæ-angliæ,	*New-England Sedge*(3). - -	Cabinet.
1287	Carex filiformis,	*Slender-leaved Sedge*(3). - -	Cabinet.
1288	Carex lanuginosa,	*Woally-fruited Sedge*(9). -	Cabinet.
1289	Carex vestita,	*Short Woolly-spiked Sedge*(4).	Cabinet.
1290	Carex pubescens,	*Pubescent Sedge*(3). - - -	Cabinet.

	Latin Names.	English Names.	
1291	CAREX LIMOSA,	*Mud Sedge*(12). - - - -	Cabinet.
1292	CAREX LIVIDA,	*Livid Sedge*(8). - - - -	Cabinet.
1293	CAREX FLAVA,	*Large Yellow Sedge*(6). - -	Cabinet.
1294	CAREX ŒDERI,	*Œder's Sedge*(2). - - - -	Cabinet.
1295	CAREX PALLESCENS,	*Pale Pubescent Sedge*(5). -	Cabinet.
1296	CAREX TORREYI,	*Torrey's Sedge.*	
1297	CAREX STRIATA,	*Striated Sedge*(2). - - - -	Cabinet.
1298	CAREX GRANULARIS,	*Granular-spiked Sedge*)4). -	Cabinet.
1299	CAREX LAXIFLORA,	*Loose-flowered Sedge.*	
1300	CAREX CONOIDEA,	*Conical-fruited Sedge*(2). -	Cabinet.
1301	CAREX DIGITALIS,	*Slender Sedge*(7). - - - -	Cabinet.
1302	CAREX OLIGOCARPA,	*Small Few-fruited Sedge*(9).	Cabinet.
1303	CAREX TETANICA,	*Crooked-necked Sedge*(3). -	Cabinet.
1304	CAREX ANCEPS,	*Two-edged Sedge*(14). - -	Cabinet.
1305	CAREX BLANDA,	*Pale Smooth Sedge.*	
1306	CAREX CRAWEI,	*Crawe's Sedge*(2). - - - -	Cabinet.
1307	CAREX PLANTAGINEA,	*Plantain-leaved Sedge*(4). -	Cabinet.
1308	CAREX CAREYANA,	*Carey's Sedge*(2). - - - -	Cabinet.
1309	CAREX EBURNEA,	*Bristle-leaved White Sedge*(5).	Cabinet.
1310	CAREX FLEXILIS,	*Fringed Sedge*(4). - - - -	Cabinet.
1311	CAREX ARCTATA,	*Short-beaked Wood Sedge*(3).	Cabinet.
1312	CAREX DEBILIS,	*Weak Sedge*(3). - - - -	Cabinet.
1313	CAREX MILIACEA,	*Millet-like Sedge*(5). - - -	Cabinet.
1314	CAREX LACUSTRIS,	*Lake Sedge*(3). - - - -	Cabinet.

Vol. 43.] ORDER CXXV. GRAMINEÆ.

1315	LEERSIA ORYZOIDES,	*Cutgrass*, or *Whitegrass*(2).	Cabinet.
1316	LEERSIA VIRGINICA,	*Small-flowered Whitegrass*(2).	Cabinet.
1317	ZIZANIA AQUATICA,	*Wild Rice*(2). - - - - -	Cabinet.
1318	ALOPECURUS PRATENSIS,	*Common Foxtail-grass.*	
1319	ALOPECURUS GENICULATUS,	*Water Foxtail-grass*(3). - -	Cabihet.
1320	PHLEUM PRATENSE,	*Timothy*, or *Herdsgrass*(2). -	Cabinet.
1321	PHALARIS ARUNDINACEA,	*Reed Canary-grass*(2). - -	Cabinet.

	Latin Names.	English Names.	
1322	Phalaris canariensis,	*Common Canary-grass*(1). -	Cabinet.
1323	Holcus lanatus,	*Meadow Softgrass*(3). - -	Cabinet.
1324	Hierochloa borealis,	*Seneca or Vanilla Grass*(2). -	Cabinet.
1325	Hierochloa alpina,	*Alpine Holygrass*(4). - - -	Cabinet.
1326	Anthoxanthum odoratum,	*Sweetscented Vernal-grass*(5).	Cabinet.
1327	Paspalum læve,	*Smooth Erect Paspalum*(2). -	Cabinet.
1328	Paspalum setaceum,	*Hairy Slender Paspalum*(2).	Cabinet.
1329	Milium effusum,	*Millet-grass*(2). - - - -	Cabinet.
1330	Panicum sanguinale,	*Common Crabgrass*(1). - -	Cabinet.
1331	Panicum glabrum,	*Smooth Crabgrass*(2). - -	Cabinet.
1332	Panicum filiforme,	*Slender Crabgrass*(2). - -	Cabinet.
1333	Panicum crus-galli,	*Barnyard-grass*(4). - - -	Cabinet.
1334	Panicum virgatum,	*Tall Smooth Panicgrass*(2).	Cabinet.
1335	Panicum latifolium,	*Broad-leaved Panicgrass*(3).	Cabinet.
1336	Panicum clandestinum,	*Hidden-flowered Panicgrass*(6).	Cabinet.
1337	Panicum xanthophysum,	*Yellow Panicgrass*(2). - -	Cabinet.
1338	Panicum capillare,	*Hair-stalked Panicgrass*(5).	Cabinet.
1339	Panicum depauperatum,	*Few-flowered Panicgrass*(4).	Cabinet.
1340	Panicum dichotomum,	*Polymorphous Panicgrass*(22).	Cabinet.
1341	Panicum verrucosum,	*Warty-flowered Panicgrass*(3).	Cabinet.
1342	Panicum agrostoides,	*Agrostis-like Panicgrass*(3).	Cabinet.
1343	Panicum proliferum,	*Proliferous Panicgrass*(2). -	Cabinet.
1344	Pennisetum glaucum,	*Foxtail*, or *Bottlegrass*(2). -	Cabinet.
1345	Pennisetum viride,	*Green Bottlegrass*(1). - - -	Cabinet.
1346	Cenchrus tribuloides,	*Burgrass*(4). - - - - -	Cabinet.

Vol. 44.]

1347	Oryzopsis asperifolia,	*White-grained Mountain-rice*(4).	Cabinet.
1348	Oryzopsis melanocarpa,	*Black-fruited Mountain-rice*(2).	Cabinet.
1349	Oryzopsis canadensis,	*Smallest Mountain-rice*(2). -	Cabinet.
1350	Stipa avenacea,	*Black Oatgrass*(1). - - -	Cabinet.
1351	Aristida dichotoma,	*Dichotomous Threeawned-grass*(2).	Cabinet.
1352	Aristida gracilis,	*Slender Threeawned-grass*(3).	Cabinet.

	Latin Names.	English Names.	
1353	Muhlenbergia diffusa,	*Dropseed-grass*(3). - - - -	Cabinet.
1354	Muhlenbergia cinna,	*Tall Muhlenbergia.*	
1355	Muhlenbergia willdenovii,	*Willdenow's Muhlenbergia*(3).	Cabinet.
1356	Muhlenbergia sylvatica,	*Wood Muhlenbergia*(3). - -	Cabinet.
1357	Muhlenbergia sobolifera,	*Awnless Muhlenbergia.*	
1358	Muhlenbergia glomerata,	*Cluster-spiked Muhlenbergia*(3).	Cab.
1359	Muhlenbergia mexicana,	*Mexican Muhlenbergia*(2). -	Cabinet.
1360	Vilfa vaginæflora,	*Hidden-flowered Vilfa*(4). -	Cabinet.
1361	Vilfa aspera,	*Rough-leaved Vilfa*(2). - -	Cabinet.
1362	Vilfa serotina,	*Late-flowering Vilfa*(3). - -	Cabinet.
1363	Vilfa heterolepis,	*Strong-scented Vilfa.*	
1364	Vilfa cryptandra,	*Large-panicled Vilfa*(1). - -	Cabinet.
1365	Agrostis vulgaris,	*Herdsgrass.*	
1366	Agrostis alba,	*Fiorin-grass.*	
1367	Agrostis laxiflora,	*Hairgrass*(6). - - - - -	Cabinet.
1368	Agrostis stricta,	*Upright-flowered Bentgrass*(2).	Cabinet.
1369	Agrostis canina,	*Bentgrass*(3). - - - - -	Cabinet.
1370	Brachyelytrum aristatum,	*Awned Brachyelytrum*(2).	Cabinet.
1371	Calamagrostis canadensis,	*Canadian Smallreed*(5). -	Cabinet.
1372	Calamagrostis coarctata,	*Glaucous Smallreed*(2). -	Cabinet.
1373	Calamagrostis inexpansa,	*Close-flowered Smallreed*(2).	Cabinet.
1374	Ammophila arundinacea,	*Common Seareed*(2). - - -	Cabinet.
1375	Phragmites communis,	*Common Reed*(1). - - - -	Cabinet.
1376	Eleusine indica,	*Dogstail-grass*, or *Yard-grass*(3).	Cabinet.
1377	Spartina cynosuroides,	*Tall Marshgrass*(2). - - -	Cabinet.
1378	Spartina juncea,	*Rush-like Marshgrass*(3). -	Cabinet.
1379	Spartina alternifolia,	*Smooth Marshgrass*(2). - -	Cabinet.
1380	Bouteloua racemosa,	*Racemed Bouteloua*(2). - -	Cabinet.
1381	Aira flexuosa,	*Common Hairgrass*(3). -	Cabinet.
1382	Aira atropurpurea,	*Purple Alpine Hairgrass*(3).	Cabinet.
1383	Aira cæspitosa,	*Tufted Hairgrass*(5). - - -	Cabinet.
1384	Trisetum molle,	*Soft Trisetum*(3). - - - -	Cabinet.

	Latin Names.	English Names.	
1385	Avena pennsylvanicum,	*Pennsylvanian Wildoat*(3). -	Cabinet.
1386	Avena striata,	*Purple Wildoat*(2). - - -	Cabinet.
1387	Arrhenatherum avenaceum,	*Grass-of-the-Andes*(2). -	Cabinet.
1388	Danthonia spicata,	*Wild Oatgrass*(3). - - -	Cabinet.
1389	Uralepis aristulata,	*Short-awned Uralepis*(3). -	Cabinet.

Vol. 45.]

1390	Poa annua,	*Annual Meadowgrass*(5). -	Cabinet.
1391	Poa laxa,	*Few-flowered Alpine Meadowgrass*(3).	Cabinet.
1392	Poa trivialis,	*Rough Meadowgrass*(1). - -	Cabinet.
1393	Poa pratensis,	*Smooth-stalked Meadowgrass*(3).	Cabinet.
1394	Poa compressa,	*Bluegrass*, or *Wiregrass*(7).	Cabinet.
1395	Poa pungens,	*Sharp-leaved Meadowgrass*(2).	Cabinet.
1396	Poa nemoralis,	*Wood Meadowgrass*(1). - -	Cabinet.
1397	Poa serotina,	*Redtop*(2). - - - - - - -	Cabinet.
1398	Poa debilis,	*Weak Meadowgrass*(3). - -	Cabinet.
1399	Poa eragrostis,	*Strongscented Meadowgrass*(1).	Cabinet.
1400	Poa pilosa,	*Slender Meadowgrass*(2). -	Cabinet.
1401	Poa reptans,	*Creeping Meadowgrass*(4). -	Cabinet.
1402	Poa hirsuta,	*Hairy Meadowgrass*(1). - -	Cabinet.
1403	Poa capillaris,	*Hair-panicled Meadowgrass*(2).	Cabinet.
1404	Poa dentata,	*Toothed Meadowgrass*(2). -	Cabinet.
1405	Poa michauxii,	*Spiked Saltmarsh Poa*(3). -	Cabinet.
1406	Tricuspis seslerioides,	*Tall Redtop*(2). - - - -	Cabinet.
1407	Glyceria fluitans,	*Common Mannagrass*(1). -	Cabinet.
1408	Glyceria acutiflora,	*Sharp-flowered Mannagrass*(2).	Cabinet.
1409	Glyceria aquatica,	*Reed Mannagrass*(1). - - -	Cabinet.
1410	Glyceria nervata,	*Nerved Mannagrass*(6). - -	Cabinet.
1411	Glyceria elongata,	*Long-panicled Mannagrass*(2).	Cabinet.
1412	Glyceria canadensis,	*Rattlesnake-grass*(2). - - -	Cabinet.
1413	Dactylis glomerata,	*Cocksfoot-grass*(2). - - - -	Cabinet.
1414	Bromus secalinus,	*Cheat*, or *Chess*(2). - - - -	Cabinet.
1415	Bromus ciliatus,	*Fringed Bromegrass*(4). - -	Cabinet.
1416	Bromus purgans,	*Hairy-flowered Bromegrass*(2).	Cabinet.

	Latin Names.	English Names.	
1417	BROMUS STERILIS,	*Barren Bromegrass*(1). - -	Cabinet.
1418	KŒLERIA PENNSYLVANICA,	*Pennsylvanian Kœleria*(2). -	Cabinet.
1419	KŒLERIA TRUNCATA,	*Truncated Kœleria*(2). - -	Cabinet.
1420	FESTUCA DURIUSCULA,	*Hard Fescuegrass*(3). - - -	Cabinet.
1421	FESTUCA TENELLA,	*Slender Fescuegrass*(2). - -	Cabinet.
1422	FESTUCA NUTANS,	*Nodding Fescuegrass*(2). - -	Cabinet.
1423	FESTUCA ELATIOR,	*Tall Fescuegrass*(1). - - -	Cabinet.
1424	FESTUCA PRATENSIS,	*Meadow Fescuegrass*(2). - -	Cabinet.
1425	DIPLACHNE FASCICULARIS,	*Cluster-flowered Diplachne*(2).	Cabinet.
1426	UNIOLA GRACILIS,	*Slender Spikegrass*(2). - -	Cabinet.
1427	LOLIUM PERENNE,	*Common Darnel*(1). - - -	Cabinet.
1428	TRITICUM REPENS,	*Couchgrass*, or *Quitchgrass*(2).	Cabinet.
1429	TRITICUM CANINUM,	*Fibrous-rooted Wheatgrass*(2).	Cabinet.
1430	ELYMUS VIRGINICUS,	*Virginian Lymegrass*(2). -	Cabinet.
1431	ELYMUS CANADENSIS,	*Canadian Lymegrass*(2). - -	Cabinet.
1432	ELYMUS VILLOSUS,	*Slender-hairy Lymegrass*(2).	Cabinet.
1433	ELYMUS HYSTRIX,	*Bottlebrush-grass*(4). - - -	Cabinet.
1434	ANDROPOGON NUTANS,	*Indian Beardgrass.*	
1435	ANDROPOGON SCOPARIUS,	*Purple Woodgrass*(2). - -	Cabinet.
1436	ANDROPOGON FURCATUS,	*Finger-spiked Woodgrass*(2).	Cabinet.
1437	ANDROPOGON VIRGINICUS,	*Virginian Beardgrass*(3). -	Cabinet.
1438	ANDROPOGON MACROURUS,	*Cluster-flowered Beardgrass*(2).	Cabinet.

ADDITIONS.

PLANTS DISCOVERED DURING THE PRINTING OF THE FLORA,

And described in Vol. ii, pp. 515 et seq.

	Latin Names.	English Names.	
1439	Polygala lutea,	*Yellow Milkwort.*	
1440	Desmodium lævigatum,	*Rigid Upright Desmodium.*	
1441	Lythrum salicaria,	*Common Purple Loosestrife.*	
1442	Saxifraga aizoides,	*Yellow Mountain Saxifrage.*	
1443	Eupatorium hyssopifolium,	*Hyssop-leaved Hempweed.*	
1444	Eupatorium album,	*Whiteheaded Hempweed.*	
1445	Eupatorium resinosum,	*Resinous Hempweed.*	
1446	Aster concolor,	*Racemed Violet Aster.*	
1447	Oakesia conradi,	*Conrad's Oakesia*(3). - - -	Cabinet.
1448	Calypso borealis,	*Northern Calypso.*	
1449	Eleocharis melanocarpa,	*Black-fruited Eleocharis*(2).	Cabinet.

PLANTS DISCOVERED AND COLLECTED SINCE THE PUBLICATION OF THE FLORA.

1450	Robinia viscosa,	*Clammy Locust*(1). - - -	Cabinet.
1451	Vicia caroliniana,	*Carolinian Vetch*(1). - - -	Cabinet.
1452	Stellaria longipes,	*Long-stalked Stitchwort*(1). -	Cabinet.
1453	Trifolium incarnatum,	*Incarnate Clover*(2). - - -	Cabinet.
1454	Pyrus malus,	*Common Apple*(4). - - - -	Cabinet.
1455	Œnothera riparia,	*Bank Evening-primrose*(1). -	Cabinet.
1456	Galium concinnum,	*Concinnate Bluets*(1). - - -	Cabinet.

	Latin Names.	English Names.	
1457	PHLOMIS TUBEROSA,	*Tuberous Phlomis*(2). - - -	Cabinet.
1458	LITHOSPERMUM LATIFOLIUM,	*Broad-leaved Gromwell*(1).	Cabinet.
1459	ONOSMODIUM CAROLINIANUM,	*Carolina False-gromwell*(2).	Cabinet.
1460	AMARANTHUS TAMARISCINUS,	*Salt Amaranth*(1). - - -	Cabinet.
1461	CHENOPODIUM MURALE,	*Wall Goosefoot*(3). - - - -	Cabinet.
1462	SALIX FRAGILIS,	*Brittle Willow*(8). - - -	Cabinet.
1463	SALIX BABYLONICA,	*Weeping Willow*(2). - - -	Cabinet.
1464	SALIX ERIOCEPHALA,	*Woolly-head Willow*(3). - -	Cabinet.
1465	SALIX ANGUSTATA,	*Narrow-leaved Willow*(3). -	Cabinet.
1466	MELANTHIUM HYBRIDUM,	*Hybrid Melanthium*(1). - -	Cabinet.
1467	CAREX STEUDELII,	*Steudel's Sedge*(1). - - -	Cabinet.
1468	CAREX PANICULATA,	*Panicled Sedge*(1). - - -	Cabinet.
1469	CAREX VULGARIS,	*Small Black-scaled Sedge*(1).	Cabinet.
1470	CAREX TORTA,	*Twisted Sedge*(6). - - - -	Cabinet.
1471	CAREX GRISEA,	*Greyish Sedge*(4). - - - -	Cabinet.
1472	CAREX PLATYPHYLLA,	*Flat-leaved Sedge*(2). - - -	Cabinet.
1473	CAREX COMOSA,	*Cyprus-like Sedge*(3). - -	Cabinet.
1474	PANICUM PAUCIFLORUM,	*Few-flowered Panicgrass*(2).	Cabinet.
1475	AVENA SATIVA,	*Common Oat*(2). - - - -	Cabinet.
1476	SPARTINA POLYSTACHYA,	*Tall Saltmarsh-grass*(2). -	Cabinet.
1477	CINNA PENDULA,	*Pendulous Cinna*(2). - - -	Cabinet.
1478	CINNA ARUNDINACEA,	*Reed-like Cinna*(2). - - -	Cabinet.

BOTANY OF NEW-YORK,

OR THE

New-York Flora.

BY JOHN TORREY.

DIVISION II. CRYPTOGAMOUS PLANTS.

BOTANY.

DIVISION II. CRYPTOGAMOUS PLANTS.

Vol. 46.] ORDER CXXVI. EQUISETACEÆ.

	Latin Name.	English Name.	In the
1	EQUISETUM ARVENSE,	*Field Horsetail.*	
2	EQUISETUM SYLVATICUM,	*Wood Horsetail*(7). - - -	Cabinet.
3	EQUISETUM LIMOSUM,	*Smooth Swamp Horsetail*, or *Pipes*(3).	Cabinet.
4	EQUISETUM HYEMALE,	*Scouring Rush*(4). - - - -	Cabinet.
5	EQUISETUM VARIEGATUM,	*Variegated Rough Horsetail*(5)	Cabinet
6	EQUISETUM SCIRPOIDES,	*Smallest Rough Horsetail*(3).	Cabinet.

ORDER CXXVII. FILICES.

	Latin Name.	English Name.	In the
7	POLYPODIUM VULGARE,	*Common Polypody*(2). - -	Cabinet.
8	POLYPODIUM PHEGOPTERIS,	*Beech Polypody*(2). - - -	Cabinet.
9	POLYPODIUM HEXAGONOPTERUM,	*Winged Polypody*(1). - -	Cabinet.
10	POLYPODIUM DRYOPTERIS,	*Three-branched Polypody*(2).	Cabinet.
11	STRUTHIOPTERIS GERMANICA,	*Common Ostrichfern*(4). - -	Cabinet.
12	ALLOSORUS GRACILIS,	*Slender Allosorus*(4). - - -	Cabinet.
13	ADIANTUM PEDATUM,	*Maidenhair*, or *Mohair*(1). -	Cabinet.
14	PTERIS AQUILINA,	*Common Brake*, or *Bracken*(2).	Cabinet.
15	PLATYLOMA ATROPURPUREA,	*Purple-stalked Rockbrake*(2).	Cabinet.
16	DOODIA VIRGINICA,	*Virginian Doodia*(1). - - -	Cabinet.
17	WOODWARDIA ANGUSTIFOLIA,	*Narrow-leaved Woodwardia*(2).	Cabinet.
18	SCOLOPENDRUM OFFICINARUM,	*Common Houndstongue*(2). -	Cabinet.
19	ASPLENIUM TRICHOMANES,	*Small Rock Spleenwort*(3). -	Cabinet.

	Latin Names.	English Names.	
20	Asplenium ebeneum,	*Screwfern*(3). - - - - -	Cabinet.
21	Asplenium angustifolium,	*Narrow-leaved Spleenwort*(2).	Cabinet.
22	Asplenium ruta-muraria,	*Wall-rue Spleenwort*(3). - -	Cabinet.
23	Asplenium thelypterioides,	*Silvery Spleenwort*(1). - -	Cabinet.
24	Asplenium filix-fœmina,	*Female-fern*(1). - - - -	Cabinet.
25	Antigramma rhizophylla,	*Walking-fern*(5). - - - -	Cabinet.
26	Aspidium marginale,	*Marginal Shieldfern*(1). - -	Cabinet.
27	Aspidium goldianum,	*Goldie's Shieldfern*(2). - -	Cabinet.
28	Aspidium cristatum,	*Crested Shieldfern*(1). - -	Cabinet.
29	Aspidium dilatatum,	*Dilated Shieldfern*(1). - -	Cabinet.
30	Aspidium thelypteris,	*Meadow Shieldfern*(1). - -	Cabinet.
31	Aspidium noveboracense,	*New-York Shieldfern*(1). -	Cabinet.
32	Aspidium acrostichoides,	*Terminal Shieldfern*(2). - -	Cabinet.
33	Aspidium aculeatum,	*Prickly Shieldfern.*	
34	Onoclea sensibilis,	*Sensitive-fern*(4). - - - -	Cabinet.
35	Woodsia ilvensis,	*Rusty Rock Polypody.*	
36	Woodsia obtusa,	*Obtuse Woodsia*(3). - - -	Cabinet.
37	Cystopteris fragilis,	*Brittle Bladderfern*(4). - -	Cabinet.
38	Cystopteris bulbifera,	*Bulb-bearing Bladderfern*(2).	Cabinet.
39	Dicksonia pilosiuscula,	*Hairy Dicksonia*(2). - - -	Cabinet.
40	Osmunda claytoniana,	*Interrupted Flowering-fern*(1).	Cabinet.
41	Osmunda cinnamomea,	*Woolly Flowering-fern*(2). -	Cabinet.
42	Osmunda spectabilis,	*Showy Flowering-fern*(2). -	Cabinet.
43	Lygodium palmatum,	*Climbing-fern*(1). - - - -	Cabinet.
44	Ophioglossum vulgatum,	*Common Adderstongue*(2). -	Cabinet.
45	Botrychium virginicum,	*Rattlesnake-fern*(1). - - -	Cabinet.
46	Botrychium lunarioides,	*Tall Smooth Moonwort*(2). -	Cabinet.
47	Botrychium simplex,	*Dwarf Moonwort*(1). - - -	Cabinet.

ORDER CXXVIII. LYCOPODIACEÆ.

48	Lycopodium selago,	*Fir Clubmoss*(3). - - - -	Cabinet.
49	Lycopodium lucidulum,	*Shining Clubmoss*(3). - - -	Cabinet.
50	Lycopodium inundatum,	*Low Marsh Clubmoss*(7). - -	Cabinet.

	Latin Names.	English Names.	
51	LYCOPODIUM ANNOTINUM,	*Interrupted Clubmoss*(2). - -	Cabinet.
52	LYCOPODIUM OBSCURUM,	*Groundpine*(2). - - - - -	Cabinet.
53	LYCOPODIUM CLAVATUM,	*Common Clubmoss*(2). - - -	Cabinet.
54	LYCOPODIUM COMPLANATUM,	*Festoon Groundpine*(2). - -	Cabinet.
55	SELAGINELLA RUPESTRIS,	*Small Rock Clubmoss*(4). -	Cabinet.
56	SELAGINELLA APUS,	*Moss-like Selaginella*(4). - -	Cabinet.

ORDER CXXIX. SALVINIACEÆ.

57	SALVINIA NATANS,	*Floating Salvinia.*	
58	AZOLLA CAROLINIANA,	*Carolinian Azolla*(3). - - -	Cabinet.

ORDER CXXX. ISOETACEÆ.

59	ISOETES LACUSTRIS,	*Common Quillwort*(1). - -	Cabinet.

MINERALOGY OF NEW-YORK,

BY LEWIS C. BECK.

MINERALOGY.

CLASS I. GASEOUS MINERALS.

ORDER I. COMBUSTIBLE GASES.

Names of Species. Localities.

1 Hydrogen (Not found pure).

2 Carburetted hydrogen (See Mineralogy, p. 128).

3 Sulphuretted hydrogen (See Mineralogy, p. 141).

4 Phosphuretted hydrogen (Sometimes found in marshes).

ORDER II. NON-COMBUSTIBLE GASES.

5 Oxygen (Sometimes found to predominate in the air given out by springs).

6 Nitrogen (See Mineralogy, p. 133).

7 Carbonic acid (See Mineralogy, p. 134).

8 Atmospheric air (Sometimes evolved from springs).

CLASS II. LIQUID MINERALS, NOT COMBUSTIBLE.

ORDER I. LIQUID ACIDS.

9 Hydrous sulphuric acid (See Mineralogy, p. 150).

ORDER II. LIQUID MINERALS, NOT ACID.

10 Atmospheric water (See Mineralogy, p. 178).

11 Sea water (See Mineralogy, p. 179).

CLASS III. COMBUSTIBLE MINERALS, NOT GASEOUS.

	Names.	Localities.	In the
12	SULPHUR (1 specimen),	Springport, Essex county. - -	Cabinet.
13	BITUMEN : *Petroleum*(1),	Erie county. - - - - - - -	Cabinet.
14	AMBER,	Rossville, Richmond county.	
15	GRAPHITE (19 specimens),	- - - - - - - - - - - -	Cabinet.
	—	Rogersrock, Essex, 2 specimens;	
	—	Ticonderoga, Essex, 3;	
	—	Port Henry, Essex, 2;	
	—	Fishkill, Dutchess, 4;	
	—	Brown's quarry, Putnam, 1;	
	—	Edenville, Orange, 2;	
	—	Saltus's quarry, Essex, 1;	
	—	Rossie, St. Lawrence, 1;	
	—	Johnsburgh, Warren, 2;	
	— ARTIFICIAL,	Rossie furnace, St.Lawrence, 1.	
16	ANTHRACITE(5);	- - - - - - - - - - - -	Cabinet.
	—	Littlefalls, Herkimer, 2;	
	—	Sprakers, Montgomery, 2;	
	—	Middleburgh, Schoharie, 1.	
17	COAL (See Mineralogy, p. 190).		
18	LIGNITE (See Mineralogy, p. 191).		
19	PEAT(1),	Lansingburgh, Rensselaer. -	Cabinet.

CLASS IV. ALKALINE MINERALS.

ORDER I. AMMONIA.

20 CARBONATE OF AMMONIA, In New-York city.

ORDER II. SODA.

21 GLAUBER'S SALT, In Rochester, Monroe.

22 NATRON, New-York city, etc.

23 COMMON SALT (See Mineralogy, p. 99).

24 HYDRIODATE OF SODA, Probably in the brine springs of Onondaga.

ORDER III. POTASH.

25 SULPHATE OF POTASH, Perhaps in the brine of Salina.

26 CARBONATE OF POTASH, Water of certain springs.

Names.	Localities.
27 MURIATE OF POTASH,	Water of brine springs, etc.
28 HYDROBROMATE OF POTASH,	Waters of Saratoga.
29 ALUM,	Catskill mountains, etc.

CLASS V. ALKALINE EARTHY MINERALS.

ORDER I. BARYTA.

30 HEAVY SPAR(35), - - - - - - - - - - - - Cabinet.
— Schoharie courthouse, Schoharie, 5;
— Littlefalls, Herkimer, 2;
— Middleburgh, Schoharie, 4;
— Syracuse, Onondaga, 2;
— Pillar point, Jefferson, 2:
— Rossie, St.Lawrence, 5:
— Carlisle, Schoharie, 4;
— Gouverneur, St.Lawrence, 4;
— Oxbow, Jefferson, 4;
— Wayne county, 3.

31 CELESTINE(8), - - - - - - - - - - - - Cabinet.
— Stark, Herkimer, 3;
— Syracuse, Onondaga, 2;
— Lockport, Niagara, 2.

ORDER II. STRONTIAN.

32 STRONTIANITE(12), - - - - - - - - - - - - Cabinet.
— Schoharie courthouse, Schoharie, 11;
— Antwerp, Jefferson, 1.

33 BARYSTRONTIANITE, Near Hamilton College, Oneida.

ORDER III. LIME.

34 CALCAREOUS SPAR(157), - - - - - - - - - - - Cabinet.
— Gouverneur, St.Lawrence, 5;
— Diana, Lewis, 2;
— Antwerp, Jefferson, 11;
— Oxbow, Jefferson, 9;
— Littlefalls, Herkimer, 3;
— Middleville, Herkimer, 3;
— Camillus, Onondaga, 3;
— Haverstraw, Rockland, 5;
— Warwick, Orange, 2:
— Amity, Orange, 4;

Names.		Localities.
CALCAREOUS SPAR :		
—		Newburgh, Orange, 1;
—		Martinsburgh, Lewis, 4;
—		Rossie, St.Lawrence, 33;
—		Catskill, Greene, 11;
—		Canaan, Columbia, 1;
—		Middleburgh, Schoharie, 2;
—		Cobleskill, Schoharie, 3:
—		Diamond point, Warren, 3;
—		Fort-Ann, Washington, 1;
—		Parish mine, St.Lawrence, 5;
—		Monroe, Orange, 2;
—		Port Henry, Essex, 9;
—		Ball's cave, Schoharie, 4;
—		Schoharie courthouse, Schoharie, 1;
—		Glenville, Schenectady, 1;
—		Rogersrock, Essex, 1;
—		Yonkers, Westchester, 1;
—		O'Niel mine, Orange, 1;
—		Muscolunge lake, Jefferson, 1;
—		Nethaway's cave, Schoharie, 1;
—		Young's cave, Schoharie, 1;
—		Caldwell, Warren, 1;
—		Lockport, Niagara, 2;
—	WHITE,	Catskill, Greene, 2;
—	WHITE,	Edenville, Orange, 1;
—	RED,	Cornwall, Orange, 4;
—	RED,	Monroe, Orange, 3;
—	BLUE,	Naturalbridge, Lewis, 1;
—	BLUE,	Diana, Lewis, 2;
—	GREEN,	Schroon, Essex, 1;
—	BROWN,	Flat creek, Montgomery, 1;
—	STALACTITE,	Ball's cave, Schoharie, 1;
—	STALAGMITE,	Ball's cave, Schoharie, 1;
—	DOGTOOTH,	Cheshire, Ontario, 1;
—	SATIN,	Rossie, St.Lawrence, 1.
35 MARBLE(5),		- - - - - - - - - - - Cabinet.
—		Montagne's quarry, Rockland, 1;
—		Hastings, Westchester, 1;
—		Haverstraw, Rockland, 1;
—		Grassy point, Rockland, 1;
—		Pleasant-valley, Dutchess, 1.

Names.	Localities.	
36 FIBROUS LIMESTONE(11),	- - - - - - - - - - - -	Cabinet.
—	Camillus, Onondaga, 6;	
—	Naturalbridge, Jefferson, 1;	
—	Ball's cave, Schoharie, 1;	
—	Carlisle, Schoharie, 1;	
—	Rossie, St.Lawrence, 2.	
37 CONCRETED CARBONATE OF LIME(22),	- - - - - -	Cabinet.
— AGARIC MINERAL,	Cobleskill, Schoharie, 1;	
— OOLITIC LIMESTONE,	Warwick, Orange, 2;	
— OOLITIC LIMESTONE,	Greenfield, Saratoga, 2;	
— CALCAREOUS SINTER,	Newburgh, Orange, 1;	
— CALCAREOUS TUFA,	Jamesville, Onondaga, 4;	
— CALCAREOUS TUFA,	Lenox, Madison, 2;	
— CALCAREOUS TUFA,	Rochester, Monroe, 1;	
— CALCAREOUS TUFA,	Syracuse, Onondaga, 1;	
— CALCAREOUS TUFA,	Chittenango, Madison, 1;	
— CALCAREOUS TUFA,	Martinsburgh, Lewis, 1;	
— CALCAREOUS TUFA,	Marcellus, Onondaga, 1;	
— FERRUGINOUS,	Johnsburgh, Warren, 3;	
— CRYSTALLIZED,	Anthony's Nose, Putnam, 2.	
38 MARL(5),	- - - - - - - - - - - -	Cabinet.
—	Dewitt, Onondaga, 1;	
—	Syracuse, Onondaga, 3;	
—	Salina, Onondaga, 1.	
39 ARRAGONITE(6),	- - - - - - - - - - - -	Cabinet.
—	Monroe, Orange, 1;	
—	Patterson, Putnam, 1;	
—	O'Niel mine, Orange, 2;	
—	Edenville, Orange, 1;	
—	How's cave, Schoharie, 1.	
40 GYPSUM(32),	- - - - - - - - - - - -	Cabinet.
—	Stark, Herkimer, 2;	
—	Lockport, Niagara, 2;	
—	Lenox, Madison, 1;	
—	Onondaga county, 2;	
—	Syracuse, Onondaga, 4;	
—	Dewitt, Onondaga, 6;	
—	Manlius, Onondaga, 4;	
—	Camillus, Onondaga, 7;	
—	Cayuga county, 1;	
— SELENITE,	Lockport, Niagara, 1;	
— SELENITE,	O'Niel mine, Orange, 1.	

	Names.		Localities.
41	ANHYDRITE,		Lockport, Niagara.
42	APATITE(13),		- - - - - - - - - - - Cabinet.
	—		Rossie, St.Lawrence, 1;
	—		Hammond, St.Lawrence, 1;
	—		Hall mine, Essex, 3;
	—		Edenville, Orange, 4;
	—		Westfarms, Westchester, 1;
	—		Diana, Lewis, 2;
	—	EUPYRCHROITE,	Crownpoint, Essex, 3.
43	FLUOR SPAR(15),		- - - - - - - - - - - Cabinet.
	—		Lowville, Lewis, 2;
	—		Amity, Orange, 2;
	—		Niagara, Niagara, 4;
	—		Schoharie courthouse, Schoharie, 3;
	—		Alexandria, Jefferson, 2;
	—		Manlius, Onondaga, 2.
44	MURIATE OF LIME,		Water of several mineral springs.
45	DATHOLITE,		Piermont, Rockland, etc.
46	PHARMACOLITE,		Monroe, Orange.

ORDER IV. MAGNESIA.

	Names.		Localities.
47	BRUCITE,		Quarantine, Richmond, etc.
48	CARBONATE OF MAGNESIA,		Staten island, etc.
49	EPSOM SALT,		Bethlehem, Albany, etc.
50	MAGNESIAN CARBONATE OF LIME(27),		- - - - - - - Cabinet.
	—	PEARL SPAR,	Lockport, Niagara, 1;
	—	PEARL SPAR,	Littlefalls, Herkimer, 2;
	—	PEARL SPAR,	Niagara falls, Niagara, 2;
	—	PEARL SPAR,	Rossie, St.Lawrence, 4;
	—	PEARL SPAR,	Theresa, Jefferson, 1;
	—	BROWN SPAR,	Diamond island, Warren, 2;
	—	BROWN SPAR,	Parish mine, St.Lawrence, 3;
	—	DOLOMITE,	Kingsbridge, New-York, 2;
	—	DOLOMITE,	Amenia, Dutchess, 1;
	—	GURHOFITE,	Phillipstown, Putnam, 5;
	—	GURHOFITE,	Quarantine, Richmond, 4.
51	HYDRAULIC LIMESTONE(3),		- - - - - - - - - - - Cabinet.
	—		Schoharie courthouse, Schoharie, 1;
	—		Van Eps's quarry, Montgomery, 1;
	—		Lockport, Niagara, 1.
52	HYDROBROMATE OF MAGNESIA,		In sea water, etc.

CLASS VI. EARTHY MINERALS.

ORDER I. SILICA.

Names.		Localities.	
53 QUARTZ(65),		- - - - - - - - - - - -	Cabinet.
—		Middleville, Herkimer, 2;	
—		Littlefalls, Herkimer, 1;	
—		Port Richmond, Richmond, 3;	
—		Diamond point, Warren, 3;	
—		Craigville, Orange, 2;	
—		Ellenville, Ulster, 3;	
—		Oxbow, Jefferson, 2;	
—		Redbridge, Ulster, 4;	
—		Sterling mine, Jefferson, 2;	
—		Diana, Lewis, 4;	
—		Wurtzborough mine, Sullivan, 2;	
—		Catskill, Greene, 1;	
—		Ticonderoga, Essex, 1;	
—		Rossie, St.Lawrence, 3;	
—		Root, Montgomery, 2;	
—		Shawangunk mountains, Sullivan, 1;	
—		Saratoga springs, Saratoga, 2;	
—		Warwick, Orange, 3;	
—		Hastings, Westchester, 1;	
—		Leyden, Lewis, 1;	
—	MASSIVE,	New-Rochelle, Westchester, 1;	
—	MASSIVE,	Yonkers, Westchester, 3;	
—	BLACK,	Littlefalls, Herkimer, 2;	
—	ROSE,	Port Henry, Essex, 3;	
—	FERRUGINOUS,	Quarantine, Richmond, 2;	
—	FERRUGINOUS,	Warwick, Orange, 1;	
—	HORNSTONE,	New-Rochelle, Westchester, 1;	
—	HORNSTONE,	Sprakers, Montgomery, 2;	
—	JASPER,	Warwick, Orange, 2;	
—	CALCEDONY,	Warwick, Orange, 3;	
—	HYALITE,	Phillips's mine, Putnam, 2.	
54 TABULAR SPAR(7),		- - - - - - - - - - - -	Cabinet.
—		Lewis, Essex, 6;	
—		Diana, Lewis, 1.	
55 NEMALITE,		Piermont, Rockland.	

Names.		Localities.	
56 SERPENTINE(107),		- - - - - - - - - - - -	Cabinet.
—		Syracuse, Onondaga, 8;	
—		New-Rochelle, Westchester, 8;	
—		Rye, Westchester, 3;	
—		Monroe, Orange, 1;	
—		Rossie, St.Lawrence, 4;	
—		Port Henry, Essex, 2;	
—		Phillipstown, Putnam, 4;	
—		New-York, New-York, 2;	
—		Diana, Lewis, 2;	
—		Quarantine, Richmond, 2;	
—		Gouverneur, St.Lawrence, 3;	
—		Antwerp, Jefferson, 1;	
—		Warwick, Orange, 1:	
—		Amity, Orange, 2;	
—		Oxbow, Jefferson, 5;	
—		Natural-dam, St.Lawrence, 2;	
—	BLACK,	Warwick, Orange, 2;	
—	BLACK,	Forshee mine, Monroe, Orange, 2;	
—	BLACK,	Southeast, Putnam, 1;	
—	DARK,	Brown's quarry, Putnam, 3;	
—	GREEN,	Fort-Ann, Washington, 4;	
—	GREY,	Fort-Ann, Washington, 2;	
—	YELLOW,	Phillipstown, Putnam, 4;	
—	MARMOLITE,	New-Rochelle, Westchester, 1;	
—	MARMOLITE,	Rye, Westchester, 1;	
—	MARMOLITE,	Phillipstown, Putnam, 2;	
—	SOAPSTONE,	Warwick, Orange, 3;	
—	SOAPSTONE,	Fort-Ann, Washington, 1;	
—	SOAPSTONE,	Wilks mine, Monroe, Orange, 1;	
—	SOAPSTONE,	Amity, Orange, 1;	
—	SOAPSTONE,	Diana, Lewis, 1;	
—	SOAPSTONE,	Gouverneur, St.Lawrence, 2;	
—	VERD ANTIQUE,	Port Henry, Essex, 5;	
—	VERD ANTIQUE,	Amity, Orange, 6;	
—	VERD ANTIQUE,	Gouverneur, St.Lawrence, 2;	
—	CRYSTALLIZED,	Greenwood, Orange, 1.	
57 MAGNESITE(4),		Stony point, Rockland. - -	Cabinet.
58 CHONDRODITE(37),		- - - - - - - - - - - -	Cabinet.
—		Southeast, Putnam, 1;	
—		Port Henry, Essex, 3;	
—		Rossie, St.Lawrence, 8;	
—		Amity, Orange, 12;	

Names.		Localities.
CHONDRODITE :		
—		Edenville, Orange, 5;
—		Naturalbridge, Orange, 2;
—		Monroe, Orange, 3;
—	CRYSTALLIZED,	Edenville, Orange, 2;
—	CRYSTALLIZED,	Monroe, Orange, 1.
59 BOLTONITE,		Several places in Orange county.
60 TALC(12),		- - - - - - - - - - - Cabinet.
—		Quarantine, Richmond, 3;
—		Amity, Orange, 5;
—		Fishkill, Dutchess, 4.
61 PYROXENE(72),		- - - - - - - - - - - Cabinet.
—		Edenville, Orange, 6;
—		O'Niel mine, Monroe, Orange, 1;
—		Rogersrock, Essex, 2;
—		Ticonderoga, Essex, 4;
—		Greenwood, Monroe, Orange, 4;
—		Warwick, Orange, 3;
—		Gouverneur, St.Lawrence, 2;
—		Rossie, St.Lawrence, 2;
—	WHITE,	Yonkers, Westchester, 1;
—	WHITE,	Patterson, Putnam, 3;
—	WHITE,	Kingsbridge, New-York, 2;
—	BLUISH,	Haverstraw, Rockland, 2;
—	BLACK,	Crag harbor, Essex, 1;
—	GREY,	Richville, St.Lawrence, 2;
—	COCCOLITE,	Monroe, Orange, 5;
—	COCCOLITE,	Rogersrock, Essex, 2;
—	COCCOLITE,	Lewis corners, Essex, 2;
—	COCCOLITE,	Phillipstown, Putnam, 2;
—	COCCOLITE,	Diana, Lewis, 2;
—	COCCOLITE,	Carmel, Putnam, 1;
—	COCCOLITE,	Port Henry, Essex, 1;
—	SAHLITE,	Monroe, Orange, 5;
—	SAHLITE,	Moriah, Essex, 1;
—	DIOPSIDE,	Phillipstown, Putnam, 1;
—	RENSSELAERITE,	Oxbow, Jefferson, 2.
62 HORNBLENDE(194),		- - - - - - - - - - - Cabinet.
—		Carmel, Putnam, 2;
—		Lewis, Essex, 2;
—		Monroe, Orange, 13;
—		Amity, Orange, 29;

Names.		Localities.
HORNBLENDE :		
—		Peckville, Fishkill, Dutchess, 1;
—		Yonkers, Westchester, 3;
—		Edenville, Orange, 13;
—		Warwick, Orange, 8;
—		Southeast, Putnam, 14;
—		Gouverneur, St.Lawrence, 2;
—		Stony point, Rockland, 1;
—		Florida, Orange, 4;
—		Moriah, Essex, 5;
—		Piermont, Rockland, 2;
—	BOWLDER,	Nyack, Rockland, 1;
—	BLACK,	New-Rochelle, Westchester, 3;
—	BLACK,	Ticonderoga, Essex, 2;
—	BLACK,	Crag harbor, Essex, 1;
—	GREY,	Monroe, Orange, 4;
—	BROWN,	Amity, Orange, 4;
—	GRANULAR,	Crag harbor, Essex, 2;
—	PARGASITE,	Whitehall, Washington, 2;
—	PARGASITE,	Rossie, St.Lawrence, 1;
—	EDENITE,	Warwick, Orange, 3;
—	ACTINOLITE,	Cornwal, Orange, 1;
—	ACTINOLITE,	Fishkill, Dutchess, 2;
—	ACTINOLITE,	Rye, Westchester, 1;
—	ACTINOLITE,	Grassy point, Rockland, 1;
—	ACTINOLITE,	Kent, Putnam, 2;
—	ASBESTUS,	Quarantine, Richmond, 4;
—	ASBESTUS,	Stony point, Rockland, 1;
—	ASBESTUS,	Monroe, Orange, 6;
—	ASBESTUS,	Patterson, Putnam, 2;
—	ASBESTUS,	Newburgh, Orange, 3;
—	ASBESTUS,	Phillipstown, Putnam, 4;
—	ASBESTUS,	Oxbow, Jefferson, 1;
—	TREMOLITE,	Patterson, Putnam, 4;
—	TREMOLITE,	Gouverneur, St.Lawrence, 2;
—	do.	Richville, St.Lawrence, 3;
—	do.	Hastings, Westchester, 6;
—	do.	Dover, Dutchess, 3;
—	do.	Edenville, Orange, 2;
—	do.	Kingsbridge, New-York, 4;
—	do.	Amity, Orange, 4;
—	do	Phillipstown, Putnam, 3;
—	do.	Port Henry, Essex, 2;
—	do.	New-Rochelle, Westchester, 3;
—	do.	Rossie, St.Lawrence, 3;

Names.	Localities.	
HORNBLENDE :		
— PSEUDOMORPHS,	Edenville, Orange, 2;	
— PSEUDOMORPHS,	Amity, Orange, 3.	
63 ARFWEDSONITE?(1)	Carmel, Putnam. - - - -	Cabinet.
64 HYPERSTHENE(1),	Putnam, Washington. - - -	Cabinet.
65 SCHILLER SPAR,	Carmel in Putnam, and Amity in Orange.	
66 ANTHOPHYLLITE(5),	- - - - - - - - - - - -	Cabinet.
—	Rye, Westchester, 2;	
—	New-Rochelle, Westchester, 3.	
67 HYDROUS ANTHOPHYLLITE(5),	- - - - - - - - -	Cabinet.
—	New-York island, 2;	
—	New-Rochelle, Westchester, 2;	
—	Fishkill, Dutchess, 1.	

ORDER II. ALUMINA.

68 CORUNDUM,	Near Amity, Orange.	
69 SPINELLE(40);	- - - - - - - - - - - -	Cabinet.
—	Amity, Orange, 19;	
—	Edenville, Orange, 10;	
—	Mount Eve, Orange, 2;	
—	Warwick, Orange, 3;	
—	Oxbow, Jefferson, 4;	
—	Gouverneur, St.Lawrence, 1;	
—	Rossie, St.Lawrence, 1.	
70 AUTOMOLITE,	Rossie, St.Lawrence.	
71 GIBBSITE(1),	Unionvale, Dutchess.	
72 ALUMINITE,	In the clay of Staten island, etc.	
73 IDOCRASE(6),	- - - - - - - - - - - -	Cabinet.
—	Amity, Orange, 4;	
—	Antwerp, Jefferson, 2.	
74 GARNET(50),	- - - - - - - - - - - -	Cabinet.
—	Amity, Orange, 3;	
—	Rogersrock, Essex, 12;	
—	Greenfield, Saratoga, 1;	
—	Lewis, Essex, 5;	
—	New-Rochelle, Westchester, 2;	
—	Hague, Warren, 1;	
—	Sprakers, Montgomery, 4;	
—	Westfarms, Westchester, 1;	

Names.		Localities.	
GARNET :			
—		Monroe, Orange, 4;	
—		Dover, Dutchess, 3;	
—		Yonkers, Westchester, 1;	
—	COLOPHONITE,	Lewis, Essex, 2;	
—	COLOPHONITE,	Carmel, Putnam, 1;	
—	COLOPHONITE,	Rogersrock, Essex, 2;	
—	COLOPHONITE,	Sterling mountain, 1;	
—	CINNAMON-STONE,	Amity, Orange, 1.	
75 SCAPOLITE(30),		- - - - - - - - - - -	Cabinet.
—		Amity, Orange, 1;	
—		Monroe, Orange, 6;	
—		Twoponds, Orange, 1;	
—		Edenville, Orange, 1;	
—		Ticonderoga, Essex, 2;	
—		Oxbow, Jefferson, 3;	
—		Lewis, Essex, 2;	
—		Diana, Lewis, 1;	
—		Gouverneur, St.Lawrence, 1;	
—	NUTTALLITE,	Naturalbridge, Lewis, 1;	
—	PSEUDOMORPH.	Oxbow, Jefferson, 1.	
76 STAUROLITE(1),		Dover, Dutchess. - - - -	Cabinet.
77 FELDSPAR(46),		- - - - - - - - - - - -	Cabinet.
—		Warwick, Orange, 2;	
—		Monroe, Orange, 10;	
—		Edenville, Orange, 2;	
—		Cornwal, Orange, 1;	
—		Southfield furnace, Orange, 2;	
—		Greenfield, Saratoga, 1;	
—		Cheever mine, Moriah, Essex, 3;	
—		New-York island, 3;	
—		Rogersrock, Essex, 1;	
—		Ticonderoga, Essex, 2;	
—		Westfarms, Westchester, 1;	
—		Yonkers, Westchester, 3;	
—		Hammond, St.Lawrence, 1;	
—		Rossie, St.Lawrence, 3;	
—		French mountain, Warren, 2;	
—		Putnam, Washington, 2;	
—		Diana, Lewis, 2;	
—		Palmer mine, Clinton, 1;	
—		Littlefalls, Herkimer, 2;	
—		Phillipstown, Putnam, 1;	
—		Grassy point, Rockland, 1.	

Names.	Localities.	
78 LABRADORITE(8),	- - - - - - - - - -	Cabinet.
—	Lewis corners, Essex, 2;	
—	Moriah, Essex, 4;	
—	Ogdensburgh, St.Lawrence, 1;	
— BOWLDER,	Hamptonburgh, Orange, 1.	
79 ALBITE(1),	Granville, Washington. - -	Cabinet.
80 STELLITE(4),	Piermont, Rockland. - - -	Cabinet.
81 MESOTYPE,	Harlem, New-York.	
82 STILBITE(9),	- - - - - - - - - - -	Cabinet.
—	Harlem, New-York, 5;	
—	Peekskill, Westchester, 4.	
83 HEULANDITE,	Near Westfarms, Westchester.	
84 EPISTILBITE,	In Rockland county?	
85 APOPHYLLITE,	Harlem, New-York.	
86 PREHNITE(1),	Westport, Essex. - - - -	Cabinet.
87 THOMSONITE,	Piermont, Rockland.	
88 LAUMONITE,	Phillipstown, Putnam (exhausted).	
89 ANALCIME,	Near Yonkers, Westchester.	
90 CHABAZITE,	Piermont, Rockland.	
91 EPIDOTE(15),	- - - - - - - - - - -	Cabinet.
—	Harlem, New-York, 4;	
—	Carmel, Putnam, 2;	
—	Cornwal, Orange, 1;	
—	Warwick, Orange, 3;	
—	Ticonderoga, Essex, 2;	
—	Westport, Essex, 2;	
—	Putnam, Washington, 1.	
92 TOURMALINE(25),	- - - - - - - - - - -	Cabinet.
—	Port Henry, Essex, 2;	
—	Gouverneur, St.Lawrence, 1;	
—	Yonkers, Westchester, 2;	
—	Harlem, New-York, 2;	
—	Edenville, Orange, 3;	
—	Warwick, Orange, 2;	
—	Amity, Orange, 2;	
—	Greenfield, Saratoga, 1;	
—	Richfield, St.Lawrence, 1;	
—	Ticonderoga, Essex, 1;	
— SCHORL,	Essex county, 1.	

	Names.	Localities.	
93	CLINTONITE(2),	Amity, Orange. - - - - -	Cabinet.
94	ANDALUSITE,	Near Nyack, Rockland.	
95	BUCHOLZITE(5),	- - - - - - - - - - - -	Cabinet.
	—	Cornwal, Orange, 1;	
	—	Monroe, Orange, 3.	
96	KYANITE,	Near New-York city.	
97	ACHMITE,	Lockport, Niagara.	
98	PITCHSTONE,	Dykes in Essex and Warren.	
99	SPODUMENE,	Near Saratoga springs.	
100	PYROPHYLLITE,	Near Westpoint, Orange.	
101	MICA(73),	- - - - - - - - - - - -	Cabinet.
	—	Ticonderoga, Essex, 1;	
	—	Antwerp, Jefferson, 5;	
	—	Oxbow, Jefferson, 2;	
	—	Rossie, St.Lawrence, 2;	
	—	Edwards, St.Lawrence, 2;	
	—	Gouverneur, St.Lawrence, 2;	
	—	Diana, Lewis, 1;	
	—	Greenfield, Saratoga, 5;	
	—	Putnam, Washington, 1;	
	—	Monroe, Orange, 12;	
	—	Edenville, Orange, 8;	
	—	Amity, Orange, 1;	
	—	Warwick, Orange, 4;	
	—	Kane's quarry, Westchester, 2;	
	—	Westfarms, Westchester, 1;	
	—	New-Rochelle, Westchester, 2;	
	—	Rye, Westchester, 1;	
	—	Southeast, Putnam, 1;	
	— BLACK,	Yonkers, Westchester, 1;	
	— YELLOW,	Warwick, Orange, 1;	
	— GREEN,	Greenwood, Monroe, Orange, 1;	
	— GREEN,	Yonkers, Westchester, 4;	
	— SILVERY,	Edwards, St.Lawrence, 2;	
	— SILVERY,	Amity, Orange, 1;	
	— COPPER,	Edenville, Orange, 3;	
	— LITHION?	Edenville, Orange, 2;	
	— CRYSTALLIZED,	Antwerp, Jefferson, 5.	

ORDER III. GLUCINA.

	Names.	Localities.	
102	EMERALD,	Near New-York city, and near Singsing in Westchester.	
103	CHRYSOBERYL(2),	Greenfield, Saratoga. - - -	Cabinet.

ORDER IV. ZIRCONIA.

104	ZIRCONITE(18),	- - - - - - - - - - -	Cabinet.
	—	Warwick, Orange, 8;	
	—	Edenville, Orange, 1;	
	—	Cornwal, Orange, 3;	
	—	Canterbury, Orange, 1;	
	—	Delong's mill, St.Lawrence, 1;	
	—	Hall mine, Moriah, Essex, 2.	

CLASS VII. METALLIC MINERALS.

ORDER I. IRON.

105	NATIVE IRON,	Near Penn-Yan, Yates?	
106	MAGNETIC IRON ORE(83),	- - - - - - - - - - -	Cabinet.
	—	Moriah, Essex, 15;	
	—	Ticonderoga, Essex, 2;	
	—	Crownpoint, Essex, 3;	
	—	Crag harbor, Essex, 2;	
	—	Clinton county, 5;	
	—	Antwerp, Jefferson, 1;	
	—	French mountain, Warren, 2;	
	—	Jessup's landing, Saratoga, 2;	
	—	Salisbury, Herkimer, 2;	
	—	Monroe, Orange, 37;	
	—	Cornwal, Orange, 6;	
	—	Canterbury, Orange, 1;	
	—	Phillipstown, Putnam, 4;	
	—	Southeast, Putnam, 3;	
	—	Haverstraw, Rockland, 2;	
	— IRON SAND,	Port Henry, Essex, 2;	
	— IRON SAND,	Duck pond, Suffolk, 1;	
	— IRON SAND,	Lyonsdale, Lewis, 1;	
	— IRON SAND,	Diana, Lewis, 1;	
	— IRON SAND,	Gouverneur, St.Lawrence, 1.	

Names.		Localities.	
107 SPECULAR IRON ORE(25),		- - - - - - - - - - - -	Cabinet.
—		Hermon, St.Lawrence, 6;	
—		Gouverneur, St.Lawrence, 2;	
—		Edwards, St.Lawrence, 3;	
—		Antwerp, Jefferson, 2;	
—		Theresa, Jefferson, 2;	
—		Naturalbridge, Jefferson, 2;	
—		Port Henry, Essex, 1;	
—	RED,	Oxbow, Jefferson, 1;	
—	LENTICULAR,	Rochester, Monroe, 2;	
—	JASPERY,	Hall mine, Moriah, Essex, 1;	
—	JASPERY,	Parish mine, St.Lawrence, 1;	
—	HEMATITE,	Ticonderoga, Essex, 1;	
—	CRYSTALLIZED,	Gouverneur, St.Lawrence, 1.	
108 LIMONITE(36),		- - - - - - - - - - - -	Cabinet.
—		Oxbow, Jefferson, 2;	
—		Port Henry, Essex, 1;	
—		Whitehall, Washington, 2;	
—		Fishkill, Dutchess, 2;	
—		Unionvale, Dutchess, 5;	
—		Amenia, Dutchess, 1;	
—		Monroe, Orange, 7;	
—		Near Canterbury, Orange, 3;	
—		Warwick, Orange, 1;	
—		Edenville, Orange, 2;	
—		Wurtzborough, Sullivan, 1;	
—		Near Quarantine, Richmond, 3;	
—		Peekskill, Westchester, 2;	
—	UMBER,	Monroe, Orange, 3;	
—	OCHRE,	Greig, Lewis, 2.	
109 IRON PYRITES(20),		- - - - - - - - - - - -	Cabinet.
—		Rossie, St.Lawrence, 1;	
—		Port Henry, Essex, 2;	
—		Diana, Lewis, 2;	
—		Martinsburgh, Lewis, 3;	
—		Flat creek, Montgomery, 1;	
—		Yonkers, Westchester, 1;	
—		Schoharie courthouse, Schoharie, 2;	
—		Kingsbridge, New-York, 1;	
—		Wurtzborough, Sullivan, 1;	
—		Newburgh, Orange, 2;	
—		Warwick, Orange, 1;	
—		Theresa, Jefferson, 1;	
—	SULPHURET,	Gouverneur, St.Lawrence, 2.	

Names.	Localities.	
110 MAGNETIC IRON PYRITES(3),	- - - - - - - - - -	Cabinet.
—	Monroe, Orange, 1;	
—	Port Henry, Essex, 2.	
111 WHITE IRON PYRITES,	Near Warwick in Orange, etc.	
112 ARSENICAL IRON PYRITES(10),	- - - - - - - - -	Cabinet.
—	Brown's quarry, Putnam, 3;	
—	Edenville, Orange, 6;	
—	Amity, Orange, 1.	
113 SCORODITE,	Warwick, Orange.	
114 IRON SINTER(3),	Edenville, Orange.	
115 SPATHOSE IRON(5),	- - - - - - - - - - - -	Cabinet.
—	Parish mine, St.Lawrence, 4;	
—	Dodge mine, Hermon, St.Lawrence, 1.	
116 ANKERITE,	Johnsburgh, Warren.	
117 COPPERAS,	Not referred to.	
118 ALUMINA-SULPHATE OF IRON,	Rossville, Richmond.	
119 CHROME-IRON ORE(2),	- - - - - - - - - - - -	Cabinet.
—	Quarantine, Richmond, 1;	
—	Rye, Westchester, 1.	
120 VIVIANITE,	Harlem, New-York.	
121 CACOXENITE(2),	Sterling mine, Antwerp, Jefferson.	Cabinet.
122 ILVAITE,	In Essex county?	
123 SILICATE OF IRON,	Ramapo, Rockland.	
124 HUDSONITE(1),	Cornwal, Orange. - - - -	Cabinet.

ORDER II. MANGANESE.

125 OXIDE OF MANGANESE(5),	- - - - - - - - - - -	Cabinet.
—	Unionvale, Dutchess, 1;	
—	Warwick, Orange, 2;	
—	Sprakers, Montgomery, 1;	
—	Crownpoint, Essex, 1.	
126 MANGANESE SPAR,	In Essex and Warren counties.	
127 BABINGTONITE,	Gouverneur, St.Lawrence.	

ORDER III. ZINC.

128 ZINC BLENDE(10),	- - - - - - - - - - - -	Cabinet.
—	Flat creek, Root, Montgomery, 1;	
—	Ellenville, Ulster, 2;	

Names.	Localities.
ZINC BLENDE :	
—	Wurtzborough, Sullivan, 4;
—	Lockport, Niagara, 2;
—	Niagara falls, Niagara, 1.

ORDER IV. LEAD.

129 GALENA(22),	- - - - - - - - - - - Cabinet.
—	Old Rossie mine, St.Lawrence, 2;
—	Mineral point, St.Lawrence, 3;
—	Martinsburgh, Lewis, 8;
—	Flat creek, Root, Montgomery, 3;
—	Wurtzborough, Sullivan, 5;
—	Macomb, St.Lawrence, 1.
130 WHITE LEAD ORE,	In St.Lawrence and Westchester counties.
131 ANGLESITE,	Rossie, St.Lawrence.
132 YELLOW LEAD ORE,	Ancram, Columbia.
133 PYROMORPHITE,	Near Singsing, Westchester.
134 VAUQUELINITE,	Near Singsing, Westchester.

ORDER V. BISMUTH.

135 NATIVE BISMUTH,	In Essex county?

ORDER VI. COPPER.

136 NATIVE COPPER,	In Washington county?
137 RED COPPER ORE,	Ladenton, Rockland.
138 VITREOUS COPPER,	In Columbia and Dutchess counties.
139 COPPER PYRITES(6),	- - - - - - - - - - - Cabinet.
—	Rossie, St.Lawrence, 1;
—	Wurtzborough, Sullivan, 1;
—	Kane's quarry, Westchester, 1.
140 GREEN MALACHITE(2),	- - - - - - - - - - - Cabinet.
—	Phillips mine, Putnam, 1;
—	Theresa, Jefferson, 1.
141 AZURITE,	Singsing, Westchester.

ORDER VII. TITANIUM.

142 NATIVE TITANIUM,	Furnaces of St.Lawrence county, etc.
143 ANATASE(1),	Phillipstown, Putnam. - - Cabinet.

Names.	Localities.	
144 Rutile(2),	Amity, Orange. - - - -	Cabinet.
145 Ilmenite(7),	- - - - - - - - - - - -	Cabinet.
—	Warwick, Orange, 4;	
—	Stirling mine, Monroe, Orange, 2;	
—	Cornwal, Orange, 1.	
146 Sphene(17),	- - - - - - - - - - - -	Cabinet.
—	Diana, Lewis, 2;	
—	Phillips mine, Putnam, 2;	
—	Warwick, Orange, 2;	
—	Amity, Orange, 2;	
—	Bush mine, Cornwal, Orange, 2;	
—	Gouverneur, St.Lawrence, 3.	
147 Warwickite(4),	- - - - - - - - - - - -	———
—	Warwick, Orange, 2;	
—	Edenville, Orange, 2.	

ORDER VIII. MOLYBDENUM.

148 Molybdenite(1),	23d-street, New-York city. -	Cabinet.

ORDER IX. ARSENIC.

149 Orpiment,	Near Carmel, Putnam.

ORDER X. CERIUM.

150 Allanite,	Monroe, Orange.

ORDER XI. SILVER.

151 Native silver,	Singsing, Westchester.
152 Vitreous silver,	Livingston's mine, Columbia.

ADDITIONS.

MINERALS FOUND SINCE THE MINERALOGY WAS PUBLISHED.

Names.	Localities.	
153 Terenite,	Antwerp, Jefferson.	
154 Columbite,	Greenfield, Saratoga.	
155 Loxoclase,	Rossie, St.Lawrence.	
156 Monazite,	Yorktown, Westchester.	
157 Nitrate of lime,	Marbletown, Ulster.	
158 Phyllite,	Clove iron mine, Dutchess.	
159 Yttro-cerite,	Amity, Orange.	
160 Dysintribite(1),	Theresa, Jefferson. - - - -	Cabinet.
161 Houghite(3),	Gouverneur, St.Lawrence. -	Cabinet.
162 Millerite(2),	Antwerp, Jefferson. - - -	Cabinet.

GEOLOGY OF NEW-YORK,

BY

WILLIAM W. MATHER, EBENEZER EMMONS, LARDNER VANUXEM, AND JAMES HALL.

GEOLOGY.

[All the specimens enumerated under this division of the Catalogue are in the Cabinet, unless specially cited as *missing*.]

I. CRYSTALLINE AND METAMORPHIC ROCKS OF THE ANTE-SILURIAN PERIOD.

FIRST TABLE CASE.

	Names of Specimens.	Localities.
1	GRAPHIC GRANITE.	Staten island.
2	GRANITE.	Westchester county.
3	GRAPHIC GRANITE.	
4	GRANITE.	Stony point, Rockland county.
5	GRANITE (gneissoid).	Dean's bridge, Westchester co.
6	GRANITE (fine-grained).	
7	GRANITE (gneissoid).	Near Clove mine, Monroe, Orange co.
8	GRANITE.	Buttermilk falls, Cornwal, Orange.
9	GRANITE (sienitic).	
10	GRANITE.	East of Boonville, Lewis.
11	GRANITE (red).	Near Boonville, Lewis.
12	GRANITE (felspathic and decomposing).	
13	KAOLIN (from decomposing granite).	
14	GRANITE (red).	Head of feeder, Boonville, Lewis.
15	GRANITE (sienitic).	Highlands.
16	GNEISS.	Near Peekskill, Westchester.

Names.	Localities.
17 & 18 GNEISS.	Near Coldspring, Putnam.
19 GNEISS.	Above Tarrytown, Westchester.
20 GNEISS (with calcareous matter).	Littlefalls.
21 & 22 GNEISS.	Littlefalls.
23 GNEISS.	Two miles south of Cranberry creek.
24 GNEISS.	South of Westpoint.
25 GNEISS.	Northeast of Fourth lake, Hamilton.
26 & 27 GNEISS.	
28 GNEISS.	Trenton village, near Remsen.
29 GNEISS.	Between Kingsborough and Clarke's.
30 GNEISS.	Salisbury, Herkimer.
31 GNEISS (epidotic).	Yorktown, Westchester.
32 HORNBLENDE.	Near New-Rochelle, Westchester.
33 – 36 MAGNETIC OXIDE OF IRON.	Monroe, Orange.
37 & 38 HYPERSTHENE ROCK.	Moriah, Essex.
39 RED GRANITE.	Lewisburgh, Lewis.
40 BLUE CRYSTALLINE LIMESTONE.	Naturalbridge, Jefferson.
41 CRYSTALLINE LIMESTONE.	Northeast of Fourth lake, Hamilton.
42 MICACEOUS LIMESTONE.	Northeast of Lewisburgh, Lewis.
43 CRYSTALLINE LIMESTONE (with quartz and augite).	N.E. Fourth lake.
44 CRYSTALLINE LIMESTONE.	Northeast of Lewisburgh, Lewis.
45 FUSED QUARTZ.	Rossie, St.Lawrence.
46 QUARTZ and MICA.	Northeast of Fourth lake, Hamilton.
47 COCCOLITE.	Northeast of Fourth lake, Hamilton.
48 PURPLE SCAPOLITE.	Antwerp, Jefferson.
49 IRON ORE.	Alexandria, Jefferson.
50 SPECULAR IRON ORE.	Edwards, St.Lawrence.
51 SPECULAR OXIDE OF IRON (with quartz crystals).	Fowler, St.Lawrence.
52 SPECULAR OXIDE OF IRON (with quartz and limestone).	Edwards.
53 PEROXIDE OF IRON (with cacoxene).	Sterling mine, Jefferson.
54 SULPHATE OF STRONTIAN.	
55 RENSSELAERITE.	Edwards, St.Lawrence.

Names.	Localities.
56 & 57 TALC.	Fowler, St.Lawrence.
58 & 59 TALC.	Naturalbridge, Jefferson.
60 RENSSELAERITE (with satin spar).	Fowler, St.Lawrence.
61 WHITE TALC.	Fowler, St.Lawrence.
62 CACOXENE (on gneissoid rock).	Naturalbridge, Jefferson.
63 SCAPOLITE ROCK.	In northeast part of Lewis county.
64 CRYSTALLINE LIMESTONE (with brucite).	Schroon, Essex.

FIRST WALL CASE.

65 – 67 LABRADORITE.	Adirondack, Essex.
68 LABRADORITE (sienitic).	Adirondack, Essex.
69 HYPERSTHENE ROCK (sienitic).	Moriah, Essex.
70 LABRADORITE.	Mayfield corners, Montgomery.
71 HYPERSTHENE ROCK.	Port Kent, Essex.
72 PORPHYRITIC TALCOSE SLATE.	Westport, Essex.
73 GRAPHIC GRANITE.	Warwick, Orange.
74 GRANITE IN LIMESTONE.	Warwick, Orange.
75 GRANITE.	Long mine, Monroe, Orange.
76 GRANITIC ROCK.	Mountain mine, Monroe, Orange.
77 GRANITE.	Royahook, Westchester.
78 GRANITE.	Saw-works, Monroe, Orange.
79 GRANITE.	Patterson mine, Monroe, Orange.
80 GRANITE (sienite).	Near Fort Montgomery, Orange.
81 GRANITE.	Tenth avenue, New-York city.
82 FELSPATHIC GRANITE.	Tarrytown, Westchester.
83 GNEISS (with magnetic oxide of iron).	Shenadone, Dutchess.
84 GNEISS (junction of hypersthene rock).	
85 GNEISS (with garnet).	O'Niel mine, Orange.
86 GNEISS.	Fort Montgomery, Orange.
87 GNEISS.	Coldspring, Putnam.
88 GNEISS.	Carmel, Putnam.
89 & 90 GNEISS.	Near Singsing, Westchester.
91 – 93 GNEISS.	Near Westpoint, Orange.

	Names.	Localities.
94	Gneiss.	Near Dobbs's ferry, Westchester.
95	Gneiss.	Royahook, Westchester.
96	Gneiss.	Mountpleasant, Westchester.
97	Gneiss.	Near Westpoint, Orange.
98	Gneiss.	Stormville, Dutchess.
99	Gneiss.	Somerstown plains, Westchester.
100 – 102	Hypersthene rock passing into gneiss.	Moriah, Essex.
103	Gneiss.	Shenadone, Dutchess.
104 & 105	Gneiss.	Herkimer county.
106	Mica slate.	Whiteplains, Westchester.
107	Mica slate (with staurotide).	Hurd's corners, Dutchess.
108	Mica.	Clove mine, Monroe, Orange.
109	Sienite (primitive greenstone).	Cortland, Westchester.
110	Sienite.	Moriah, Essex.
111	Hornblende.	Warwick, Orange.
112	Hornblende.	Westport, Essex.
113	Kaolin.	
114	Kaolin (or porcelain clay).	Johnsburgh, Warren.
115	Felspar.	Westport, Essex.
116	Sahlite (in hypersthene).	Westport, Essex.
117	Scapolite rock.	Ausable, Essex.
118	Magnetic oxide of iron.	Sanford ore bed, Essex.
119 & 120	Magnetic oxide of iron.	Salisbury, Herkimer.
121	Magnetic oxide (in limestone).	Near Coldspring, Putnam.
122 – 125	Magnetic oxide of iron.	Monroe, Orange.
126	Magnetic oxide (with arragonite).	O'Niel mine, Monroe, Orange.
127	Black oxide of manganese.	Crownpoint, Essex.
128	Copper pyrites (in limestone).	Paradox lake, Essex.
129	Rose quartz.	Moriah, Essex.
130	White augite.	Near Phillipstown, Putnam.
131	Epidote.	Westport, Essex.
132	Epidote (boulder).	In place in Vermont.
133	Obsidian.	Johnsburgh, Warren.

Names.	Localities.
134 Colophonite.	Johnsburgh, Warren.
135 Crystalline limestone.	Port Henry, Essex.

136 Crystalline limestone (with an unknown mineral). Port Henry.

137 Crystalline limestone (with graphite). Port Henry, Essex.

138 & 139 Crystalline limestone (ferruginous). Johnsburgh, Warren.

140 Crystalline limestone (with mica and brucite). Schroon, Essex.

141 Crystalline limestone (with graphite).

142 Crystalline limestone (with quartz and pyroxene). Moriah, Essex.

143 Crystalline limestone (with serpentine). Bolton, Warren.

144 – 147 Crystalline limestone (with serpentine). Moriah, Essex.

148 Crystalline limestone (with serpentine). Port Henry, Essex.

149 Serpentine. Warrensburgh, Warren.

150 Serpentine and limestone. 58th-street, New-York city.

151 Limestone with brucite. Near Putnam courthouse, Putnam.

152 Crystalline limestone (with mica).

153 Crystalline limestone. Near Putnam courthouse, Putnam.

154 – 156 Crystalline limestone (flesh-colored). Monroe, Orange.

157 Crystalline limestone (white).

158 White limestone. Edenville, Orange.

159 White limestone (with plumbago). Monroe, Orange.

160 Pyroxene or augite. Twoponds, Monroe, Orange.

161 Limestone (with augite and crystallized iron ore). Monroe, Orange.

162 Limestone (with mica). Monroe, Orange.

163 Limestone (with pargasite and meionite). Monroe, Orange.

164 Limestone (with pargasite). Island pond, Monroe, Orange.

165 Limestone (with serpentine or boltonite). Monroe, Orange.

166 Crystalline limestone. Near Westfarms, Westchester.

167 Granular limestone. Near Somerstown plains, Westchester.

168 Crystalline limestone. North-Salem, Westchester.

169 Limestone (with tremolite). Near North-Salem, Westchester.

170 Serpentine. Forshee's mine, Monroe, Orange.

171 Serpentine (black).

172 Serpentine (with amianthus). O'Niel mine, Monroe, Orange.

	Names.	Localities.
173	Serpentine (striated surface).	
174	Primitive greenstone.	Near Peekskill, Westchester.
175 & 176	Dendritic porphyry.	Essex, Essex.
177	Trap and limestone.	Near Saw-works, Monroe.
178	Trap (striated surface).	Near Ross's bridge, Essex.
179	Veinstone.	Near Singsing, Westchester.
180	Trap.	
181	Trap.	Near Fort-Ann, Washington.
182	Trap	Near Saw-works, Monroe, Orange.
183	Trap.	Near Greenwood furnace, Monroe, Orange.
184	Trap (vesicular).	Parish ore bed, St.Lawrence.
185	Augite.	Sparta, Westchester.

SECOND WALL CASE.

186	Calcareous spar.	Rossie lead mine, St.Lawrence.
187	Calcareous spar (purple).	Oxbow, Jefferson.
188	Calcareous spar (with chalcedony).	Fowler, St.Lawrence.
189	Crystalline limestone.	
190	Quartz crystals (in limestone).	Laidlaw lake, Oxbow, Jefferson.
191	Granite (graphic).	Gouverneur, St.Lawrence.
192	Felspar and trap.	Alexandria, Jefferson.
193	Gneiss.	Lewisburgh furnace, Lewis.
194	Gneiss.	Rossie lead mine, St.Lawrence.
195	Mica slate.	Northeast of Fourth lake, Hamilton.
196 & 197	Crystalline limestone.	Lewisburgh, Lewis.
198	Crystalline limestone.	Gouverneur, St.Lawrence.
199	Crystalline limestone (with magnesian nodules).	Gouverneur.
200	Primary limestone (brecciated).	Gouverneur, St.Lawrence.
201	Crystalline limestone (with hornblende).	Gouverneur.
202	Crystalline limestone (with crystals of mica).	Antwerp, Jefferson.
203	Limestone (with quartz).	Fourth lake, Jefferson.
204	Limestone (with quartz and felspar).	Fourth lake, Jefferson.
205	Serpentine (with quartz).	Sterling's mine, Antwerp, Jefferson.

Names.	Localities.
206 Serpentine.	Sterling mine, Antwerp, Jefferson.
207 Rensselaerite.	Naturalbridge, Jefferson.
208 Rensselaerite.	Edwards, St.Lawrence.
209 & 210 Silvery talc.	Fowler, St.Lawrence.
211 Scapolite.	Gouverneur, St.Lawrence.
212 Brown mica.	Edwards, St.Lawrence.
213 Brown mica (in crystals).	Pope's mills, St.Lawrence.
214 Fluor spar.	Muscalunge lake, Jefferson.
215 Fused quartz.	Hammond, St.Lawrence.
216 Quartz in chlorite.	Brant lake, Essex?
217 Iron ore (scoriaceous).	Lewisburgh, Lewis.
218 Iron ore (compact).	Lewisburgh, Lewis.
219 Iron ore (specular).	Lewisburgh, Lewis.
220 Iron ore.	Reamer's ore bed, Lewisburgh, Lewis.
221 Limestone with iron ore.	Lewisburgh ore bed, Lewis.
222 Limestone (ferruginous).	Lewisburgh, Lewis.
223 Crystalline limestone.	Lewisburgh, Lewis.
224 Ferruginous limestone.	Near Lewisburgh, Lewis.
225 Impure limestone with iron ore.	Lewisburgh, Lewis.
226 & 227 Iron pyrites.	Indian lake, Lewis.
228 Ferruginous limestone.	Lewisburgh, Lewis.
229 Specular iron ore.	Harrisville, Jefferson.
230 & 231 Specular iron ore (with quartz).	Edwards, St.Lawrence.
232 Specular iron ore (with quartz crystals).	Edwards, St. Lawrence.
233 Specular iron ore.	Edwards, St.Lawrence.
234 Specular iron ore (with cacoxene).	Sterling mine, St.Lawrence.
235 Specular iron ore.	Harrisville, Jefferson.
236 Gneiss (sienitic).	Near Harrisville, Jefferson.
237 Siliceous limestone.	Harrisville, Jefferson.
238 Iron pyrites (in trap).	Naturalbridge, Jefferson.
239 Chlorite (the silver ore).	Naturalbridge, Jefferson.
240 Serpentine.	Naturalbridge, Jefferson.
241 Serpentine (brecciated).	Antwerp, Jefferson.

II. METAMORPHIC ROCKS OF THE MOHAWK GROUP.

SECOND TABLE CASE.

Names.	Localities.
1 Quartz rock.	Stanford, Dutchess.
2 Granular quartz.	Amenia, Dutchess.
3 Compact quartz rock.	Poughquaick, Dutchess.
4 Granular quartz.	Near Peekskill, Westchester.
5 Ferruginous quartz.	Williamstown, Massachusetts.
6 & 7 Granular limestone.	Dover plains, Westchester.
8 Granular limestone.	Williamstown, Massachusetts.
9 & 10 Granular limestone.	Hillsdale, Columbia.
11 – 13 Granular limestone.	Amenia, Dutchess.
14 Granular limestone (clouded).	Northeast, Dutchess.
15 Granular limestone (grey).	Cortland, Westchester.
16 Granular limestone (variegated).	Peekskill, Westchester.
17 Granular limestone (blue).	Peekskill, Westchester.
18 Granular limestone (striped).	Near Peekskill, Westchester.
19 Granular limestone (compact).	Stormville, Dutchess.
20 Talcy limestone.	Stormville, Dutchess.
21 Talco-slaty limestone.	Stormville, Dutchess.
22 & 23 Talcy limestone.	Unionvale, Dutchess.
24 Slaty limestone.	Ancram lead mine, Columbia.
25 Sparry limestone.	Unionvale, Dutchess.
26 Sparry limestone.	Bloomingrove, Orange.
27 Sparry limestone.	Warwick, Orange.
28 – 30 Sparry limestone.	Hoosick, Rensselaer.
31 Slaty-talcy limestone.	Arthursburgh, Dutchess.
32 Talco-slaty limestone.	Lebanon springs, Columbia.

Names.	Localities.
33 Slaty limestone.	Williamstown, Massachusetts.
34 Slaty limestone.	Cortland, Westchester.
35 Slaty limestone.	Ashford, Massachusetts.
36 Slaty limestone.	Stanford, Dutchess.
37 Mica slate (with garnets).	Dover, Dutchess.
38 Mica and talcy slate.	Amenia, Dutchess.
39 Slate.	Montrose, Dutchess.
40 Talcose slate.	Near Peekskill, Westchester.
41 Slate (black).	Clinton, Dutchess.
42 Slate (green).	Clinton, Dutchess.
43 Mica slate (the alum rocks).	Near Ameniaville, Dutchess.
44 & 45 Slate.	Near Canaan centre, Columbia.
46 Slate (green).	Near Washington-hollow, Dutchess.
47 Talcose slate.	Canaan-gap, Columbia.
48 Talcose slate.	Hillsdale, Columbia.
49 Slate.	Hillsdale, Columbia.
50 Micaceous slate.	Taghkanic falls, Rensselaer.
51 Talco-micaceous slate.	Richmond, Vermont.
52 Chlorite slate.	Canaan, Columbia.
53 Purple slate.	Petersburgh, Rensselaer.
54 - 57 Slate.	Hoosick, Rensselaer.
58 Talcose slate (greenish).	Saddle mountain, Massachusetts.
59 Talcose slate.	Taconic mountain, Rensselaer.
60 Talco-fibrous slate.	Taconic mountain, Rensselaer.
61 Mica slate.	Taconic mountain, Rensselaer.
62 Slaty sandstone.	Williamstown, Massachusetts.
63 Crystalline quartz (veins in slate).	Ancram, Columbia.
64 Crystalline quartz (with copper ore).	Washington, Dutchess.
65 Quartz in chlorite (with oxide of manganese).	Taconic mountain.
66 Carbonate of iron.	Stockbridge, Massachusetts.
67 Limestone (with iron ore).	Stockbridge, Massachusetts.
68 Talc and mica cemented by oxide of iron.	Stockbridge, Mass.
69 Hematitic iron ore (stalactitic).	Stockbridge, Massachusetts.

SECOND WALL CASE.

	Names.	Localities.
70	Limestone (with talc).	Williamstown, Massachusetts.
71	White limestone.	New-Ashford, Massachusetts.
72	White limestone.	Near East-Dover, Dutchess.
73	Crystalline limestone.	Singsing, Westchester.
74	Crystalline limestone (dolomitic).	Singsing, Westchester.
75	Dolomitic limestone (grey).	Singsing, Westchester.
76	Granular limestone (blue).	Singsing, Westchester.
77 & 78	Crystalline limestone.	Whiteplains, Westchester.
79	Compact limestone.	Beekmanville, Dutchess.
80 & 81	Crystalline limestone.	Bedford, Westchester.
82 & 83	Crystalline limestone (white).	Eastchester, Westchester.
84	Crystalline limestone (bluish).	Westfarms, Westchester.
85 & 86	Crystalline limestone (white).	Kingsbridge, New-York.
87 & 88	Granular limestone (white).	Verplanck, Westchester.
89	Granular limestone (grey).	Dover plains, Dutchess.
90	Slaty and clouded limestone.	Amity, Orange.
91	Grey lamininated limestone.	Adams, Massachusetts.
92	White limestone (with talc).	New-Ashford, Massachusetts.
93	White limestone (sawed slab).	New-Ashford, Massachusetts.
94	Limestone (with talc).	New-Ashford, Massachusetts.
95	Buff-colored limestone.	Williamstown, Massachusetts.
96	Milky quartz.	Williamstown, Massachusetts.
97	Hornstone in limestone.	Williamstown, Massachusetts.
98 – 100	Limestone with serpentine.	Near Putnam courthouse.
101	Talco-serpentine rock.	Near Peekskill, Westchester.
102	Serpentine rock.	Phillipstown, Putnam.
103	Fibrous serpentine.	Troy, Vermont.
104	Mica slate.	Near Verplanck, Westchester.
105	Black slate.	Bennington, Vermont.
106	Talco-slate (greenish).	Taconic mountain.
107	Slate with quartz veins.	Williamstown, Massachusetts.

Names.	Localities.
108 SLATE.	Williamstown, Massachusetts.
109 TALCO-SLATE (greenish).	Richmond, Vermont.
110 SLATE.	Taconic mountain.
111 GREEN SLATE.	
112 HEMATITIC IRON ORE.	Stockbridge, Massachusetts.
113 RED CHALK.	Cortland, Westchester.
114 SLATY QUARTZ.	Williamstown, Massachusetts.

III. NEW-YORK SYSTEM.

1. POTSDAM SANDSTONE.

THIRD TABLE CASE.

	Names.		Localities.
1	POTSDAM SANDSTONE	(red).	Dekalb, St.Lawrence.
2	do	(grey).	Moira, Clinton.
3	do	(conglomerate).	Near Plattsburgh, Clinton.
4	do	(red).	West-Chazy, Clinton.
5	do	(with ripplemarks).	Port Kent, Clinton.
6	do	(red).	West-Chazy, Clinton.
7	do	(fragmentary, red).	Dekalb, St.Lawrence.
8	do		Keeseville, Clinton.
9	do	(grey).	Klip hill, Johnstown, Montgomery.
10	do		Lewisburgh furnace, Lewis.
11	do	(conglomerate).	Near Lewisburgh furnace.
12	do	(conglomerate, grey).	
13	do	(red).	Military road west of Plattsburgh.
14	do	(metamorphic).	
15	do	(grey).	
16	do	(ripplemarks).	
17	do		Near Lewisburgh furnace, Lewis.
18	do	(conglomerate).	Near Lewisburgh furnace.
19	do		Lewisburgh ore bed.
20	do		Lafarge's, near Harrisville.
21 & 22	do		West of Johnstown, Montgomery.
23	do		Klip hill, Johnstown, Montgomery.
24	do		Near Lewisburgh furnace, Lewis.
25	do	(with lingulæ).	Birmingham, Clinton.

	Names.	Localities.
26	POTSDAM SANDSTONE.	Chazy, Clinton.
27	do	Keeseville, Essex.
28	do	(with lingulæ). French creek, St.Lawrence.
29	do	(with *Lingula antiqua*).
30	do	(with lingulæ : spotted with manganese).
31 & 32	do	Near Lewisburgh furnace, Lewis.
33	do	Port Kent, Essex.
34	do	(containing concretions).
35	do	(concretion).
36	do	Potsdam.
37	do	Saranac.
38	do	(colored with vegetable matter). Keeseville, Essex.
39 & 40	do	(containing concretionary carbonate of lime).
41	do	(red).
42	do	(brecciated).
43	do	(fucoidal).
44	do	(brecciated). Chazy, Clinton.
45	do	(weathered surface). French creek, Jefferson.
46 & 47	do	(metamorphic).

THIRD WALL CASE.

48	POTSDAM SANDSTONE	(lowest layer brecciated). Dekalb, St.Lawrence.
49	do	(massive). Potsdam, St.Lawrence.
50	do	(ripplemarks). Keeseville, Essex.
51	do	(with casts of mud furrows).
52	do	Washington county.
53	do	(lowest layer conglomeritic). Lewisburgh, Lewis.
54 – 56	do	Lewisburgh, Lewis.
57	do	Dekalb, St.Lawrence.
58	do	Washington county.
59	do	Chazy, Clinton.
60	do	Keeseville, Essex.
61 & 62	do	Galway, Saratoga.
63	do	(with fragments of impure limestone). Chazy.
64	do	(columnar from artificial heat). Keeseville, Essex.

2. CALCIFEROUS SANDSTONE.

FOURTH TABLE CASE.

	Names.	Localities.
1 – 3	CALCIFEROUS SANDSTONE	(conglomeritic). Spruce creek, Salisbury, Herkimer.
4 – 6	do	Spruce creek, Herkimer.
7 & 8	do	(porphyritic). Lead mine, Salisbury, Herkimer.
9 & 10	do	(erratic). East creek, Herkimer.
11	do	(brown). East of Amsterdam, Montgomery.
12 & 13	do	East of Canajoharie, Montgomery.
14 & 15	do	(with calcareous spar). East of Canajoharie.
16	do	(with calcareous spar). Railroad, Tripe's hill.
17 & 18	do	Canal west of Littlefalls, Herkimer.
19	do	(with globules of anthracite). Littlefalls.
20	do	(with anthracite and calcareous spar). Creek at Spraker's basin, Montgomery.
21	do	(anthracite from). Middleville, Herkimer.
22	do	West of Littlefalls, Herkimer.
23	do	(calcareous, with fossils). Quarry at Canajoharie.
24	do	(calcareous, greenish). Canajoharie.
25	do	Near Amsterdam, Montgomery.
26	do	(with quartz crystals, brown).
27	do	(with quartz crystals). Middleville, Herkimer.
28	do	(crystals of quartz from). Middleville, Herkimer.
29	do	(with calcareous spar). Littlefalls, Herkimer.
30	do	(with drops of anthracite). Littlefalls, Herkimer.
31	do	(calcareous, with *Ophileta*). Canajoharie.
32	do	(calcareous, with fossils).
33	do	(with *Lingula*). Canajoharie, Montgomery.
34	do	(with *Orthoceras primigenium*). Opposite Fort-plain, Montgomery.
35	do	(with *Fucoides*). Canajoharie, Montgomery.
36	do	(upper part of mass). Canajoharie, Montgomery.

	Names.	Localities.
37	CALCIFEROUS SANDSTONE	(shaly, with *Palæophycus tubularis*). Opposite Fortplain, Montgomery.
38	do	(brecciated). East-Canada creek, Montgomery.
39	do	(casts of mud cracks). Creek S. of Canajoharie.
40 – 44	do	(from the altered rocks on the Hudson river.)
45	do	(calcareous).

I do not regard it as proved that the last six specimens belong to the Calciferous sandstone proper. J. H.

THIRD WALL CASE.

46	CALCIFEROUS SANDSTONE	(a red siliceous limestone?). Bellvale, Orange.
47	do	(with drusy quartz). Littlefalls, Herkimer.
48	do	Littlefalls, Herkimer.
49	do	(with anthracite). Littlefalls, Herkimer.
50	do	Glensfalls, Warren.
51	do	(with anthracite).
52	do	(with trap). Canajoharie, Montgomery.
53	do	Canajoharie, Montgomery.
54	do	(upper part of the rock). Canajoharie.
55	do	Littlefalls, Herkimer.
56 & 57	do	Canajoharie, Montgomery.
58	do	Newport, Herkimer.
59	do	(with anthracite). Littlefalls, Herkimer.
60	do	(with calcareous spar).
61	do	(trap dyke in).
62	do	(with anthracite). North of Littlefalls, Herkimer.
63	do	(trap in). Wellsborough falls.
64	do	(greenstone trap in).
65	do	
66	do	(with pearl spar).
67	do	(with *Orthoceratite*). Fortplain, Montgomery.
68	do	(cherty) Galway, Saratoga.
69 & 70	do	Galway, Saratoga.

	Names.	Localities.
71 & 72	CALCIFEROUS SANDSTONE.	Canajoharie, Montgomery.
73 & 74	do	Chazy, Clinton.
75	do	(with sulphate of iron).
76	do	(with lenticular carbonate of lime). Middleville.
77	do	(with crystals of quartz and lime).
78	do	(hexahedral prism of carbonate of lime from).
79	do	(with pearl spar and lenticular carbonate of lime).
80 & 81	do	(with pearl spar). Littlefalls, Herkimer.
82	do	(coarse oolite from). Littlefalls, Herkimer.
83	do	Washington, Dutchess.
84	do	(*Ophileta*). Near East-Canada creek.
85	do	Galway, Saratoga.
86 & 87	do	Fortplain, Montgomery.
88	do	(chert from). Herkimer, Herkimer.
89	do	(drab-colored layer, with spar). Depeauville.
90	do	Warwick, Orange.
91	do	Amity, Orange.
92	do	Littlefalls, Herkimer.
93	do	Ogdensburgh, St.Lawrence.
94	do	Galway, Saratoga.
95	do	Glensfalls, Warren.
96	do	(oolitic). Galway, Saratoga.
97	do	(oolitic). Chazy, Clinton.
98	do	Glensfalls, Warren.
99 & 100	do	Galway, Saratoga.
101	do	(oolitic). Whitehall, Washington.
102	do	(encrinal mass in). Chazy, Clinton.
103	do	(encrinal layer in). Chazy, Clinton.
104	do	Fortplain, Montgomery.
105	do	(with *Orthis*). Chazy, Clinton.

3. BLACK-RIVER LIMESTONE GROUP,

INCLUDING THE CHAZY, BIRDSEYE AND BLACK-RIVER LIMESTONES.

FIFTH TABLE CASE.

	Names.	Localities.
1 & 2	CHAZY LIMESTONE	(lower layers). Chazy, Clinton.
3	do	(encrinal layers). Chazy, Clinton.
4	do	(encrinal mass). Chazy, Clinton.
5	do	(encrinal layer with discs and plates). Chazy.
6	do	(with fossil shells). Chazy.
7	do	(oolitic). Chazy.
8	do	(oolitic). Big island, Orange.
9	do	(compact). Mount Lookout, Orange.
10	POLISHED SURFACE	of the Encrinal layer. Chazy, Clinton.
11 & 12	CHAZY LIMESTONE	(with *Maclurea magna*). Chazy.
13 & 14	do	(with fragments of fossils). Chazy.
15	do	(two specimens, with fragments of shells). Chazy.
16	do	(two, with *Maclurea* and *Raphistoma*). Chazy.
17	do	(with *Atrypa* and crinoidal columns). Chazy.
18	BIRDSEYE LIMESTONE	(with *Orthoceras* and *Phytopsis*). Great bend of the Black river.
19	do	(with fossils). Creek near Spraker's basin.
20	do	(with fragments of trilobites). Watertown, Jefferson.
21	do	(with obscure fossils). Sugar river near Boonville.
22	do	(with *Phytopsis cellulosum*). Near Watertown.
23 - 26	do	(with *Phytopsis tubulosum*). Fortplain.
27	do	(with *P. tubulosum*). Near Boonville, Lewis.
28 - 30	do	Fortplain, Montgomery.
31	do	(polished surface, exhibiting transverse sections of *P. tubulosum*). Fortplain.
32 - 34	do	Near Boonville, Lewis.
35	do	(with *Phytopsis*). Near Boonville, Lewis.
36	do	(with *Phytopsis*). Near Amsterdam, Fulton.

	Names.	Localities.
37	BASE of *Phytopsis*).	Fortplain, Montgomery.
38	BIRDSEYE LIMESTONE.	
39	BLACK-RIVER LIMESTONE (with *Columnaria alveolata*).	Watertown.
40	do (with *C. alveolata*).	Amsterdam.
41	do (concretionary).	North of Amsterdam, Fulton.
42	do (concretionary).	Goshen, Orange.
43	do (with *Ormoceras tenuifilum*).	Watertown.
44 – 46	do (with *O. tenuifilum*).	Near Littlefalls, Herkimer.

FOURTH WALL CASE.

	Names.	Localities.
46 – 49	CHAZY LIMESTONE (with *Atrypa*, etc.).	Chazy, Clinton.
50	do (with *Scolithus*).	Clinton.
51	do (with *Maclurea*).	Chazy.
52	do (with coral and *Maclurea*).	Chazy.
53	do (with *Maclurea*).	Chazy.
54	do (remains of *Atrypa*, etc.).	Chazy.
55 & 56	do (marble).	Isle Lamotte.
57	do (with *Orthoceratite*).	Chazy.
58	do (with remains of fossils).	Chazy.
59 & 60	do (with *Orthoceras*).	Chazy.
61 & 62	do (with *Maclurea*).	Chazy.
63	do (with remains of *Atrypa*, etc.).	Chazy.
64	do (with traces of *Maclurea*).	Chazy.
65	BIRDSEYE LIMESTONE (weathered surface).	Mohawk valley.
66	do (with *Maclurea*).	Amsterdam, Fulton.
67	do (remains of fossils).	Near Watertown, Jefferson.
68	do (with *Phytopsis*).	Chazy? Clinton.
69	do (with *Leptæna sericea*).	Near Middleville.
70	do	Chazy, Clinton.
71	do (with *Streptelasma*).	Dunkirk, Lewis.
72	do (with *Phytopsis*, etc.).	Watertown, Jefferson.
73	do (with coral).	Lafargeville, Jefferson.

	Names.	Localities.
74	HORNSTONE (position uncertain).	Goshen, Orange.
75	BIRDSEYE LIMESTONE.	Chazy, Clinton.
76	do (with *Phytopsis*).	Watertown, Jefferson.
77	do (with *Phytopsis*).	Fortplain, Montgomery.
78	do (with *Phytopsis tubulosum*).	Watertown.
79	do (with *Phytopsis cellulosum*).	Fortplain.
80	do	Fortplain.
81	LIMESTONE (with scratches).	Crownpoint, Essex.
82	LIMESTONE (with drift scratches).	Pillarpoint, Jefferson.
83 – 85	LIMESTONE (with drift scratches).	Amsterdam, Fulton.

The last four specimens apparently belong to the Trenton and Black-river limestones.

86 & 87	BLACK-RIVER LIMESTONE (with *Columnaria*).	Chazy, Clinton.
88	do (with *Columnaria*).	Dry Moose river, Lewis.
89	do (with *Columnaria*).	Watertown, Jefferson.
90 – 93	do (with *Orthoceras*).	Watertown.
94	do (iridescent).	
95	do (with concretions).	St.Johnsville, Montgomery.
96	do	Tripeshill, Montgomery.
97	do (with *Orthoceras*).	Watertown, Jefferson.
98	do (with *Columnaria*).	Watertown.
99	do	St.Johnsville, Montgomery.
100	do (concretionary).	St.Johnsville, Montgomery.
101	do (concretionary).	
102	do (concretionary).	Littlefalls, Herkimer.
103	do (concretionary).	Amsterdam, Fulton.
104	do (concretionary).	Littlefalls, Herkimer.
105	do (striated from movement of strata).	
106	do (with *Columnaria*).	

4. TRENTON LIMESTONE.

SIXTH TABLE CASE.

Names.		Localities.
1 – 3	TRENTON LIMESTONE	(with *Chætetes*). Newport, Herkimer.
4	Large hemispherical form of *Chætetes lycoperdon*.	Newport.
5	The same (weathered specimen).	Middleville, Herkimer.
6	TRENTON LIMESTONE	(with *Chætetes*). Middleville.
7 & 8	*Chætetes* (hemispherical form).	
9	TRENTON LIMESTONE	(with branching forms of *Chætetes lycoperdon*). Sugar river, Boonville, Lewis.
10	do	(with branching or ramose forms of *C. lycoperdon*). Herkimer, Herkimer.
11	do	(with similar forms). Lowville, Lewis.
12	do	(with *Streptelasma corniculum*).
13	do	(encrinal). Creek at Spraker's basin.
14	do	(encrinal). Remsen, Oneida.
15	do	(with fragments of trilobites).
16	do	(with fragments of *Trinucleus*). Near Middleville.
17	do	(with head of *Calymene senaria*). Middleville.
18	do	(with *Calymene senaria*). Middleville.
19	do	(with fragments of *Calymene*).
20 & 21	do	(with caudal shield of *Isotelus gigas*). Middleville.
22	do	(with fragments of *Isotelus* and *Ceraurus*). One mile east of Florida, Fulton.
23	do	(with *Isotelus gigas*). Quarry north of Littlefalls.
24 & 25	do	(caudal shield of *I. gigas*). Middleville.
26	do	(with middle lobe of the buckler of *Isotelus gigas*). Middleville.
27	do	(with *Avicula trentonensis*). Middleville.
28	do	(with fossils). Middleville.
29	do	(with *Leptæna sericea*). Fortplain, Montgomery.
30	do	(with *Leptæna sericea*). Middleville, Herkimer.

	Names.	Localities.
31 – 33	TRENTON LIMESTONE	(with *Leptæna*, etc.). Middleville.
34	do	(with *L. sericea*). Fortplain, Montgomery.
35 & 36	do	(with *L alternata*). Near Middleville, Herkimer.
37 & 38	do	(with *Orthis pectinella*). Middleville.
39	do	(with *O. pectinella* and fragments). Middleville.
40	do	(with *O. testudinaria*). North of Littlefalls.
41	do	(with *O. testudinaria*). Watertown, Jefferson.
42	do	(with *Delthyris lynx*).
43	do	(with *Atrypa extans* and impressions of *Orthis*). Near Boonville.
44	do	(with *Atrypa extans*). Watertown, Jefferson.
45	do	(with *Pleurotomaria*, etc.). Watertown.
46	do	(with *Pleurotomaria* and *Subulites*). Watertown.
47	do	(with *Endoceras proteiforme*). Middleville.
48	do	(with fragment of an *Orthoceras*). Watertown.
49	do	(with fragment of *Orthoceras*). Middleville.
50	do	(with fragment of *Orthoceras*). Fortplain.
51 – 53	do	(with fragments of *Orthoceras*). Middleville.
54	do	(with fragments of *Endoceras proteiforme*). Middleville.
55	do	(with fragments of *O. junceum*). Watertown.

56 *Endoceras* of the Trenton limestone.

57 TRENTON LIMESTONE (with fragment of *Orthoceras?*).

FIFTH WALL CASE.

58 TRENTON LIMESTONE (with *Isotelus*). Creek at Spraker's basin, Fulton.

59 Fragment of *Orthoceras*.

60 TRENTON LIMESTONE (with *Leptæna*, etc.).

61 Fragments of *Orthoceras* from the Trenton limestone.

62 TRENTON LIMESTONE (with fossils).

63	do	(with *Isotelus*). Glensfalls, Warren.
64	do	(with *Isotelus*). Middleville, Herkimer.
65 – 67	do	Glensfalls, Warren.

	Names.	Localities.
68	TRENTON LIMESTONE.	Baker's falls, Washington.
69	do	(with *Trinucleus*). Locality unknown.
70	do	(with fossils). Locality unknown.
71	do	(with *Chætetes lycoperdon*). Jacksonburgh, Herkimer.
72	do	(with *Trinucleus* and other fossils). Near Boonville?
73	do	(with *Chætetes lycoperdon*).
74	do	(with *Calymene senaria*). Below Middleville.
75	do	(with *Calymene senaria*).
76 & 77	do	(with *Chætetes*).
78 – 81	Hemispherical *Chætetes* from the Trenton limestone.	
82	TRENTON LIMESTONE (with *Orthoceras*).	
83	*Orthoceras.*	
84	TRENTON LIMESTONE (with *Orthoceras*).	Dry Moose river, Lewis.
85	do	(with *Orthoceras*). Middleville, Herkimer.
86	do	(with *Orthoceras*). Watertown, Jefferson.
87	do	(with *Subulites*). Watertown, Jefferson.
88	do	Sugar river near Boonville, Oneida.
89	do	(with *Pleurotomaria*, *Murchisonia*, etc.). Trenton.
90	do	(with remains of *Trinucleus*, etc.). Tribeshill.
91	do	(with *Orthoceras*).
92	do	(with fragments of fossils).
93	do	(with *Orthis pectinella*).
94	do	(with *Leptæna alternata*, young shell).
95	do	(with *Atrypa extans*).
96	do	(with *Pleurotomaria lenticularis*).
97	do	(with *Leptæna sericea*).
98	do	(with *L. sericea* and others).
99	do	(with *Orthis testudinaria*). West-Canada creek.
100	do	(with *Leptæna alternata*).
101	do	(with *Orthis* and *Leptæna*). Near Boonville.
102	do	(with *Leptæna alternata*). Below Middleville.

	Names.	Associated fossils and localities.
103	TRENTON LIMESTONE	(with *Orthis* and *Leptæna*). Dry Moose river, Lewis.
104	do	(with fragments of fossils).
105	do	(with *Chætetes lycoperdon*).
106	do	(with remains of fossils).
107	do	(hemispherical form of *Chætetes* from).
108	do	(with *Conularia*). Sugar river near Boonville.
109	do	(with remains of *Leptæna*).
110	do	(with *L. sericea*). Sugar river, Boonville.
111	do	(with *Orthis pectinella*). Middleville.
112	do	(with *Leptæna sericea*). Dry Moose river.
113	do	(with graptolites). Trenton falls.
114	do	(with spar). Sugar river, Boonville.
115	do	(with *Orthis testudinaria*). Fortplain.
116	do	(with *O. testudinaria*).
117	do	(with encrinal and other remains).
118	do	(with obscure *Leptæna alternata*). Martinsburgh.
119	do	(polished specimen). Boonville, Sugar river.
120	do	(with encrinal stems).
121	do	(with caudal shield of *Illænus crassicauda*).
122	do	(with encrinal fragments). Near Trenton village.
123	do	(with fragment of *Isotelus gigas*). Near Boonville.
124	do	(with fragments of *Calymene*). Middleville.
125	do	(with encrinal and other remains).
126	do	(with fragments of *Orthoceras*, etc.). Watertown.
127	do	(with *Orthis*, etc.). Watertown.
128	do	(with crinoidal fragments and concretions). Creek at Spraker's basin.
129	do	(with casts of *Isotelus gigas*). Plattsburgh.
130	do	(with *Orthis pectinella*).
131	do	(with obscure fossils). Dry Moose river.
132	do	(with *Orthis*). Falls of Sugar river, Boonville.
133	do	(with fragments of *Pleurotomaria*). Watertown.
134	do	(with fragments of fossils, crystalline).

Names.		Associated fossils and localities.
135	TRENTON LIMESTONE	(with *Orthoceras*). Middleville.
136	do	(with spar). Middleville.
137	do	(with fragments of fossils). Middleville.
138	do	(with calc spar). Falls at Lowville.
139	do	(with base of *Chætetes* and shells).
140	do	(with fragments of fossils, crystalline). Hawkins's mill, Boonville road.
141	do	(with *Leptæna* and fragments of other fossils). Lower falls of Lansing's kill.
142 – 145	do	(crinoidal fragments). Quarry near Trenton village.
146 & 147	do	(mass of fossil fragments, crystalline). Near Trenton village.
148	do	(with fossils and concretions). Amsterdam.
149	do	(with spar). Martinsburgh.
150	do	(with lead ore). Martinsburgh.
151	do	(with *Chætetes*, branched variety).
152	TRAP DYKE	(in Trenton limestone). East-Canada creek.
153 & 154	PORPHYRY	(in Trenton limestone). Essex.

---

5. UTICA SLATE.

SEVENTH TABLE CASE.

1	UTICA SLATE	(with graptolites). East-Canada creek.
2	do	(with fragments of *Calymene beckii*). Mohawk valley.
3	do	(with *Leptæna sericea*). Creek at Johnstown.
4	do	(with *Orthis testudinaria*). Creek at Johnstown.
5	do	(with heads of *Calymene beckii*). Oxtungo creek, south of Fortplain.
6	do	(with *Calymene beckii*). Oxtungo creek.
7	do	(with *Graptolithus lævis*). Turin, Lewis.
8	do	(with graptolites). Johnstown creek.

	Names.	Associated fossils and localities.
9 & 10	UTICA SLATE	(with graptolites). Oxtungo creek.
11	do	(with graptolites). Creek north of Herkimer.
12	do	(with *Orthoceras*). Turin.
13	do	(with *Orthoceras*). East-Canada creek.
14	do	(with graptolites and *Pleurotomaria*). Coldspring.
15	do	(with *Calymene*). Near Amsterdam.
16	do	(with fragments of graptolites).
17	do	(with head of *Calymene beckii*). Turin.
18	do	(with *Calymene beckii*). Whetstone creek, Lewis.
19	do	(with fragments of *Calymene*). Whetstone creek.
20	do	(with fragments of *C. beckii*). Pulaski, Oswego.
21	do	(with fragment of *Orthoceras*). East-Canada creek.
22 & 23	do	(with fragments of *Orthoceras*). Whetstone creek.
24	do	Loraine, Jefferson.
25	do	(with fragments of *Calymene*, *Graptolithus*, etc.). Pulaski and Loraine.
26	do	(with fragments of fossils). Loraine.
27	do	(with fossils in an erratic mass). Near Littlefalls.
28	do	(with *Orthoceras*). Whetstone creek, Lewis.
29	do	(compact, with iron pyrites). East-Canada creek.
30	do	(compact, with a concretion). Near Middleville.
31	do	Canajoharie.
32	do	(with graptolites).
33 & 34	do	(with graptolites and crystals of gypsum). Baker's falls, Washington.
35	do	(glazed). Chatham, Columbia.
36	do	(glazed). Near Poughkeepsie.
37	do	Reed's spring, Washington.
38	do	(with graptolites). Kinderhook creek, Columbia.
39	do	(metamorphic). Near Hudson.

6. HUDSON-RIVER GROUP.

EIGHTH TABLE CASE.

	Names.	Associated fossils and localities.
1	HUDSON-RIVER SLATE	(with *Chætetes*, branched form). Loraine, Jefferson.
2	do	(with encrinal stems and obscure fossils). Loraine.
3	do	(with encrinal fragments). Lee centre.
4	do	(with obscure remains). Loraine.
5	HUDSON-RIVER SHALE	(with fragments of fossils). Pulaski, Oswego.
6	do	(calcareous, with encrinal stems and fragments). Pulaski.
7 & 8	do	(calcareous, with *Leptæna alternata*). Pulaski.
9	HUDSON-RIVER CALCAREOUS SANDSTONE	(with *Modiolopsis*). Pulaski.
10	do	(with *Ambonychia* and *Orthis*). Turin, Lewis.
11	do	(with fragments of fossils). Walden.
12	do	(with *Modiolopsis*). Loraine.
13	HUDSON-RIVER SANDSTONE, calcareous and shaly, decomposing	(with shells). Pulaski.
14	do	(with fragments of *Leptæna*, etc.). Pulaski.
15	do	(with obscure impressions of *Tentaculites* and *Leptæna*). Whetstone creek, Lewis.
16	do	(shaly and calcareous, decomposing, with *Ambonychia* and numerous other fossils). Pulaski.
17	SHALY & CALCAREOUS SANDSTONE	(with *Modiolopsis*, etc.). Pulaski.
18	HUDSON-RIVER CALCAREOUS SANDSTONE	(with fossil fragments). Pulaski.
19	do	(decomposing, with impressions of *Orthis testudinaria*). Pulaski.
20	do	(with encrinal joints, *Orthis*, etc.). Loraine.
21	do	(with encrinal joints, *Ambonychia*, etc.). Loraine.
22	do	(with *Ambonychia radiata*). Loraine.
23	HUDSON-RIVER CALCAREOUS SHALE	(with encrinal columns and other fossils). Loraine.

Names. Associated fossils and localities.

24 HUDSON-RIVER SANDSTONE (with obscure remains of *Chætetes*, *Orthis*, etc.). Loraine.

25 do (with *Ambonychia* and *Orthonota*). Talcott's quarry, near Rome, Oneida.

26 do (with *Ambonychia*). Talcott's quarry.

27 do (with *Modiolopsis*). Talcott's quarry.

28 & 29 HUDSON-RIVER CALCAREOUS SANDSTONE (with *Leptæna alternata*). Pulaski, Oswego.

30 HUDSON-RIVER CALCAREOUS SANDSTONE (with obscure fossil impressions). Falls of Salmon river.

31 HUDSON-RIVER CALCAREOUS SHALE (with obscure fossils). Northwest corner of Columbia county.

32 HUDSON-RIVER CALCAREOUS SHALE (with crinoidal plates and shells). Pulaski, Oswego.

33 HUDSON-RIVER DECOMPOSING SHALY SANDSTONE (with *Cyrtolites ornatus*). Loraine, Jefferson.

34 HUDSON-RIVER CALCAREOUS SANDSTONE (with *Bellerophon bilobatus*). Loraine.

35 HUDSON-RIVER SANDSTONE (with *Orthoceras*). Oneida.

36 & 37 HUDSON-RIVER SHALY SANDSTONE, decomposing (with *Leptæna*, etc.). Pulaski.

38 HULSON-RIVER CALCAREOUS SANDSTONE (with fossil fragments). Pulaski.

39 HUDSON-RIVER SANDSTONE (with *Leptæna alternata*, etc.). Loraine.

40 HUDSON-RIVER CALCAREOUS SANDSTONE (with *Chætetes* & fragments). Talcott's quarry.

41 HUDSON-RIVER CALCAREOUS SANDSTONE (with *Ambonychia*). Oneida.

42 HUDSON-RIVER CALCAREOUS SANDSTONE (with obscure impressions).

SIXTH WALL CASE.

43 SHALY SANDSTONE. Snake hill, Saratoga.

44 GREEN SHALE. Snake hill.

45 GRAY SANDSTONE. Redhook, Dutchess.

46 GREEN SHALE. Snake hill, Saratoga.

47 & 48 BLACK SLATE (with graptolites). Columbia county.

49 SHALE. Banks of North river, Dutchess.

	Names.	Localities.
50	GREEN SLATE.	Cornwall, Orange.
51	GREEN (calcareous) SHALE (with fossils, *Nucula*, etc.).	Whitt's quarry.
52	SILICEOUS BLACK SLATE.	Clermont, Columbia.
53	GREEN SILICEOUS SLATE.	Montrose, Dutchess.
54	SANDSTONE, slaty (slaty graywacke).	Redhook.
55	SHALY SANDSTONE.	Stockport, Columbia.
56	BLACK SLATE.	Hydepark, Dutchess.
57	SANDSTONE (compact and partially altered).	Bloomingrove, Orange.
58	SILICEOUS SLATE.	Cornwall, Orange.
59	SANDSTONE (laminated and micaceous).	Minisink, Orange.
60	SLATE, black (thinly laminated).	Clermont, Columbia.
61	SLATE, black (thinly laminated).	Sugarloaf, Orange.
62	SANDSTONE (laminated and micaceous).	Walden, Orange.
63	SLATY SANDSTONE (with mica and grains of anthracite).	Walden.
64	FLINTY SLATE (black).	Hudson, Columbia.
65	FLINTY SLATE (greenish).	Hudson.
66	LAMINATED SANDSTONE.	Schoharie.
67	GRAY SANDSTONE.	Banks of Hudson river, Dutchess.
68	BLACK SLATE.	Hillsdale, Columbia.
69	GRAY SANDSTONE (siliceous and partially altered).	Ghent, Columbia.
70	GRAY SANDSTONE (conglomeritic).	Banks of Hudson river, Dutchess.
71	GRAY SANDSTONE (slightly conglomeritic and laminated).	Hydepark landing, Dutchess.
72	SILICEOUS SLATE (with copper and iron pyrites).	Near Lower Redhook.
73	FLINTY SLATE.	Near Hudson, Columbia.
74	BROWN JASPERY SLATE.	Near Kinderhook creek, Chatham, Columbia.
75	GLAZED SLATE.	Near Rider's mills, Chatham.
76	GLAZED SLATE.	South of Hudson, Columbia.
77	GLAZED SLATE, greenish (shining argillite).	Rider's mills, Chatham.
78	SILICEOUS and GLAZED SLATE (with limestone).	Chatham.
79	QUARTZ CRYSTALS, in cavities of quartz.	Near Lansingburgh.
80	RED SLATE.	South of Hampton, Washington.
81	SILICEOUS SLATE.	Lower Redhook landing, Dutchess.

Names.	Localities.
82 SLATE.	Union corner, Hydepark, Dutchess.
83 SILICEOUS SLATE (greenish).	Banks of Hudson river, Dutchess.
84 SLATE with iron pyrites (thinly laminated).	Hillsdale, Columbia.
85 BLACK SLATE (thinly laminated).	Hillsdale.
86 ROOFING SLATE.	Gillet's quarry, Lebanon, Columbia.
87 SLATE (micaceous and laminated).	Redhook, Dutchess.
88 & 89 TALCOSE SLATE (contorted).	Whiting's pond, Canaan, Columbia.
90 GREEN SLATE, siliceous.	Near Albany.
91 RED JASPERY SLATE.	Lower Redhook landing, Dutchess.
92 BROWN JASPERY SLATE.	Bloomingrove, Orange.
93 SLATE with cast of mud-furrows.	Frankfort creek, Herkimer.
94 SILICEOUS SLATE with irregular surface (mud markings).	Oneida.
95, 96, 97 BLACK SLATE (with satin spar).	St.Albans, Vermont.
98 SILICEOUS SLATE (altered).	Willsborough, Essex.
99 SANDSTONE (gray, siliceous).	Oneida creek.
100 RED SLATE.	Washington?
101 GREENISH SANDSTONE (argillaceous).	Falls of Salmon river, Oswego.
102 GREENISH SANDSTONE (with surface markings).	Falls of Salmon river.
103 FERRUGINOUS SANDSTONE (with quartz veins).	
104 GREEN SLATE.	Ridge mill near Rome, Oneida.
105 SHALY SANDSTONE (with quartz crystals).	
106 & 107 GREEN SHALY SANDSTONE (with calcareous spar).	
108 & 109 GREEN SHALE.	Barney's, north of Rome, Oneida.
110 COMPACT DARK SLATE.	Summit pond, Argyle, Washington.
111 DARK GREEN SLATE.	Wynn creek.
112 BLACK THINLY LAMINATED SLATE.	Vanhorn's mill near Rome.
113 COMPACT SILICEOUS SLATE.	Near Rome, Oneida.
114 ARENACEOUS LIMESTONE (with *Ambonychia* and *Cyrtolites*).	Lewis.
115 ORTHOCERATITE.	Lewis county.
116 SHALY SANDSTONE (with *Ambonychia radiata*).	Loraine, Jefferson.
117, 118, 119 SANDY SHALE (with crinoidal joints, *Orthis*, etc.).	Loraine.
120 SHALY LIMESTONE (with *Orthis*, *Orthoceras*, etc.).	Loraine.

Names. Associated fossils and localities.

121 GRAY SANDSTONE (with fossils). West of Constableville, Lewis.

122 SILICEOUS MASS in black shale. Lansingburgh, Rensselaer.

123 SLATY ARGILLACEOUS LIMESTONE. Greenwich, Washington.

124 SANDSTONE (with small branching *Chætetes lycoperdon*). Oswego.

125 CALCAREOUS SANDSTONE (with *Ambonychia radiata*).

126 GRAY SANDSTONE (with *Ambonychia*, etc.). Near Rome, Oneida.

127 BLACK SLATE (thinly laminated). Vanhorn's mill near Rome.

128 GRAYISH GREEN SHALE. Snake hill, Saratoga.

129 CALCAREOUS SHALE (with columns of *Heterocrinus*). Oneida.

130 SHALY SANDSTONE (with *Orthoceras*). Loraine, Jefferson.

131 SHALY SANDSTONE (with *Modiolopsis ovata*). Loraine.

132 CALCAREOUS SANDSTONE (with *Ambonychia radiata*). Pulaski.

133 SHALY SANDSTONE (with *Leptæna sericea*). Near Copenhagen, Lewis.

134 COMPACT SANSTONE. Talcott's quarry near Rome.

135 GREEN SHALE. Saugerties, Ulster.

136 GRAY SANDSTONE (with concretion). Near Rome, Oneida.

137 LIMESTONE with fossils (intercalated with the Hudson-river shales). Near Barnegate, Dutchess.

138 SANDSTONE (with *Orthoceratites*, *Cyrtolites*, etc.). Turin, Lewis.

139 SHALY SANDSTONE (ferruginous and decomposing). Loraine?

140 GRAY SANDSTONE (with fragments of fossils). Near Constableville.

141 GREEN SILICEOUS SLATE (whetstone slate). Columbia county.

142 COMPACT SHALY SANDSTONE (with quartz crystals). Near Albany.

143 GLAZED SLATE. Near Hudson.

144 THINBEDDED SANDSTONE (with fossils). Near Russia, Herkimer.

145 SLATY CALCAREOUS ROCK (with *Orthis testudinaria*). Lewis.

146 SILICEOUS LIMESTONE (interstratified with slate). Columbia.

147 SHALY SANDSTONE. Rogers's creek, Oneida.

7. GREY SANDSTONE.

SEVENTH TABLE CASE.

Names. Localities, etc.

1 Roof slate. Rowley's quarry, New-Lebanon, Columbia county.

2 Slate. One mile west of Hillsdale, Columbia.

3 Glazed slate. One mile south of Hudson, at the supposed coal mine.

4 Red slate. Near Kinderhook, Chatham, Columbia.

5 Red slate. One mile southwest of Washington-hollow, Dutchess.

6 Millstone grit. Steel's creek.

7, 8, 9 Shaly sandstone (with fragments of fossils).

10 Shaly sandstone (with impressions of *Modiolopsis modiolaris*).

11 Shaly sandstone.

12 Concretionary sandstone.

13 Gray shaly sandstone. Two and a half miles north of Rome.

14, 15, 16 Gray sandstone. Woodruff's, south of Rome.

17 Greenish glazed slate.

18, 19 Gray sandstone. Salmon creek, village of Florence.

20 Gray sandstone. Falls of Stony brook, Redfield.

21 Gray sandstone. Village of Florence.

22 Gray sandstone (with water-marked surface). Falls of Salmon creek.

23 Gray sandstone. West of Oswego village.

24 Gray sandstone. Woodruff's quarry, south of Rome.

25 Gray sandstone. Below the dam on Mad river, Camden.

26 Gray sandstone. Dam at Mad river, near Camden.

27 Gray sandstone. Upper falls of Mad river, Redfield.

28 Gray sandstone. Road to Loraine from Redfield.

29 Gray sandstone. West of Ghent meeting-house, Columbia.

30 Gray sandstone. Road south of Rome, Oneida.

31 Gray sandstone. Tippler's quarry.

32, 33, 34 Gray sandstone (with *Strophomena alternata*).

35 Gray siliceous sandstone (with shaly nodules, and containing galena).

Names. Localities, etc.

36 Contorted limestone. Near Stanfordville, Dutchess.

37 Millstone grit. Bloggs's clove, Bloomingrove, Orange.

38 Compact sandstone. Twoponds, Monroe, Orange.

39 Millstone grit (boulder). Hamptonburgh, Orange.

40 Millstone grit. Deerpark, foot of Shawangunk mountain range.

41 Graywacke. Two miles west of Woodbury, Monroe, Orange.

42 Millstone grit. Deerpark, Orange.

43 Conglomerate. Canterbury, Orange.

44 Finegrained grit rock. Shawangunk mountain, Rochester, Ulster.

45 Grit rock. Walls of the Shawangunk lead vein, Sullivan.

46 Millstone grit. Deerpark, Orange.

47 Breccia. Two miles northeast of Craigville, Orange.

48 Yellowish sandstone. Stockport landing, Columbia.

49 Compact shaly sandstone. Near Hydepark, Dutchess.

50 A metamorphic slaty and crystalline rock. ——?

51 Compact metamorphic grit rock. ——?

52 Brownish siliceous limestone (metamorphic). ——?

53 Compact shaly sandstone.

54 Shaly sandstone (with thin layers of shale). ——?

55 Siliceous limestone.

56 Limestone. Bloggs's clove, Bloomingrove, Orange.

57 Limestone. Warwick, Orange.

SEVENTH WALL CASE.

58 Grey sandstone. Three miles north of Salem, Washington.

59 Black slate. Hoosick, Rensselaer.

60 Limestone. West of Granville, Washington.

61, 62 Limestone. Snakehill, Saratoga.

63 Red shale. Eaton, Washington.

64, 65 Shale. Sugarloaf, Orange.

66 Compact sandstone. Bellvale, Warwick, Orange.

67 Red slate. Bloomingrove, Orange.

68 Millstone grit (compact). Canterbury, Orange.

69 Red shaly sandstone. Canterbury.

70 Red sandstone. Pine hill, Cornwal, Orange.

71 Red millstone grit. Carpenter's point, Deerpark, Orange.

72 Red shale. Cambridge, Washington.

EIGHTH TABLE CASE.

	Names.	Localities, etc.
1, 2, 3	ONEIDA CONGLOMERATE.	Steel's creek, Herkimer.
4	ONEIDA CONGLOMERATE.	Cleveland, Oneida lake.
5, 6	do	Mason's quarry, southwest of Utica.
7	do	Mansfield, south of Hampton.
8	do	South of New-Hartford, Oneida.
9	do	Mason's quarry.
10, 11	do	Near Starch-factory creek, Oneida.
12	do	Steel's creek, Herkimer.
13	do	Mansfield, south of Hampton.
14	MILLSTONE GRIT.	Hill near Starch-factory creek, Oneida.

---

8. MEDINA SANDSTONE.

EIGHTH TABLE CASE.

	Names.	Localities, etc.
15, 16	MEDINA SANDSTONE (gray beds).	Lewiston, Niagara county.
17	MEDINA SANDSTONE (with ripplemarks).	Lewiston, high bank of river.
18	do (gray beds).	Lewiston.
19	do (with undulating lines of deposition).	Martville, Cayuga.
20	do	Wayne county.
21 - 23	do	Near Martville, Cayuga.
24	do	Hulme's quarry, Sterling, Cayuga.
25	do (with *Dictuolites beckii*).	Medina, Orleans.
26	do (upper mass).	Hulme's quarry, Sterling.
27, 28	do (upper mass).	Cental's mill, Wayne.
29, 30	do	Hulme's quarry, Sterling.
31, 32	do	Near Martville, Cayuga.
33	do (upper gray mass).	Medina.
34	do (upper gray mass).	Lewiston.
35	do (upper gray mass).	Rochester.
36	do (variegated).	Rochester.

NINTH TABLE CASE.

Names.		Localities, etc.
1 – 5	MEDINA SANDSTONE.	Sterling centre, Cayuga county.
6	MEDINA SANDSTONE.	Park's milldam, Amboy, Oswego.
7	do	(with concretionary markings). Oswego village.
8	do	(with mud cracks). Oswego village.
9, 10	do	(with *Pleurotomaria pervetusta*). Medina.
11	do	(with *P. pervetusta* & *Lingula cuneata*). Medina.
12 – 14	do	(with *P. pervetusta*). Medina.
15	do	East side of Irondequoit bay.
16	do	(with *Palæophycus tortuosus*). Brighton, Monroe.
17 – 22	do	(with *Lingula cuneata*). Medina.
23	do	(with *Palæophycus*). Medina.
24	do	(with *Modiolopsis primigenius*). Medina.
25 – 28	do	(with fucoids). —— ?
29	do	(with *Arthrophycus harlani*, loose). Near Cleveland, Oneida lake.
30	do	(with *A. harlani*). Medina.
31	do	Near Sterling, Cayuga.
32	do	(with *Arthrophycus harlani*). Medina.
33	do	(with *A. harlani* & *Fucoides? auriformis*). Medina.
34	do	(with *Dictuolites beckii*). Medina.

SEVENTH WALL CASE.

35	MEDINA SANDSTONE	(with *Lingula cuneata*, showing current markings). Lockport, Niagara county.
36	do	(geode). Lockport.
37	do	(upper gray layers). Medina, Orleans.
38	do	(variegated). Rochester, Monroe.
39	do	Lewiston, Niagara.
40	do	(upper gray layer). Lewiston.
41	do	(conglomerate). Wolcott, Wayne.
42	do	(with water-markings). Lewiston.
43	do	(showing diagonal lines of lamination). Rochester.

	Names.	Localities, etc.
44	MEDINA SANDSTONE.	Martville, Cayuga.
45	do	(inclosing nodules of shale). Rochester.
46	do	(with *Arthrophycus harlani*). Wayne.
47	do	(variegated and shaly). Medina.
48	do	(shaly). Lewiston.
49	do	Redfield, Oneida.
50	do	(upper shaly layers). Medina.
51	do	(variegated). Lewiston.
52 & 53	do	(upper greenish layers). Lewiston.
54	do	(upper gray layers, with *Cytherina cylindrica*). Medina.
55	do	(variegated). Near Martville, Cayuga.
56	do	(variegated). Lewiston, Niagara.
57	do	Rochester, Monroe.
58	do	(very shaly). Irondequoit bay, Monroe.
59	do	Medina, Orleans.
60	do	(with *Lingula cuneata* and *Cytherina cylindrica*). Medina.
61 & 62	do	(with nodules of shale enclosed). Medina.
63 & 64	do	(with *Lingula cuneata*). Lockport and Medina.
65	do	(with *L. cuneata* and *Pleurotomaria pervetusta*). Medina.
66	do	(with *L. cuneata*). Medina.
67	do	Clarendon, Orleans.
68	do	(with tortuous lamination). Rochester.
69 – 71	do	(shaly variety). Lewiston.
72	do	(shaly). Rochester, Monroe.
73	do	(shaly). Martville, Cayuga.
74	do	(with *C. cylindrica* and *L. cuneata*). Medina.
75	do	(with concretionary surface). Oswego.
76	do	(with *Arthrophycus harlani*). Medina.
77	do	(with *A. harlani*). Adams's basin, Monroe.
78	do	(with *Fucoides? heterophyllus*). Adams's basin.
79 & 80	do	(with *F.? heterophyllus*). Medina.

Names.		Localities, etc.
81	MEDINA SANDSTONE	(with *F.? heterophyllus*). Rochester.
82 & 83	do	(with fucoidal markings). Medina.
84	do	(with fucoidal markings). Martville.
85	do	(variegated). Philipsburgh, Oswego.
86	do	(with fucoidal markings). Lewiston.
87	do	(with *Arthrophycus harlani*, and conglomerate). Oswego county.
88	do	(with *A. harlani*). Medina, Orleans.
89	do	(with ripplemarks). Medina.
90	do	(with *A. harlani*). Sodus, Wayne.
91 & 92	do	(upper gray layers). Medina.
93	do	Medina.

---

9. CLINTON GROUP.

TENTH TABLE CASE.

1 CONGLOMERATE (with shaly surface). Blackstone's quarry, New-Hartford, Oneida county.

2 SHALY SANDSTONE (with *Buthotrephis palmata*). Blackstone's quarry.

3 SHALY SANDSTONE (with *Rusophycus bilobatus*). Gaylord and Norton's quarry, New-Hartford.

4 SHALY SANDSTONE (with *Buthotrephis gracilis*). Blackstone's quarry.

5 SANDSTONE (with *Beyrichia*). New-Hartford.

6 CONGLOMERATE. Stebbins's creek, near Clinton village, Oneida.

7 CONGLOMERATE (with iridescent surface). Blackstone's quarry.

8, 9, 10 OOLITIC IRON ORE. Bennett's ore bed, west of Clinton village.

11	OOLITIC IRON ORE.	Wadsworth's quarry, New-Hartford.
12	do	(with crinoidal joints). Eames's quarry, Verona.
13	do	(with crinoidal joints). Parsons's quarry, Verona.
14	do	Hammond's ore bed, Westmoreland, Oneida.
15	do	Parsons's quarry.
16	do	(with *Leptæna sericea*). Bennett's ore bed.

Names. Associated fossils and localities.

17 SHALY SANDSTONE (with *L. sericea*). South of Verona, Oneida.

18, 19 LIMESTONE (with *Pentamerus oblongus*). Rochester, Monroe.

20 SILICEOUS LIMESTONE (with *P. oblongus*). Wolcott, Wayne.

21 LIMESTONE (with *Atrypa hemispherica*). Below Martville, Cayuga.

22 LIMESTONE (with fragments of *P. oblongus*). Sodus, Wayne.

23 OOLITIC IRON ORE. Rochester.

24 OOLITIC IRON ORE (2 specimens). Stebbins's creek, Oneida.

25 LIMESTONE (with *Leptæna rugosa*). Donnelly's quarry, Madison.

26 OOLITIC IRON ORE. Wolcott, Wayne.

27 do (with fragments of shells). Donnelly's quarry.

28 do (with *Pentamerus oblongus*). Donnelly's quarry.

29 & 30 do (with *Spirifer radiatus*). Donnelly's quarry.

31 FERRUGINOUS LIMESTONE (with *P. oblongus*). Donnelly's quarry.

32, 33 SHALY SANDSTONE (with *Rusophycus pudicus*). Gaylord's quarry.

34 *Atrypa congesta.* Reynale's basin, Niagara.

35 *Atrypa plicatella.* Reynale's basin.

36 SHALE (with *Graptolithus clintonensis*). Sodus.

37 LIMESTONE (with *Atrypa hemispherica*). Rochester.

38 LIMESTONE (with *A. reticularis* and *P. oblongus*). Donnelly's quarry.

39 GRAY SANDSTONE (with fragments of *Homalonotus delphinocephalus*). Steel's creek, Herkimer.

40 GRAY SANDSTONE (upper mass of group). Steel's creek.

41 SHALE (with *Atrypa congesta*). Reynale's basin, Niagara.

42 *Atrypa plicatella.* Reynale's basin.

43 *Chætetes lycoperdon.* Reynale's basin.

44 UPPER GRAY SANDSTONE (with *Modiolopsis ovata*). Remington's quarry.

45 LIMESTONE (with *Atrypa congesta*). Medina.

46 *Caninia bilateralis* (2 specimens). Reynale's basin.

47 *Atrypa congesta.*

48 FIBROUS SULPHATE OF STRONTIAN. Stark, Herkimer.

49 FIBROUS SULPHATE OF STRONTIAN (with carbonate of lime, etc.). Stark.

50 CRYSTALLIZED SULPHATE OF STRONTIAN. Stark.

51 GYPSUM. Stark.

EIGHTH WALL CASE.

Names. Associated fossils and localities.

52 Shaly sandstone (with fucoidal markings). Blackstone's quarry.

53 Shale (with obscure fossil markings). Blackstone's quarry.

54 Green shale. Martville, Cayuga.

55 Ferruginous sandstone (with *Beyrichia*). New-Hartford.

56 Shaly sandstone (with *Rusophycus subangulatus*). Blackstone's.

57 Shaly sandstone (with fucoidal markings). Blackstone's quarry.

58 Shale (with *Buthotrephis gracilis*). Near Clinton village.

59 Sandstone (with *B. palmata*). Fox-hollow, Herkimer.

60 Shaly sandstone (with organic markings). Blackstone's quarry.

61 Shaly sandstone (with *Rusophycus bilobatus*). Gaylord's quarry.

62, 63 Shale (with fragments of *B. ramosa*). Blackstone's quarry.

64 Shaly sandstone (with fucoidal fragments). Near Verona.

65 Conglomerate (with iron pyrites). Blackstone's quarry.

66 do (with iridescent surface). Blackstone's quarry.

67 do (with shaly surface). Stebbins's creek.

68 do (with shaly surface). Rogers's creek.

69 do Blackstone's quarry.

70 Shaly sandstone (with fucoidal markings). Near Clinton village.

71 Shaly sandstone (with fucoidal markings). North of Martville.

72 Shale. A quarry north of Martville.

73 Shaly sandstone (2 specimens, with fucoidal remains). Clinton.

74 Hornstone (composed of fragments of shells). Rochester.

75 Sandstone (with *Beyrichia*). New-Hartford.

76 Grey sandstone (with *Lingula oblonga*). Quarry north of Martville.

77 Ferruginous sandstone (with organic remains). New-Hartford.

78 Ferruginous sandstone. Stark, Herkimer.

79 Ferruginous sandstone. Steel's creek, Herkimer.

80 Shaly sandstone. Vanhornsville, Herkimer.

81 Shaly limestone. Bushnell's, Oneida lake.

82 do Quarry near Verona.

83 do (with *Fenestella prisca?*). Near Verona.

Names. Associated fossils, and localities.

84 SHALY LIMESTONE (with *Fenestella prisca?*). Martville, Cayuga.

85 SHALY LIMESTONE. Martville.

86 GREEN SHALE. Martville.

87 GREEN SHALE. Swift's creek.

88 LIMESTONE. Near Verona, Oneida.

89 SHALY LIMESTONE. Near Verona.

90 OOLITIC IRON ORE (with *Beyrichia*). Vanhornsville, Herkimer.

91 do Swift's creek.

92 & 93 do Bennett's ore bed, Clinton, Oneida.

94 do (with concretions and crinoidal joints). Pearson's ore bed, near Verona.

95 RED SANDSTONE. Steel's creek, Herkimer.

96 RED CONGLOMERATE. Steel's creek.

97 OOLITIC IRON ORE (with limestone). Wolcott, Wayne.

98 LIMESTONE (with *Pentamerus oblongus*). Sodus, Wayne.

99, 100 LIMESTONE (with *P. oblongus*). Rochester, Monroe.

101 SHALE (with *Leptæna rugosa*). Donnelly's quarry, Madison.

102 OOLITIC IRON ORE (with calcareous spar). Wolcott.

103 SHALY LIMESTONE (with *Fenestella prisca*). Taberg furnace.

104 SHALE (with *Atrypa plicatella*). Taberg furnace.

105 SHALE (with *Beyrichia* and *Tentaculites*). Taberg furnace.

106 OOLITIC IRON ORE (with fragments of fossils). Stebbins's creek.

107 do Stebbins's creek.

108 do (with fragments of fossils). Near Clinton village.

109 do Quarry north of Clinton village.

110 do Hammond's quarry.

111 do (with *Phenoptera constellata*). Wolcott, Wayne.

112 do (with sulphate of baryta). Wolcott.

113 do (with *Pentamerus oblongus*). Donnelly's quarry.

114 LIMESTONE (with fragments of fossils). Near Martville, Cayuga.

115 SANDSTONE (with iron pyrites). Stebbins's quarry, Clinton, Oneida.

116 SHALY SANDSTONE (with casts of *Leptæna*). Near Blackstone's quarry.

117 FERRUGINOUS SANDSTONE (with cast of *L. subplana*). Near Clinton.

Names. Associated fossils, and localities.

118 SHALY SANDSTONE (with *L. rugosa*). Near Tippler's quarry.

119 SILICEOUS LIMESTONE (with *L. rugosa*). Munger's quarry.

120 SILICEOUS LIMESTONE (with *L. rugosa*). Oneida lake.

121 SILICEOUS AND SHALY LIMESTONE. Swift's creek, Oneida.

122 SHALY LIMESTONE (with *L. corrugata* and *Pyrenomœus cuneatus*). Clinton, Oneida.

123 SHALY SANDSTONE (with *Avicula emasculata*). Munger's quarry.

124 do (with imperfect fossils). Gaylord's quarry, near Utica.

125 – 127 do (with *Rusophycus bilobatus*). Gaylord and Norton's quarry, New-Hartford.

128 do (with *B. palmata*). Gaylord and Norton's quarry.

129 do (with roots of marine plants).

130 GRAY SANDSTONE (with concretions).

131 SHALY SANDSTONE (with fucoidal markings). Vanhornsville, Herkimer.

132 SHALY SANDSTONE. Stark, Herkimer.

133 & 134 SILICEOUS LIMESTONE (with sulphate of strontian in crystals). Stark, Herkimer.

135 GYPSUM. Stark.

136 DARK-COLORED GYPSUM. Stark.

137 SANDSTONE AND GYPSUM. Stark.

138 & 139 SHALE WITH GYPSUM. Stark.

---

10. NIAGARA GROUP.

ELEVENTH TABLE CASE.

1 SHALE (with *Phacops limulurus*). Lockport, Niagara.

2 do (with impression of *P. limulurus*). Lockport.

3 do (with *Homalonotus delphinocephalus*). Lockport.

4 do (with *Dictyonema retiformis*). Lockport.

5 do (with *Caryocrinus ornatus*). Lockport.

6, 7 do (with *Spirifer niagarensis*). Lockport.

Names. Associated fossils, and localities.

8 Shale (with *Leptæna subplana*). Lockport.

9 do (with *Atrypa nitida*). Lockport.

10 Limestone composed of crinoidal joints. Lockport.

11 Anhydrous gypsum.

12 White gypsum (or alabaster). Lockport.

13 Encrinal limestone (polished). Lockport.

14 Limestone (with crystallized coral). Lockport.

15 Siliceous limestone. Niagara falls.

16 Dark limestone (with *Cytherina*). Wayne county.

17, 18 Dark bituminous limestone. Wayne.

19 Pearl spar. Lockport, Niagara.

20 Dogtooth spar. Lockport.

21 Pearl spar and dogtooth spar. Lockport.

22 Dogtooth spar. Lockport.

23 Limestone (with small geodes of pearl spar). Lockport.

24 do (with galena, sulphuret of lead). Rochester.

25 do (with zinc blende). Niagara falls.

26 do (with crystals of zinc blende). Niagara falls.

27, 28 Fragments of *Orthocera*. Wayne county.

29, 30 Sulphate of strontian. Lockport.

31 Pearl spar with dogtooth spar. Lockport.

32 Dark limestone (with cavities). Barre, Orleans.

33 Dark limestone (upper part of rock). Niagara falls.

34 Encrinal limestone. Niagara falls.

35 Limestone (with *Cladopora seriata*). Lockport.

36 Dark limestone. Near Lenox, Madison.

37 Brecciated limestone. Oneida county.

38 Brecciated limestone. Ham's quarry.

39 – 42 Conglomerate limestone.

43 Conglomerate limestone. Ham and Bigelow's quarries.

NINTH WALL CASE.

	Names.	Associated fossils, and localities.
44	SHALE	(with nodules of gypsum replacing *Caryocrinus ornatus*). Lockport, Niagara county.
45	do	(with *Orthoceras undulatus*). Lockport.
46	do	(with *Dictyonema retiformis*). Lockport.
47	do	(with *Leptæna striata*). Lockport.
48	do	(with *L. rugosa* and *L. striata*). Lockport.
49	do	(with *Orthis elegantula*). Lockport.
50	do	(with *O. testudinaria* and *L. rugosa*). Lockport.
51	do	(with *O. testudinaria*). Lockport.
52	do	(with *Bumastis barriensis*). Lockport.
53	do	(with fragments of various fossils). Lockport.
54	do	(with *O. testudinaria* and *L. rugosa*). Lockport.
55	do	(with *Avicula emacerata*). Lockport.
56	do	(with *Leptæna subplana*). Lockport.
57	ENCRINAL LIMESTONE.	Near Lewiston, Niagara.
58	SHALE	(with *Caryocrinus ornatus*, and cavities filled with calcareous spar). Lockport.
59	LIMESTONE	(with crinoidal columns). Lockport.
60	*Astrocerium venustum*	(polished specimen from the original excavation of the Erie canal, 1825). Lockport.
61	LIMESTONE	(with striated surface, lignilite). Lockport.
62	LIMESTONE	(with *Atrypa reticularis*). Lockport.
63	BROWN BITUMINOUS LIMESTONE.	Rochester.
64	LIMESTONE	(with *Trematopora ostiolata*). Rochester.
65	do	(with *Atrypa neglecta*). Rochester.
66	do	(with vertically striated surface, lignilites). Lockport.
67	BRECCIATED LIMESTONE.	Near Rochester.
68	WHITE GYPSUM	(alabaster, polished specimens). Lockport.
69	GEODE OF DOGTOOTH SPAR.	Lockport.
70	ENCRINAL LIMESTONE.	Lockport.
71	ENCRINAL LIMESTONE	(polished specimen). Lockport.
72	LIMESTONE	(with dogtooth and pearl spar). Lockport.

Names. Associated fossils, and localities.

73 LIMESTONE (with dogtooth spar). Lockport.

74 do (with pearl spar). Lockport.

75 do (with geode of dogtooth spar). Lockport.

76 SULPHATE OF STRONTIAN. Lockport.

77 LIMESTONE (with pearl spar and dogtooth spar). Lockport.

78 do (with geode of pearl spar with selenite). Rochester.

79 ANHYDROUS GYPSUM. Lockport.

80 SULPHATE OF STRONTIAN. Lockport.

81, 82 LIMESTONE (with pearl spar). Lockport.

83 LIMESTONE (with geode filled with bituminous coal). Lockport.

84 do (with dogtooth spar). Lockport.

85 do (with pearl spar and dogtooth spar). Lockport.

86, 87 do (with dogtooth spar). Lockport.

88 PEARL SPAR (a geode). Lockport.

89 PEARL SPAR and DOGTOOTH SPAR. Lockport.

90 PEARL SPAR (rose-colored). Lockport.

91 LIMESTONE (with rose-colored pearl spar and dogtooth spar). Lockport.

92 do (with dogtooth spar and sulphate of strontian). Lockport.

93 do (with dogtooth spar). Lockport.

94 PEARL SPAR in geode of limestone. Lockport.

95 DOGTOOTH SPAR. Lockport.

96 DOGTOOTH SPAR and PEARL SPAR (replacing *Astrocerium venustum*). Lockport.

97 BROWN SPAR. Lockport.

98 LIMESTONE (with *Euomphalus hemispherica*). Lockport.

99 CONCRETIONARY LIMESTONE. North of Manchester.

100 LIMESTONE (with concretionary nodes upon surface). Niagara falls.

101 GEODE (with pearl spar and crystals of sulphate of strontian). First excavation of Erie canal, 1825. Lockport.

102 LIMESTONE (a concretion). Near Skonondoa, Oneida.

103 DARK BITUMINOUS LIMESTONE. Between Lenox basin and Canastota.

104 LIMESTONE (with cavity showing laminæ of growth of *Astrocerium venustum*). Rochester.

105 COMPACT LIMESTONE (with *Cytherina*). Ham's quarry, Cayuga.

Names. Associated fossils, and localities.

106 CONCRETIONARY LIMESTONE. Four miles north of Manchester.

107, 108 COMPACT DARK-COLORED LIMESTONE. Wolcott. Wayne.

109 LIMESTONE (with *Cladopora seriata*). Sweden, Monroe.

110 LIMESTONE (with *Diplophyllum cæspitosum*). Lockport.

111 COMPACT LIMESTONE (with *Cytherina*). Butler, Wayne.

112 LIMESTONE (with cavities lined with crystals of calcareous spar).

113 SHALY LIMESTONE (with *Spirifer crispus* and minute cytherinæ).

114 COMPACT BROWN LIMESTONE. Rochester.

115 COMPACT LIMESTONE. North of Manchester, Ontario.

116 CONCRETIONARY LIMESTONE. Steel's creek, Herkimer.

117 BRECCIATED LIMESTONE. Steel's creek.

118 LIMESTONE (with surface markings). Ham's quarry, Cayuga.

119 REDDISH COMPACT LIMESTONE. Steel's creek.

120 CONCRETIONARY LIMESTONE. Near Skonondoa, Oneida.

121 – 124 BRECCIATED LIMESTONE. Near Skonondoa.

125 CONCRETIONARY LIMESTONE. Near Skonondoa.

---

11. ONONDAGA-SALT GROUP.

TWELFTH TABLE CASE.

1 COMPACT RED SHALE. Cruger's mill, Herkimer county.

2 VARIEGATED SHALE. Chittenango, Madison.

3 RED SHALE. Between Sauquoit creek and Paris hill, Oneida.

4 VARIEGATED SHALE. Baldwinsville, Onondaga.

5 RED SHALE (with green spots). Baldwinsville.

6 RED SHALE (with green spots). Oneidacastle, Oneida.

7 GREENISH GRAY SHALE. North of Chittenango village.

8 GREY SHALE. South of Port Byron, Cayuga.

9 GREEN SHALE. Churchville, Monroe.

10 GREEN SHALE (with seams of gypsum). Near Lake Sodom.

11 RED SELENITE (with green shale). Clyde, Wayne.

Names. Associated fossils, and localities.

12 Red gypsum (with green shale). Lake Sodom.

13 Compact gypsum (with green shale). Monroe county.

14 Grey shale (with cavities of crystals). Near Lake Sodom.

15 do (with remains of *Cytherina*). Near Peru, Livingston.

16 do (with cavities of crystals). Near Lake Sodom.

17 Calcareous infiltrations between layers of gypsum. Allen's creek.

18 Gypseous marl. Newark, Wayne.

19, 20 Gypsum. Allen's creek, Monroe.

21 Gypseous marl (with seams of fibrous gypsum). Monroe county.

22 Selenite. Nine-mile creek.

23, 24 do (with fragments of marl enclosed). Newark, Wayne.

25 do (with fragments of marl enclosed). Camillus, Onondaga.

26 Gypseous marl (with marks of pseudomorphic crystals of common salt). South of Syracuse, Onondaga.

27 do (with ditto). Hill southeast of Chittenango, Madison.

28, 29 do (with ditto). Bull's quarry, Lenox, Madison.

30 do (with ditto). Kelby's quarry, Lenox.

31 Pseudomorphic crystals of common salt. South of Syracuse.

32 do do Bull's quarry.

33 do do Nine-mile creek.

34 Gray shale. Bull's quarry, Lenox.

35 do (with obscure fossils). Near Bellisle, Onondaga.

36, 37 do (with impressions of fossil shells). Bull's quarry.

38 do (with obscure fossil shells). Bull's quarry.

39 do (with plant-like impressions). Bull's quarry.

40 do (with some plant-like impressions). Bull's quarry.

41, 42 Serpentine. Near Syracuse.

43 – 46 Calcareous serpentine. Near Syracuse.

47 Serpentine (with crystals of calcareous spar). Near Syracuse.

48 Serpentine. Syracuse.

49 Gypseous marl. Nine-mile creek.

50 Black gypseous marl (with selenite). South of Bellisle.

51 Nodule of gypsum and marl. South of Chittenango.

Names. Associated fossils, and localities.

52, 53 Selenite (with black gypseous marl). Springport, Cayuga.

54 Dark shale (with surface covered with black selenite). Port Byron.

55 Gray gypseous marl (with spherical cavities containing concretions). Lenox, Madison.

56 Impure limestone (with spherical cavities).

57 Hydraulic limestone. Throopsville, Cayuga.

58 Ash-colored hydraulic limestone (with remains of *Streptelasma*). Blackrock, Erie.

59 Hydraulic limestone (with lignilites). Canescraga creek.

60, 61 do (with lignilites). Onondaga.

62, 63 do (with lignilites). Canescraga creek.

64 Vermicular limestone. Near Syracuse.

65 Hydraulic limestone (with head of *Eurypterus remipes*). Oriskany.

TENTH WALL CASE.

66 Variegated red marl. Near Oneidacastle.

67 Red marl (with green spots). Chittenango, Madison.

68 Red shale. Between Sauquoit creek and Paris hill, Oneida.

69 Green shale. Between Sauquoit creek and Paris hill.

70 Gray shale. Near Chittenango, Madison.

71 Gray shale. Allen's creek, Monroe.

72 Gray gypseous marl. Orleans county.

73 Gray gypseous shale. Near Churchville, Monroe.

74 Gypseous marl. Allen's creek.

75 Gypseous marl. Lockville, Wayne.

76 Friable sandstone. Near Paris hill, Oneida.

77, 78 Gypseous shale. Near Paris hill.

79 Gypseous marl. Allen's creek.

80 Gypseous marl (with seams of fibrous gypsum). Monroe county.

81, 82 Greenish marl (with fibrous gypsum). Jordan, Onondaga.

83 Red gypsum (with gypseous marl). Jordan.

84 Red gypsum (nodules). Newark, Wayne.

85, 86 Gypseous marl. Clyde, Wayne.

Names. Associates and localities.

87 Marl (with red selenite). Newark.

88 Gypseous marl. Near Port Gibson, Monroe.

89 Argillaceous limestone. Near Churchville, Monroe.

90 Selenite (with decomposing iron pyrites). Newark, Wayne.

91 Gypsum. Newark.

92 Gypsum. Allen's creek.

93, 94, 95 Gypsum. Leroy, Genesee.

96 Gypsum (nodule). Monroe county.

97 Granular gypsum. Allen's creek.

98 Gypseous marl (with selenite). South of Bellisle, Onondaga.

99 Grey gypseous marl.

100 Grey argillaceous limestone.

101 Gypseous shale. Near Waterville, Oneida.

102 Compact limestone (with minute vermicular cavities). Waterville.

103 Compact limestone (with minute cavities filled with concretions). Near Waterville.

104 Grey shale (with cavities made by crystals). Near Jordan lake.

105 Dark shaly limestone. Near Waterville.

106 Compact limestone. Near Waterville.

107 Shaly limestone. Near Waterville.

108 Grey shale.

109 Gypseous marl (with selenite). Newark, Wayne.

110, 111 Gypseous marl. Near Camillus, Onondaga.

112 Selenite. Near Camillus.

113 Gypseous marl (with selenite and marks of pseudomorphic crystals). Near Camillus.

114 Gypseous marl (with marks of pseudomorphic crystals). Camillus.

115, 116, 117 Pseudomorphic crystals of common salt. Camillus.

118 Pseudomorphic crystals (with imperfect fossil shells on shale). Lenox, Madison.

119 Imperfect pseudomorphic crystals. Brown's quarry.

120 Gypseous shale (with marks of pseudomorphic crystals). Bellisle.

121 Gypseous shales (with marks of pseudomorphic crystals). Lenox.

Names. Associates and localities.

122 Gypseous shales. Near Camillus.

123 Pseudomorphic crystal of common salt. Near Camillus.

124 Gypseous shale (with pseudomorphic crystals). Near Camillus.

125 Dark-colored shale.

126 Grey shale. Near Bellisle, Onondaga.

127, 128 Dark shale (with impression of marine plants). Lenox.

129 Grey shale. Chittenango, Madison.

130, 131, 132 Serpentine and limestone. Syracuse.

133 Serpentine and limestone (polished). Syracuse.

134 Serpentine and limestone. Syracuse.

135 Serpentine (polished). Syracuse.

136 – 143 Serpentine. Syracuse.

144 Serpentine and limestone. Syracuse.

145 Sulphate of strontian in gray marl. Syracuse.

146 Gray marl (with crystals of sulphate of strontian). Syracuse.

147 Gray gypseous marl. Lenox, Madison.

148 Gray shale (with impressions of fossil shells). Lenox.

149 Shale (with obscure fossil shells). Lenox.

150 Vesicular limestone. Onondaga-hollow.

151 – 153 do Lenox.

154 & 155 do Port Byron.

156 do Near Syracuse.

157 Dark shale. Cherryvalley, Otsego.

158 Limestone. Chittenango, Madison.

159 Limestone (with drusy cavities). Oriskany-falls, Oneida.

160 Gypseous marl. Cherryvalley, Otsego.

161 Gray shaly limestone. Chittenango, Madison.

162 Gypseous marl (with calcareous incrustations). Monroe county.

163 Hydraulic limestone (with cavities).

164, 165 Gray gypseous shale. Chittenango.

166 Gypseous marl.

167 Nodule of gypsum. Near Jamesville, Onondaga.

168 Gypseous marl (with seams of fibrous gypsum). Phelps, Ontario.

Names. Associates and localities.

169 SELENITE (with compact gypsum). Phelps.

170, 171, 172 GYPSEOUS MARL (with selenite). Springport, Cayuga.

173 LIMESTONE above gypsum beds. Jamesville, Onondaga.

174 GYPSEOUS MARL (with nodules of gypsum). South of Chittenango.

175, 176 COMPACT GYPSEOUS MARL.

177 GRAVEL cemented by gypsum. Boring at Salina, Onondaga.

178 GYPSEOUS SHALE.

179 COMPACT LIMESTONE (with vesicular cavities filled with crystalline matter). Near Lanark's mill.

180 COMPACT LIMESTONE (with zinc blende). Near Lanark's mill.

181 COMPACT LIMESTONE (with irregular cavities). Near Lanark's mill.

182, 183 HYDRAULIC LIMESTONE (with lignilites). Near Lanark's mill.

184 HYDRAULIC LIMESTONE (with obscure fossils). Byron, Genesee.

185, 186 HYDRAULIC LIMESTONE (with cherty nodules). Near Camillus.

187 COMPACT SHALY LIMESTONE. Phelps, Ontario.

188 CRYSTALLIZED GYPSUM (deposits from the salt-vats, ten specimens). Syracuse, Onondaga.

189 CALCAREOUS FORMATION having oolitic structure (deposits from salt-vats, four specimens). Syracuse.

190 OOLITE (deposits from salt-vats, three specimens). Syracuse.

191 CALCAREOUS MASS showing oolitic and pitted structure (deposits from salt-vats). Syracuse.

UPPER PART OF THE ONONDAGA-SALT GROUP CONTINUED IN THE WALL CASE OF THE WATER-LIME GROUP.

1, 2, 3 HYDRAULIC LIMESTONE. Allen's creek.

4	HYDRAULIC LIMESTONE.	Clarence-hollow.
5 – 8	do	Allen's creek.
9	do	Monroe county.
10	do	Caledonia, Livingston.
11	do	Near Lewiston, Niagara.
12	do	Allen's creek.
13 & 14	do	Williamsville, Erie.
15 & 16	do	Street farm, Caledonia, Livingston

Names. Associates and localities.

17 Hydraulic limestone. Allen's creek.

18 do Street farm, Caledonia.

19 do Phelps, Ontario.

20 do One mile east of Vienna, Oneida.

21 do Near Vienna.

22 do (with sulphate of strontian). Street farm.

23 do Phelps, Ontario.

24 do (partially burned). Phelps.

25 Shaly hydraulic limestone.

26 Hylraulic limestone (with nodule of chert). Marcellus, Onondaga.

27, 28 Hydraulic limestone (with crystalline nodules). Lanark's mills.

29 Shaly hydraulic limestone.

30 Dark-colored hydraulic limestone. Marcellus, Onondaga.

31 Hydraulic limestone. Cherryvalley, Otsego.

32 Hydraulic limestone (dark colored). Near Marcellus.

33 Shaly hydraulic limestone. Near Deansville, Oneida.

34 Shaly hydraulic limestone (dark colored). Near Deansville.

35 Hydraulic limestone. Onondaga valley.

36 – 41 Hydraulic limestone (with fluor spar). Manlius, Onondaga.

42 Hydraulic limestone. Onondaga valley.

43 do Cherryvalley, Otsego.

44 do Phelps, Ontario.

45 Gypseous shaly limestone.

46 Hydraulic limestone. Near Lanark's mills.

47 do (shaly). Oriskany falls, Oneida.

48 do Chittenango, Madison.

49 do Near Manlius, Onondaga.

50 do (with anhydrite).

51 Vesicular limestone. Near Syracuse.

52 Hydraulic limestone. East Steel's creek, Herkimer.

53 do (upper part shaly, with crystals of baryta; three specimens). Phelps, Ontario.

54 do (black, shaly upper layers). Phelps.

Names.		Associates and localities.
55	Hydraulic limestone	(with lingulæ). Cherryvalley, Otsego.
56 & 57	do	(vesicular). Oriskany, Oneida.
58	do	Below Jamesville, Onondaga.
59	do	(with cavities filled with crystalline matter). Near Jamesville.
60 & 61	do	(with crystals of magnesian carbonate of lime). Near Marcellus, Onondaga.
62	do	(with nodule of chert). Near Marcellus.
63	do	(with gypsum). Near Syracuse.

NEW-YORK SYSTEM (Continued).

Name of Group.	Contained in	No. of Specimens.
13. Waterlime group.	Fifteenth table case. - - - -	58
14. Pentamerus limestone.	Sixteenth table case. - - - -	49
15. Catskill shaly limestone.	Seventeenth table case. - -	42
16. Oriskany sandstone.	Eighteenth table case. - - - -	45
17. Cauda-galli grit.	Nineteenth table case. - - - -	23
18. Schoharie grit.	Twentieth table case. - - - -	41
19. Onondaga limestone.	Twenty-first table case. - - -	67
20. Corniferous limestone.	Twenty-second table case. - -	54
21. Marcellus shale.	Twenty-third table case. - - -	55
22. Hamilton group.	Twenty-fourth table case. - - -	62
22. Hamilton group.	Twenty-fifth table case. - - -	74
23. Tully limestone.	Twenty-sixth table case. - - -	29
24. Genesee slate.	Twenty-seventh table case. - -	36
25. Portage group.	Twenty-eighth table case. - - -	32
26. Ithaca group.	Twenty-ninth table case. - - -	50
27. Chemung group.	Thirtieth table case. - - - -	50
28. Catskill group.	Thirty-first table case. - - -	55
Conglomerate.	Thirty-second table case. - - -	16
Carboniferous system (of Pennsylvania).	33d table case.	33
Miscellaneous.	Thirty-fourth table case. - - -	49
Miscellaneous.	Thirty-fifth table case. - - - -	66
Miscellaneous.	Thirty-sixth table case. - - -	77
Miscellaneous.	Thirty-seventh table case. - - -	75

Fifteen wall cases unarranged specimens.

PALÆONTOLOGY OF NEW-YORK,

BY JAMES HALL.

PALÆONTOLOGY.

1. POTSDAM SANDSTONE.

PLANTS.

		Name.	Locality.	In the
1	1	Scolithus linearis (1 specimen). - - - - - - - -		Cabinet.

BRACHIOPODA.

2	1	Lingula prima(1).	Keeseville, Essex county.	Cabinet.
3	2	Lingula antiqua(2).	Hammond, St.Lawrence.	Cabinet.

2. CALCIFEROUS SANDSTONE.

PLANTS.

4	1	Palæophycus tubularis(4).	Canajoharie and Fortplain.	Cabinet.
5	2	Palæophycus irregularis.	Near Keeseville. - - -	———
6	1	Buthotrephis antiquata(1).	Chazy, Clinton. - - -	Cabinet.

BRACHIOPODA.

7	3	Lingula acuminata (in a boulder).		

GASTEROPODA.

8	1	Euomphalus uniangulatus (plaster cast). - - - -		Cabinet.
9	1	Maclurea sordida(2).	Mohawk valley. - - -	Cabinet.
10	2	Maclurea matutina.	Canajoharie, Montgomery.	
11	1	Ophileta levata(2).	Near Fortplain. - - -	Cabinet.
12	2	Ophileta complanata(1).	Mohawk valley. - - -	Cabinet.
13	1	Turbo dilucula.	Middleville and Littlefalls.	
14	2	Turbo? obscura(1).	Fortplain, Montgomery. -	Cabinet.
15	1	Pleurotomaria? turgida.	Saratoga county.	

CEPHALOPODA.

		Names.	Localities.	
16	1	Orthoceras primigenium(1).	Near Fortplain. - -	Cabinet.
17	2	Orthoceras laqueatum(1).	- - - - - - - -	Cabinet.

---

3. CHAZY LIMESTONE.

CORALS.

18	1	Retepora incepta(1).	Chazy, Clinton. - -	Cabinet.
19	2	Retepora gracilis.	- - - - - - - -	———
20	1	Gorgonia? aspera.	Chazy.	
21	1	Stictopora fenestrata(1).	Chazy. - - - -	Cabinet.
22	2	Stictopora glomerata.	Granville (Vermont).	
23	1	Streptelasma expansa(2).	Chazy. - - - -	Cabinet.
24	1	Chætetes ———?(1).	Chazy. - - - -	Cabinet.

CRINOIDEA.

25	1	Actinocrinus tenuiradiatus(1).	Chazy. - - - -	Cabinet.
26	2	Actinocrinus? ———.	Near Chazy.	
27	1	Asterias? ———.	Chazy.	

BRACHIOPODA.

28	1	Leptæna plicifera(1).	Chazy. - - - -	Cabinet.
29	2	Leptæna incrassata(3).	Chazy. - - - -	Cabinet.
30	3	Leptæna fasciata(1).	Chazy. - - - -	Cabinet.
31	1	Orthis costalis(1).		
32	1	Atrypa dubia(1).	Chazy. - - - -	Cabinet.
33	2	Atrypa acutirostra.	Chazy. - - - -	———
34	3	Atrypa plena(1).	Chazy. - - - -	Cabinet.
35	4	Atrypa plicifera(1).	Chazy. - - - -	Cabinet.
36	5	Atrypa altilis(1).	Chazy. - - - -	Cabinet.
37	1	Orbicula? deformata.	Chazy.	
38	1	Metoptoma? dubia.	Chazy. - - - -	Cabinet.

CRUSTACEA.

39	1	Illænus arcturus(1).	Chazy. - - - -	Cabinet.
40	2	Illænus crassicauda?(1).	Chazy. - - - -	Cabinet.

		Names.	Localities.	
41	1	ASAPHUS? OBTUSUS(1).	Chazy. - - - -	Cabinet.
42	2	ASAPHUS MARGINALIS.	Chazy. - - - -	———
43	1	ISOTELUS GIGAS?(1).	Chazy. - - - -	Cabinet.
44	2	ISOTELUS CANALIS(1).	Chazy. - - - -	Cabinet.
45	1	CERAURUS? ———(1).	Chazy. - - - -	Cabinet.
		GASTEROPODA.		
46	3	MACLUREA MAGNA(8).	Chazy. - - - -	Cabinet.
47	1	SCALITES ANGULATUS(2).	Chazy. - - - -	Cabinet.
48	1	RAPHISTOMA STRIATA(1).	Chazy. - - - -	Cabinet.
49	2	RAPHISTOMA STAMINEA(1).	Chazy. - - - -	Cabinet.
50	3	RAPHISTOMA PLANISTRIA(1).	Chazy. - - - -	Cabinet.
51	4	RAPHISTOMA PLANISTRIA, *var.* PARVA.	Chazy. - - -	———
52	2	PLEUROTOMARIA BIANGULATA (fragment).	Chazy. - -	Cabinet.
53	3	PLEUROTOMARIA ———?	Chazy. - - - -	———
54	4	PLEUROTOMARIA ANTIQUATA(1).	Chazy. - - - -	Cabinet.
55	1	CAPULUS AURIFORMIS.	Galway, Saratoga. -	———
56	1	MURCHISONIA ABBREVIATA.	Chazy.	
57	1	BUCANIA SULCATINA(1).	Chazy. - - - -	Cabinet.
58	2	BUCANIA ROTUNDATA (a cast).	Chazy. - - - -	———
		CEPHALOPODA.		
59	3	ORTHOCERAS RECTIANNULATUM(1).	Chazy. - - - -	Cabinet.
60	4	ORTHOCERAS SUBARCUATUM.	Chazy. - - - -	———
61	5	ORTHOCERAS TENUISEPTUM(1).	Chazy. - - - -	Cabinet.
62	6	ORTHOCERAS BILINEATUM.	Near Albany.	
63	7	ORTHOCERAS MONILIFORME.	Chazy.	

---

4. BIRDSEYE LIMESTONE.

		PLANTS ?		
64	1	PHYTOPSIS TUBULOSUM(6).	Mohawk valley. -	Cabinet.
65	2	PHYTOPSIS CELLULOSUM(2).	Watertown & Mohawk valley.	Cabinet.
		ACEPHALA.		
66	1	MODIOLA? OBTUSA(1).	Watertown, Jefferson.	Cabinet.

GASTEROPODA.

		Names.	Localities.	
67	2	MURCHISONIA? ANGUSTATA.		
68	3	MURCHISONIA VENTRICOSA(1).	Watertown, Jefferson.	Cabinet.
69	4	MURCHISONIA PERANGULATA.	Watertown. - - -	———
70	5	MURCHISONIA VARICOSA(1).	Watertown. - - -	Cabinet.
71	1	NATICA? ———.	Watertown.	
72	5	PLEUROTOMARIA? NUCLEOLATA.	Watertown.	
73	6	PLEUROTOMARIA QUADRICARINATA(1).	Watertown. - -	Cabinet.
74	7	PLEUROTOMARIA UMBILICATA(4).	Watertown. - - -	Cabinet.
75	8	PLEUROTOMARIA? NODULOSA(1).	Watertown. - - -	Cabinet.
76	9	PLEUROTOMARIA? OBSOLETA(1).	Watertown. - - -	Cabinet.

CRUSTACEA.

77	1	CYTHERINA (fragments).	Watertown. - - -	Cabinet.

CEPHALOPODA.

78	8	ORTHOCERAS MULTICAMERATUM(1).	Watertown. - - -	Cabinet.
79	9	ORTHOCERAS RECTICAMERATUM.	Watertown.	

CORALS OF THE BIRDSEYE AND BLACK-RIVER LIMESTONES.

80	1	COLUMNARIA ALVEOLATA(3).	Mohawk valley. - -	Cabinet.
81	1	STROMATOCERIUM RUGOSUM.	Watertown, Chazy, &c.	———
82	2	CHÆTETES LYCOPERDON?	Watertown.	
83	2	STREPTELASMA PROFUNDA(6).	East-Canada creek.	Cabinet.
84	3	STICTOPORA LABYRINTHICA(1).	Chazy. - - - -	Cabinet.
85	4	STICTOPORA RAMOSA.	Watertown. - - -	———

CEPHALOPODA.

86	1	LITUITES UNDATA (plaster cast).	Watertown. - - -	Cabinet.
87	2	LITUITES CONVOLVANS?(1).	Watertown. - - -	Cabinet.
88	1	GONIOCERAS ANCEPS(1).	Watertown. - - -	Cabinet.
89	1	ORMOCERAS TENUIFILUM(4).	Watertown. - - -	Cabinet.
90	2	ORMOCERAS TENUIFILUM, *var.* DISTANS.	Watertown.	
91	3	ORMOCERAS? GRACILE.	Watertown.	
92	1	ENDOCERAS SUBCENTRALE.	Watertown. - - -	———
93	2	ENDOCERAS LONGISSIMUM.	Watertown.	
94	3	ENDOCERAS MULTITUBULATUM.	Watertown.	

		Names.	Localities.	
95	4	Endoceras gemelliparum.	Henderson's bay.	
96	10	Orthoceras fusiforme(1).	Watertown. - - -	Cabinet.

---

5. TRENTON LIMESTONE.

PLANTS.

97	2	Buthotrephis gracilis(1).	Jacksonburgh, Herkimer.	Cabinet.
98	3	Buthotrephis succulens.	Glensfalls.	
99	3	Palæophycus rugosus(1).	Below Prospect hill.	Cabinet.
100	4	Palæophycus simplex(1).	Middleville, Herkimer.	Cabinet.

CORALS.

101	2	Chætetes lycoperdon(9).	Various places. - -	Cabinet.
102	3	Chætetes rugosus.	Middleville.	
103	4	Chætetes columnaris.	Sugar river.	
104	1	Receptaculites neptunii.	Carlisle (Pennsylvania).	
105	3	Streptelasma corniculum(1).	Middleville. - - -	Cabinet.
106	4	Streptelasma crassa.	Near Middleville.	
107	5	Streptelasma multilamellosa(1).	Watertown. - -	Cabinet.
108	6	Streptelasma parvula(1).	Middleville. - - -	Cabinet.
109	1	Porites? vetusta.	Watertown.	
110	1	——— cyathiformis.	Carlisle (Pennsylvania).	
111	1	Escharopora recta(1).	Jacksonburgh. - -	Cabinet.
112	2	Escharopora recta, *var.* nodosa.		
113	5	Stictopora? acuta.	Lowville, Lewis. -	———
114	6	Stictopora elegantula.	Middleville. - - -	———
115	2	Gorgonia perantiqua.	Near Middleville.	
116	1	Aulopora arachnoidea.	Ohio and Kentucky.	
117	1	Alecto inflata.	Trenton falls, Oneida.	
118	1	Intricaria? reticulata(1).	Watertown. - - -	Cabinet
119	3	Retepora? foliacea.	Lowville.	
120	1	Stellipora antheloidea.	Lowville.	
121	1	Graptolites amplexicaule.	Trenton falls, etc.	

CRINOIDEA.

		Names.	Localities.	
122	1	Schizocrinus nodosus(3).	Glensfalls and Middleville.	Cabinet.
123	1	Poteriocrinus alternatus (fragment).	- - - - - -	———
124	2	Poteriocrinus gracilis.	Middleville.	
125	1	Scyphocrinus heterocostalis.	Middleville.	
126	2	Schizocrinus ———?(1).	Sugar river, Lewis.	Cabinet.
127	1	Echino-encrinites anatiformis.	Turin, Lewis. - -	———
128	2	Asterias matutina.	Trenton falls.	
129	1	Tentaculites? flexuosa.	Lowville.	

BRACHIOPODA.

130	4	Lingula attenuata?	Middleville, etc.	
131	5	Lingula riciniformis(2).	Middleville. - - -	Cabinet.
132	6	Lingula æqualis(1).	Middleville, etc. -	Cabinet.
133	7	Lingula quadrata(1).	Lewis county. - -	Cabinet.
134	8	Lingula elongata.	Lewis county.	
135	9	Lingula curta.	Middleville, etc.	
136	10	Lingula obtusa(1).	Middleville. - - -	Cabinet.
137	11	Lingula crassa(1).	- - - - - - - -	Cabinet.
138	2	Orbicula? filosa(1).	Middleville. - - -	Cabinet.
139	3	Orbicula lamellosa.	Middleville.	
140	4	Orbicula (Trematis) terminalis(1).	Middleville. -	Cabinet.
141	4	Leptæna alternata(8).	Middleville and Watertown.	Cabinet.
142	5	Leptæna camerata(1).	Trenton falls. - -	Cabinet.
143	6	Leptæna deltoidea(2).	Middleville and Trenton falls.	Cabinet.
144	7	Leptæna tenuistriata(1).	Middleville, etc. -	Cabinet.
145	8	Leptæna alternistriata.	Cincinnati, Ohio. -	———
146	9	Leptæna sericea(4).	Middleville and Lowville.	Cabinet.
147	10	Leptæna filitexta(2).	Middleville. - - -	Cabinet.
148	11	Leptæna planumbona.	Cincinnati, Ohio. -	———
149	12	Leptæna deflecta.	Mineral point (Wisconsin).	
150	13	Leptæna recta.	Mineral point.	
151	14	Leptæna planoconvexa.	Cincinnati (Ohio). -	———
152	15	Leptæna tenuilineata.		

		Names.	Localities.	
153	16	Leptæna subtenta.	Trenton falls?	
154	17	Leptæna ———.		
155	2	Orthis testudinaria(3).	Middleville. - - -	Cabinet.
156	3	Orthis subæquata.	Mineral point (Wisconsin).	
157	4	Orthis bella-rugosa.		
158	5	Orthis disparilis.	Mineral point (Wisconsin).	
159	6	Orthis perveta.	Mineral point.	
160	7	Orthis æquivalvis.	Middleville?	
161	8	Orthis fissicosta.	Near Cincinnati (Ohio).	
162	9	Orthis tricenaria.	Middleville. - - -	———
163	10	Orthis plicatella.	- - - - - - - - -	———
164	11	Orthis pectinella(3).	Sugar river, Lewis.	Cabinet.
165	12	Orthis pectinella, *var.* semiovalis(1).	Turin, etc.	Cabinet.
166	13	Orthis insculpta.	Watertown, etc.	
167	14	Orthis dichotoma.	Cincinnati (Ohio).	
168	15	Orthis subquadrata.	Cincinnati and Oxford (Ohio).	———
169	16	Orthis occidentalis(3).	Cincinnati and Oxford.	Cabinet.
170	17	Orthis sinuata.	Cincinnati and Oxford.	———
171	18	Orthis subjugata.	Cincinnati and Oxford.	———
172	1	Delthyris lynx(7).	Trenton falls, Oneida.	Cabinet.
173	6	Atrypa extans(1).	Watertown, Jefferson.	Cabinet.
174	7	Atrypa nucleus.	Middleville, Herkimer.	
175	8	Atrypa cuspidata(3).	Lowville, Lewis. -	Cabinet.
176	9	Atrypa bisulcata.	Adams, Jefferson. -	———
177	10	Atrypa deflecta.	Near Martinsburgh, Lewis.	
178	11	Atrypa recurvirostra(1).	Martinsburgh. - -	Cabinet.
179	12	Atrypa exigua.	Lowville.	
180	13	Atrypa modesta(1).	Cincinnati and Oxford (Ohio).	Cabinet.
181	14	Atrypa circulus.	Middleville, Herkimer.	
182	15	Atrypa ambigua.	Middleville.	
183	16	Atrypa hemiplicata(3).	Middleville. - - -	Cabinet.
184	17	Atrypa ———.	Middleville.	
185	18	Atrypa subtrigonalis.	Turin, Lewis.	

		Names.	Localities.	
186	19	ATRYPA INCREBESCENS(4).	Middleville. - - -	Cabinet.
187	20	ATRYPA DENTATA.	Turin.	
188	21	ATRYPA SORDIDA.		

ACEPHALA.

189	1	NUCULA LEVATA(3).	Middleville and Lowville.	Cabinet.
190	2	NUCULA POSTSTRIATA.	Carlisle (Pennsylvania).	
191	1	TELLINOMYA NASUTA (1 and a cast).	Middleville. - -	Cabinet.
192	2	TELLINOMYA SANGUINOLAROIDEA (plaster cast).	- - -	Cabinet.
193	3	TELLINOMYA GIBBOSA (1 and a plaster cast).	Middleville.	Cabinet.
194	4	TELLINOMYA DUBIA(2).	Middleville, etc. -	Cabinet.
195	5	TELLINOMYA ANATINIFORMIS(1).	Watertown. - - -	Cabinet.
196	1	CARDIOMORPHA VETUSTA.	Middleville.	
197	1	EDMONDIA VENTRICOSA(2).	Lowville. - - -	Cabinet.
198	2	EDMONDIA SUBTRUNCATA.	Watertown. - - -	———
199	3	EDMONDIA? SUBANGULATA(1).	Watertown. - - -	Cabinet.
200	1	MODIOLOPSIS MYTILOIDES(1).	Middleville. - - -	Cabinet.
201	2	MODIOLOPSIS PARALLELA.		
202	3	MODIOLOPSIS FABA(3).	Middleville and Watertown.	Cabinet.
203	4	MODIOLOPSIS NASUTUS(1).	Carlisle (Pennsylvania).	Cabinet.
204	5	MODIOLOPSIS ARCUATUS.	Herkimer. - - -	———
205	6	MODIOLOPSIS SUBSPATULATUS.	Watertown.	
206	7	MODIOLOPSIS LATUS.	Watertown.	
207	8	MODIOLOPSIS CARINATUS.	Middleville.	
208	9	MODIOLOPSIS AVICULOIDES.	Middleville.	
209	10	MODIOLOPSIS? TRENTONENSIS.		
210	1	AVICULA TRENTONENSIS(2).	Middleville. - - -	Cabinet.
211	2	AVICULA ELLIPTICA.	Middleville.	
212	1	AMBONYCHIA BELLISTRIATA (plaster cast).	Trenton falls.	Cabinet.
213	2	AMBONYCHIA ORBICULARIS(1).	Watertown. - - -	Cabinet.
214	3	AMBONYCHIA AMYGDALINA (plaster cast).	Adams. -	Cabinet.
215	4	AMBONYCHIA UNDATA(1).	Watertown. - - -	Cabinet.
216	5	AMBONYCHIA OBTUSA (plaster cast).	Watertown. - -	Cabinet.
217	6	AMBONYCHIA? ———.	Middleville.	

GASTEROPODA.

		Names.	Localities.	
218	1	Holopea symmetrica.	Middleville. - - -	———
219	2	Holopea obliqua(2).	Watertown. - - -	Cabinet.
220	3	Holopea paludiniformis(1).	Watertown. - - -	Cabinet.
221	4	Holopea ventricosa (plaster cast).	Middleville. - -	Cabinet.
222	10	Pleurotomaria subtilistriata.	Watertown.	
223	11	Pleurotomaria lenticularis(2).	Watertown. - - -	Cabinet.
224	12	Pleurotomaria rotuloides.	Middleville.	
225	13	Pleurotomaria subconica (plaster cast).	Watertown.	Cabinet.
74	7	Pleurotomaria umbilicata.	Lowville and Adams.	———
226	14	Pleurotomaria indenta(1).	Watertown. - - -	Cabinet.
227	15	Pleurotomaria ambigua (plaster cast).	Adams. - -	Cabinet.
228	16	Pleurotomaria percarinata (plaster cast).	Middleville.	Cabinet.
229	6	Murchisonia bicincta(2).	Lowville and Watertown.	Cabinet
230	7	Murchisonia tricarinata.	Mineral point (Wisconsin).	
231	8	Murchisonia perangulata.	Middleville. - - -	———
232	9	Murchisonia uniangulata.	Middleville.	
233	10	Murchisonia bellicincta(2).	Middleville, Turin, etc.	Cabinet
234	11	Murchisonia subfusiformis (1 and a cast).	Lowville.	Cabinet.
235	12	Murchisonia vittata.	Adams. - - - -	———
236	13	Murchisonia gracilis(2).	Middleville. - - -	Cabinet.
237	1	Subulites elongata(2).	Watertown. - - -	Cabinet.
238	1	Carinaropsis carinata.	Middleville and Trenton.	
239	2	Carinaropsis patelliformis.	Middleville. - - -	———
240	1	Bellerophon bilobatus(2).	Trenton falls & Middleville.	Cabinet.
241	2	Bellerophon bilobatus, *var.* acutus.	Trenton falls.	———
242	3	Bellerophon bilobatus, *var.* corrugatus.	Trenton falls.	———
243	3	Bucania expansa (plaster cast).	Watertown. - - -	Cabinet.
244	4	Bucania bidorsata.	Watertown. - - -	———
245	5	Bucania punctifrons(2).	Middleville. - - -	Cabinet.
246	1	Cyrtolites compressus(3).	Middleville. - - -	Cabinet.
247	2	Cyrtolites trentonensis.	Mohawk valley. - -	———
248	3	Cyrtolites filosum (plaster cast).	Watertown. - -	Cabinet.

CEPHALOPODA.

		Names.	Localities.		
249	1	Trocholites ammonius(1).	Middleville.	- - -	Cabinet.
250	1	Cyrtoceras lamellosum.	Middleville.		
251	2	Cyrtoceras annulatum.	Middleville.	- - -	———
252	3	Cyrtoceras macrostomum (plaster cast).	Wisconsin.		Cabinet.
253	4	Cyrtoceras constrictostriatum.	Middleville.		
254	5	Cyrtoceras multicameratum.	Middleville.	- - -	———
255	6	Cyrtoceras arcuatum.	Middleville.		
256	7	Cyrtoceras camurum.	Middleville.		
257	1	Oncoceras constrictum(2).	Watertown.	- - -	Cabinet.
258	11	Orthoceras arcuoliratum(2).	Watertown.	- - -	Cabinet.
259	12	Orthoceras teretiforme(1).	Watertown.	- - -	Cabinet.
260	13	Orthoceras textile.	Watertown.		
261	14	Orthoceras bilineatum(1).	Middleville.	- - -	Cabinet.
262	15	Orthoceras bilineatum, *var. α*.	Middleville, etc.		
263	16	Orthoceras clathratum.	Middleville.		
264	17	Orthoceras vertebrale.	Middleville.		
265	18	Orthoceras anellum.	Middleville, etc.		
266	19	Orthoceras undulostriatum.	Middleville.		
267	20	Orthoceras ———.	Middleville.		
268	21	Orthoceras latiannulatum.	Middleville.		
269	22	Orthoceras junceum.	Watertown.	- - -	———
270	23	Orthoceras amplicameratum.	Middleville.	- - -	———
271	24	Orthoceras strigatum.	Middleville.		
17	2	Orthoceras laqueatum.	Watertown & Middleville.		
272	25	Orthoceras laqueatum, *var. α*.	Middleville.		
273	5	Endoceras annulatum.	Watertown.		
274	6	Endoceras proteiforme, *var.* tenuistriatum(1).		-	Cabinet.
275	7	Endoceras proteiforme, *var.* tenuitextum(1).		- -	Cabinet.
276	8	Endoceras proteiforme, *var.* lineolatum(1).		- -	Cabinet.
277	9	Endoceras proteiforme, *var.* strangulatum(1).		-	Cabinet.
278	10	Endoceras proteiforme, *var.* elongatum(1).		- - -	Cabinet.

These five varieties of Endoceras proteiforme were all obtained in Middleville, Herkimer county.

		Names.	Localities.	
279	11	Endoceras arctiventrum.	Middleville.	
280	12	Endoceras angusticameratum.	Middleville.	
281	13	Endoceras magniventrum(1).	Near Middleville. -	Cabinet.
282	14	Endoceras magniventrum, *var.*	Near Middleville.	
283	15	Endoceras approximatum.	Near Middleville.	
284	16	Endoceras duplicatum(1).	Near Middleville. -	Cabinet.
285	17	Endoceras distans.	Turin, Lewis.	
286	1	Cameroceras trentonense.	Middleville. - - -	———
89	1	Ormoceras tenuifilum?	Turin, etc.	
287	1	Conularia trentonensis(1).	Middleville. - - -	Cabinet.
288	2	Conularia granulata.	Middleville, etc.	
289	3	Conularia papillata.	Near Middleville.	
290	4	Conularia gracile.	Near Middleville.	

CRUSTACEA OF THE BIRDSEYE AND TRENTON LIMESTONES, HUDSON-RIVER GROUP, AND UTICA SLATE.

291	1	Ogygia? vetusta.	Mohawk valley.	
292	3	Asaphus extans(1).	Lowville. - - -	Cabinet.
293	1	Calymene multicosta(1).	Isle Lamotte. - -	Cabinet.
40	2	Illænus crassicauda.	Carlisle (Pennsylvania).	———
294	3	Illænus trentonensis.	Hogansburgh, Franklin.	———
295	4	Illænus latidorsata.	Near Watertown.	
43	1	Isotelus gigas (several imperfect specimens).	Middleville.	Cabinet.
296	1	Platynotus trentonensis (plaster cast).	Middleville, etc.	Cabinet.
297	2	Calymene beckii(4).	Middleville. - - -	Cabinet.
298	3	Calymene senaria(2).	Middleville. - - -	Cabinet.
299	1	Acidaspis trentonensis.	Bay of Quinty.	
300	2	Acidaspis spiniger.	Mohawk valley.	
301	2	Ceraurus pleurexanthemus (fragments).	Middleville.	Cabinet.
302	3	Ceraurus vigilans.	Middleville. - - -	———
303	4	Ceraurus? pustulosus.	Watertown.	
304	1	Phacops callicephalus.	Middleville & Watertown.	
305	2	Phacops? laticaudus.	Turin.	

		Names.	Localities.	
306	4	Asaphus nodostriatus(1).	Watertown. - - -	Cabinet.
307	1	Trinucleus concentricus(2).	Loraine, etc. - -	Cabinet.
308	4	Calymene ——.	Canajoharie.	
309	5	Asaphus? latimarginata.	Watertown.	
310	1	Olenus asaphoides.	Greenwich, Washington.	
311	2	Olenus undulostriatus.	Snakehill, Saratoga.	——
312	1	Agnostus lobatus.	Troy, Rensselaer. -	——
313	1	Thaleops (Illænus) ovatus.	Mineral point (Wisconsin).	

---

6. HUDSON-RIVER GROUP.

PLANTS.

314	1	Sphenothallus angustifolius.	Mohawk valley.	
315	2	Sphenothallus latifolius(6).	Schoharie. - - -	Cabinet.
316	4	Buthotrephis subnodosa.	Turin, Lewis. - -	——
317	5	Buthotrephis? flexuosa.	Jackson, Washington.	——
318	5	Palæophycus virgatus(1).	Union, Washington.	Cabinet.
319	6	Palæophycus ——?(1).	Rome, Oneida. - -	Cabinet.
320	1	Gordia marina.	Jackson, Washington.	——

CORALS.

321	2	Graptolithus pristis(1).	Turin, Loraine, etc.	Cabinet.
322	3	Graptolithus secalinus(1).	Hoosick slate quarries.	Cabinet.
323	4	Graptolithus mucronatus(1).	Near Albany. - -	Cabinet.
324	5	Graptolithus bicornis(2).	Albany. - - - -	Cabinet.
325	6	Graptolithus ramosus(1).	Albany. - - - -	Cabinet.
326	7	Graptolithus scalaris(1).	West-Canada creek & Albany.	Cabinet.
327	8	Graptolithus sagittarius(1).	Albany. - - - -	Cabinet.
328	9	Graptolithus tenuis(1).	Albany. - - - -	Cabinet.
329	10	Graptolithus sextans(1).	Albany. - - - -	Cabinet.
330	11	Graptolithus furcatus.	Normanskill near Albany.	
331	12	Graptolithus serratulus.	Normanskill.	
332	13	Graptolithus gracilis(1).	Albany. - - - -	Cabinet.

		Names.	Localities.	
333	14	GRAPTOLITHUS LÆVIS.	Turin, Lewis.	
334	1	FAVISTELLA STELLATA.	Madison (Indiana).	———
101	2	CHÆTETES LYCOPERDON.	Turin, etc. - - -	———

CRINOIDEA.

335	1	DISCOPHYLLUM PELTATUM.	Near Troy, Rensselaer.	
336	1	*Undetermined.*	Turin, Pulaski, Loraine, etc.	
337	1	HETEROCRINUS HETERODACTYLUS (columns on a fragment of slate).	Near Rome, Oneida.	Cabinet.
338	2	HETEROCRINUS SIMPLEX.	Cincinnati (Ohio).	
339	3	HETEROCRINUS? GRACILIS.	Snakehill, Saratoga.	———
340	1	GLYPTOCRINUS DECADACTYLUS (columns on a fragment of slate).	Turin, Rome, etc. -	Cabinet.
129	1	TENTACULITES FLEXUOSA.	Turin. - - - -	Cabinet.

BRACHIOPODA.

133	7	LINGULA QUADRATA(1).	Loraine, Jefferson. -	Cabinet.
141	4	LEPTÆNA ALTERNATA(4).	Pulaski, Oswego. -	Cabinet.
146	9	LEPTÆNA SERICEA(1).	Turin, Lewis. - -	Cabinet.
155	2	ORTHIS TESTUDINARIA(1).	Turin, Pulaski, etc.	Cabinet.
341	19	ORTHIS? ERRATICA(2).	In southern counties.	Cabinet.
342	20	ORTHIS CENTRILINEATA.	Loraine. - - - -	———
186	19	ATRYPA INCREBESCENS(1).	Turin. - - - -	Cabinet.
343	5	ORBICULA? SUBTRUNCATA.	Loraine. - - - -	———
344	6	ORBICULA? CRASSA.	Near Troy.	
345	7	ORBICULA CÆLATA.	Near Troy.	

ACEPHALA.

346	3	AVICULA INSUETA(1).	Canajoharie. - - -	Cabinet.
347	4	AVICULA DEMISSA.	Near Rome, Oneida.	———
348	5	AVICULA? DESQUAMATA.	Near Troy.	
349	7	AMBONYCHIA RADIATA(3).	Pulaski and Turin. -	Cabinet.
350	8	AMBONYCHIA CARINATA.		
351	11	MODIOLOPSIS MODIOLARIS(3).	Loraine, Pulaski, etc.	Cabinet.
352	12	MODIOLOPSIS TRUNCATUS.	Near Rome.	

		Names.	Localities.	
203	4	Modiolopsis nasutus(1).	Pulaski. - - - -	Cabinet.
353	13	Modiolopsis curta.	Loraine. - - - -	———
354	14	Modiolopsis ———.	Cincinnati (Ohio).	
355	15	Modiolopsis anodontoides.	Pulaski. - - - -	———
202	3	Modiolopsis faba.	Pulaski. - - - -	———
356	16	Modiolopsis? nuculiformis.	Turin.	
357	1	Orthonota pholadis.	Pulaski.	
358	2	Orthonota parallela.	Pulaski. - - - -	———
359	3	Orthonota contracta.	Cincinnati (Ohio).	
360	1	Cleidophorus planulatus.	Loraine. - - - -	———
190	2	Nucula? poststriata.	Loraine and Pulaski.	———
361	1	Lyrodesma plana.	Near Rome.	
362	2	Lyrodesma pulchella.	Turin, etc.	

GASTEROPODA.

236	13	Murchisonia gracilis.	Loraine. - - - -	———
363	14	Murchisonia uniangulata, *var.* abbreviata.	Near Rome.	———
225	13	Pleurotomaria subconica.	Pulaski. - - - -	———
364	17	Pleurotomaria? bilix(2).	Indiana and Ohio. -	Cabinet.
365	18	Pleurotomaria ———(2).	Coldspring, Montgomery.	Cabinet.
366	2	Metoptoma? rugosa.	Near Troy, Rensselaer.	
239	2	Carinaropsis patelliformis.	Pulaski, Oswego. -	———
367	3	Carinaropsis orbiculatus.	Waterford, Saratoga.	———
240	1	Bellerophon bilobatus.	Turin, Loraine, etc.	———
368	4	Bellerophon cancellatus(1).	Loraine. - - - -	Cabinet.
369	4	Cyrtolites ornatus(1).	Turin, Pulaski, etc.	Cabinet.

CEPHALOPODA.

249	1	Trocholites ammonius(2).	Canajoharie, Montgomery.	Cabinet.
370	2	Trocholites planorbiformis(1).	Pulaski, Oswego. -	Cabinet.
371	18	Endoceras proteiforme?(3).	Turin, Lewis. - -	Cabinet.
372	26	Orthoceras ———.	Turin.	
373	27	Orthoceras coralliferum(2).	Turin and Pulaski. -	Cabinet.
374	28	Orthoceras lamellosum(1).	Turin, etc. - - -	Cabinet.

		Names.	Localities.	
375	2	Ormoceras crebriseptum(1).	Turin. - - - -	Cabinet.
376	1	Theca? triangularis.	Near Waterford.	
377	9	Ambonychia mytiloidea.	Chazy.	
378	2	Schizocrinus striatus.	Middleville.	
379	3	Nucula? donaciformis.		
380	6	Bucania intexta.	Near Waterford	

7. MEDINA SANDSTONE.

PLANTS.

382	1	Arthrophycus harlani.	Medina, Lockport, etc.	Cabinet.
383	2	Arthrophycus ———?	Medina and Lockport.	
384	2	Scolithus verticalis.	Monroe county. - -	Cabinet.
385	7	Palæophycus tortuosus.	Mouth of Genesee river.	Cabinet.
386	1	Dictuolites beckii(1).	Medina. - - - -	Cabinet.
387	5	Chætetes ———?	Lockport.	

BRACHIOPODA.

388	12	Lingula cuneata.	Medina, Lockport, etc.	Cabinet.
389	22	Atrypa oblata.	Lockport.	
390	23	Atrypa plicata.	Lockport.	
391	17	Modiolopsis orthonota.	Medina and Lockport.	———
392	18	Modiolopsis? primigenius.	Medina and Lockport.	Cabinet.
393	19	Pleurotomaria? pervetusta(2).	Medina and Lockport.	Cabinet.
394	20	Pleurotomaria litorea.	Lockport.	
395	15	Murchisonia? conoidea.	Lockport.	
396	7	Bucania trilobatus.	Medina.	
397	2	Oncoceras gibbosum.	Lockport.	
398	26	Orthoceras ———.	Lockport.	
399	27	Orthoceras multiseptum.	Lockport and Medina.	———
400	2	Cytherina cylindrica.	Medina.	

8. CLINTON GROUP.

PLANTS.

		Names.	Localities.	
401	6	Buthotrephis gracilis(1).	New-Hartford. - -	Cabinet.
402	7	Buthotrephis gracilis, *var.* intermedia.	New-Hartford.	
403	8	Buthotrephis gracilis, *var.* crassa.	Oneida county, etc.	
404	9	Buthotrephis gracilis?		
405	10	Buthotrephis palmata(1).	- - - - - - - -	Cabinet.
406	11	Buthotrephis impudica(1).	New-Hartford. - -	Cabinet.
407	12	Buthotrephis ramosa(1).	New-Hartford. - -	Cabinet.
408	8	Palæophycus? striatus.	Clinton.	
409	9	Palæophycus ———?	New-Hartford.	
410	10	Palæophycus ———?	New-Hartford.	
411	1	Rusophycus clavatus.	New-Hartford.	
412	2	Rusophycus subangulatus.	New-Hartford.	
413	3	Rusophycus pudicus.	New-Hartford.	
414	4	Rusophycus bilobatus(4).	Near New-Hartford.	Cabinet.
415	1	Ichnophycus tridactylus.	New-Hartford.	
		Tracks of marine animals (three specimens).	- - -	Cabinet.

CORALS.

416	15	Graptolithus clintonensis(1).	Sodus, Williamson, etc.	Cabinet.
417	16	Graptolithus venosus.	Below Rochester.	
101	2	Chætetes lycoperdon.	Sodus, Rochester, etc.	Cabinet
418	2	Favistella favosidea.	Rochester, etc.	
419	1	Caninia bilateralis(1).	Lockport, Rochester, etc.	Cabinet.
420	1	Cyclolites rotuloides.	Near Clinton village.	
421	1	Cannapora junciformis.	Ontario, Rochester, etc.	
422	1	Catenipora escharoides(1).	Clinton, Oneida. -	Cabinet.
423	1	Helopora fragilis.	Rochester, Lockport, etc.	
424	7	Stictopora crassa.	Wayne county, etc.	
425	8	Stictopora raripora.	Rochester.	
426	1	Phænopora explanata.	Probably at Lockport.	
427	2	Phænopora constellata.	Wayne county.	

		Names.	Localities.
428	3	PHÆNOPORA ENSIFORMIS.	Flamborough head (Canada West).
429	1	RHINOPORA VERRUCOSA.	Flamborough head.
430	2	RHINOPORA TUBULOSA.	Sodus, etc.
431	4	RETEPORA ANGULATA.	Sodus and Rochester.
432	1	FENESTELLA PRISCA?(1).	Ontario, Rochester, etc. Cabinet.
433	2	FENESTELLA TENUIS.	Wayne county.

BRACHIOPODA.

434	13	LINGULA OBLONGA(2).	Martville, Cayuga. - Cabinet.
435	14	LINGULA OBLATA.	Sodus and Wolcott.
436	15	LINGULA PEROVATA.	Rochester.
437	16	LINGULA LAMELLATA.	Near Clinton village.
438	17	LINGULA ACUTIROSTRA.	
439	21	ORTHIS CIRCULUS.	Niagara county.
440	22	ORTHIS ELEGANTULA? *var.*	Sodus.
441	23	ORTHIS TRINUCLEUS.	Wayne county.
442	24	ORTHIS TENUIDENS.	New-Hartford.
146	9	LEPTÆNA SERICEA.	Rochester and Sodus. Cabinet.
443	18	LEPTÆNA CORRUGATA.	Rochester, etc.
444	19	LEPTÆNA PATENTA.	Medina.
445	20	LEPTÆNA PROFUNDA.	Lockport.
446	21	LEPTÆNA OBSCURA.	Kirkland, Oneida.
447	22	LEPTÆNA ORTHIDIDEA.	Kirkland.
448	23	LEPTÆNA DEPRESSA.	Kirkland, etc.
449	1	STROPHODONTA PRISCA.	Kirkland.
450	1	CHONETES CORNUTA.	Sodus.
172	1	SPIRIFER BIFORATUS, *var.* LYNX.	Rochester, etc.
451	2	SPIRIFER ———.	Sodus.
452	3	SPIRIFER RADIATUS.	Wayne and Niagara counties.
453	24	ATRYPA CONGESTA.	Rochester, Medina, etc.
454	25	ATRYPA QUADRICOSTATA.	Lockport.
455	26	ATRYPA BIDENS.	Lockport.
456	27	ATRYPA NEGLECTA.	Niagara county(1).

		Names.	Localities.
457	28	Atrypa equiradiata.	Oneida county.
458	29	Atrypa emacerata.	Sodus, Rochester, etc.
459	30	Atrypa robusta.	Lockport.
460	31	Atrypa reticularis.	Sodus.
461	32	Atrypa plicatula.	Niagara county.
462	33	Atrypa hemispherica.	Rochester, etc.
463	34	Atrypa planoconvexa.	Flamborough head (C. W.).
464	35	Atrypa naviformis.	Sodus and Rochester.
465	36	Atrypa cylindrica.	Lockport.
466	37	Atrypa intermedia.	Lockport.
467	38	Atrypa ——— (cast).	Kirkland.
468	39	Atrypa cylindrica? (cast).	Lockport.
469	40	Atrypa gibbosa.	Near Clinton village.
470	1	Pentamerus oblongus(1).	Wayne county. - - Cabinet.
471	2	Pentamerus fornicatus.	Lockport.

ACEPHALA.

472	6	Avicula emacerata.	Kirkland and Wolcott. Cabinet.
473	7	Avicula rhomboidea.	New-Hartford and Sodus.
474	19	Modiolopsis subalatus.	Rochester, Sodus, etc.
475	6	Tellinomya lata.	Wolcott, Wayne.
476	7	Tellinomya machæriformis.	Wolcott.
477	8	Tellinomya curta.	Wolcott.
478	4	Orthonota curta.	Wolcott and Rochester.
479	1	Posidonia? alata.	Rochester.
480	1	Pyrenomœus cuneatus.	Wolcott. - - - - Cabinet.

GASTEROPODA.

481	1	Cyclonema cancellata.	Sodus, etc.
482	2	Cyclonema ventricosa.	Sodus.
483	3	Cyclonema? obsoleta.	Medina and Lockport.
484	4	Cyclonema cancellata?	Lockport.
485	1	Platyostoma ———.	Kirkland and New-Hartford.
486	16	Murchisonia subulata.	Wolcott, Medina, etc.

		Names.	Localities.
487	8	BUCANIA STIGMOSA.	Lockport.
488	9	BUCANIA? BELLA-PUNCTA.	Wolcott.
396	7	BUCANIA TRILOBATA.	New-Hartford.

CEPHALOPODA.

489	3	ONCOCERAS SUBRECTUM.	Lockport.
490	5	ORMOCERAS VERTEBRATUM.	Niagara county.
491	28	ORTHOCERAS VIRGULATUM,	Lockport, etc.
492	29	ORTHOCERAS ANNULATUM?	Wolcott.
493	30	ORTHOCERAS ABRUPTUM.	Lockport.

INCERTÆ SEDES.

494	1	CORNULITES FLEXUOSUS.	Lockport.
495	1	DISCOSORUS CONOIDEUS.	Ontario and Lockport.

UPPER GREY SANDSTONE OF THE CLINTON GROUP.

496	1	MYALINA MYTILIFORMIS.	South of Mohawk village.
497	20	MODIOLOPSIS OVATUS(2).	S. of Mohawk village. Cabinet.
498	21	MODIOLOPSIS SUBCARINATUS(4),	S. of Mohawk village. Cabinet.
499	9	TELLINOMYA ELLIPTICA.	S. of Mohawk village.
500	3	PENTAMERUS OVALIS.	New-Hartford.
446	21	LEPTÆNA OBSCURA?	New-Hartford.
501	2	PLATYOSTOMA ———.	New-Hartford.
502	31	ORTHOCERAS CLAVATUM.	South of Mohawk village.
503	1	HOMALONOTUS DELPHINOCEPHALUS(4).	S. Mohawk village. Cabinet.
504	1	ICHTHYODORULITE (fragment).	

---

9. NIAGARA GROUP.

CORALS.

505	7	STREPTELASMA CALICULA.	Lockport, Rochester, etc.
506	1	POLYDILASMA TURBINATUM.	Lockport.
419	1	CANINIA BILATERALIS.	Lockport.
507	1	CONOPHYLLUM NIAGARENSE.	Niagara county.
508	1	DIPLOPHYLLUM CÆSPITOSUM.	Lockport.

		Names.	Localities.	
509	2	Diplophyllum cæspitosum?	Lockport.	
510	1	Syringopora? multicaulis.	Lockport and Barre.	
511	1	Astrocerium venustum.	Lockport, Rochester, etc.	
512	2	Astrocerium parasiticum.	Near Lockport.	
513	3	Astrocerium pyriforme.	Rochester, Wolcott, etc.	
514	4	Astrocerium constrictum.	Lockport, etc.	
515	1	Favosites niagarensis.	Niagara falls, etc.	
516	2	Favosites favosa?	Milwaukie (Wisconsin).	
517	1	Catenipora escharoides(1).	Near Rochester. -	Cabinet.
518	2	Catenipora agglomerata.	Sweden and Ogden.	——
519	1	Heliolites elegans.	Lockport.	
520	2	Heliolites spinipora.	Lockport.	
521	3	Heliolites pyriformis?	Lockport.	
522	4	Heliolites macrostylus.	Milwaukie (Wisconsin).	
523	1	Stromatopora concentrica.	Lockport, Rochester, etc.	Cabinet.
524	1	Cladopora seriata.	Lockport, etc. - -	Cabinet.
525	2	Cladopora cespitosa.	Lockport.	
526	3	Cladopora cervicornis.	Lockport.	
527	4	Cladopora fibrosa.	Lockport.	
528	5	Cladopora multipora.	Lockport.	
529	6	Cladopora macrophora.	Lockport.	
530	7	Cladopora reticulata.	Lockport.	
531	1	Limaria ramulosa.	Lockport.	
532	2	Limaria fruticosa?	Lockport.	
533	3	Limaria laminata.	Lockport.	
534	1	Callopora elegantula.	Lockport.	
535	2	Callopora florida.	Lockport.	
536	3	Callopora laminata.	Lockport.	
537	4	Callopora aspera.	Lockport.	
538	5	Callopora nummiformis.	Lockport.	
539	1	Trematopora tuberculosa.	Lockport.	
540	2	Trematopora coalescens.	Lockport.	
541	3	Trematopora tubulosa.	Wayne county.	

		Names.	Localities.
542	4	Trematopora punctata.	Lockport.
543	5	Trematopora ostiolata.	Lockport, Rochester, etc. Cabinet.
544	6	Trematopora solida.	Lockport.
545	7	Trematopora striata.	Lockport.
546	8	Trematopora granulifera.	Lockport.
547	9	Trematopora aspera.	Lockport.
548	10	Trematopora spinulosa.	Lockport.
549	11	Trematopora sparsa.	Lockport.
550	1	Striatopora flexuosa.	Lockport.
551	9	Stictopora punctipora.	Lockport.
552	1	Diamesopora dichotoma.	Lockport.
553	1	Clathropora alcicornis.	Lockport.
554	2	Clathropora frondosa.	Lockport.
555	5	Retepora diffusa.	Lockport.
556	6	Retepora asperato-striata.	Lockport.
557	1	Hornera? dichotoma.	Lockport and Rochester.
558	3	Fenestella elegans.	Lockport, Rochester, etc.
559	4	Fenestella tenuiceps.	Lockport, Rochester, etc.
560	5	Fenestella cribrosa.	Lockport.
561	6	Fenestella ———.	Lockport.
562	1	Polypora incepta.	Lockport, Rochester, etc.
563	1	Ceramopora imbricata.	Lockport.
564	2	Ceramopora incrustans.	Lockport.
565	3	Ceramopora foliacea.	Lockport.
566	3	Rhinopora tuberculosa.	Lockport.
567	1	Lichenalia concentrica.	Rochester and Lockport.
568	1	Sagenella membranacea.	Rochester and Lockport.
569	1	Dictuonema retiformis.	Lockport, Rochester, etc. Cabinet.
570	2	Dictuonema gracilis.	Lockport.
571	1	Inocaulis plumulosa.	Lockport, Rochester, etc.

CRINOIDEA OF THE CLINTON GROUP.

		Names.	Localities.
572	1	Closterocrinus elongatus.	Lockport.
573	2	Glyptocrinus plumosus.	Oak-orchard creek.
574	3	Glyptocrinus ———?	Niagara county.
575	1	Ichthyocrinus clintonensis.	Niagara county.
576	1	Caryocrinus ornatus.	Lockport.
577	2	Tentaculites minutus.	Rochester.
578	3	Tentaculites distans.	Flamborough head (Canada West).
		Joints of undetermined crinoidea(1).	S. Mohawk village. Cabinet.

CRINOIDEA OF THE NIAGARA GROUP.

		Names.	Localities.
579	1	Homocrinus parvus.	Lockport.
580	2	Homocrinus cylindricus.	Lockport.
581	1	Glyptaster brachiatus.	Lockport.
582	1	Thysanocrinus liliiformis.	Lockport.
583	2	Thysanocrinus canaliculatus.	Lockport.
584	3	Thysanocrinus aculeatus.	Lockport.
585	4	Thysanocrinus immaturus.	Lockport.
586	1	Myelodactylus convolutus.	Lockport.
587	1	Dendrocrinus longidactylus.	Lockport.
588	2	Ichthyocrinus lævis.	Lockport.
589	1	Lyriocrinus dactylus.	Lockport.
590	1	Lecanocrinus macropetalus.	Lockport.
591	2	Lecanocrinus ornatus.	Lockport.
592	3	Lecanocrinus simplex.	Lockport.
593	4	Lecanocrinus caliculus.	Lockport.
594	1	Macrostylocrinus ornatus.	Lockport.
595	1	Saccocrinus speciosus.	Lockport.
596	1	Eucalyptocrinus decorus.	Lockport, Rochester, etc.
597	2	Eucalyptocrinus cælatus.	Lockport.
598	3	Eucalyptocrinus papulosus.	Sweden, Monroe.
599	1	Stephanocrinus angulatus.	Lockport.
600	2	Stephanocrinus gemmiformis.	Lockport.

		Names.	Localities.
601	1	Caryocrinus ornatus.	Lockport, Rochester, etc. Cabinet.
602	1	Melocrinites sculptus.	Lockport.
603	1	Heterocystites armatus.	Lockport.
604	2	Myelodactylus brachiatus.	Lockport.
605	3	Myelodactylus ———?	Lockport.
		Plates and columns of undetermined crinoidea.	

CYSTIDEÆ.

606	1	Callocystites jewettii.	Lockport.
607	1	Apiocystites elegans.	Lockport.
608	1	Hemicystites parasitica.	Lockport.

ASTERIADÆ.

609	1	Palæaster niagarensis.	Lockport.

BRACHIOPODA.

437	16	Lingula lamellata.	Lockport, Sweden, etc.
610	8	Orbicula tenuilamellata.	Lockport.
611	9	Orbicula? squamiformis.	Rochester, Sweden, etc.
612	25	Orthis pisum.	Wolcott.
613	26	Orthis pyramidalis.	Lockport.
440	22	Orthis elegantula.	Wolcott, etc.
614	27	Orthis hybrida.	Wolcott, etc.
615	28	Orthis puncto-striata.	Lockport.
616	29	Orthis flabellulum, *var.?*	Lockport, Sweden, etc.
617	30	Orthis fasciata.	Rochester and Lockport.
618	24	Leptæna transversalis.	Near Rochester, etc.
448	23	Leptæna depressa.	Lockport, Rochester, etc.
619	25	Leptæna striata.	
620	26	Leptæna subplana.	Lockport, etc.
621	4	Spirifer bilobus.	Wolcott and Lockport.
622	5	Spirifer sulcatus.	Lewiston, Lockport, etc.
623	6	Spirifer crispus.	Lockport, Lewiston, etc.
624	7	Spirifer bicostatus.	Oneida county.
625	8	Spirifer niagarensis.	Wolcott, Rochester, etc.

		Names.	Localities.
452	3	Spirifer radiatus.	Lockport, Lewiston, etc.
626	9	Spirifer pyramidalis.	Near Lewiston.
627	41	Atrypa nitida.	Lockport, etc.
628	42	Atrypa nitida, *var.* oblata.	Lockport and Sweden.
629	43	Atrypa ———.	Lockport.
630	44	Atrypa crassirostra.	Lockport.
460	31	Atrypa reticularis.	Lockport, etc.
631	45	Atrypa rugosa.	Lockport.
632	46	Atrypa nodostriata.	Lockport.
633	47	Atrypa camura.	Lockport.
456	27	Atrypa neglecta.	Wolcott, Lockport, etc.
634	48	Atrypa interplicata.	Lockport.
635	49	Atrypa bidentata.	Lockport.
636	50	Atrypa cuneata.	Lockport, etc.
637	51	Atrypa ———?	Lockport.
638	52	Atrypa disparilis.	Wolcott.
639	53	Atrypa brevirostris.	Lockport.
640	54	Atrypa obtusiplicata.	Lockport.
641	55	Atrypa plicatella?	Wolcott.
642	56	Atrypa aprinis.	Lockport.
643	57	Atrypa corallifera.	Lockport and Rochester.

ACEPHALA.

472	6	Avicula emacerata.	Lockport, Rochester, etc. Cabinet.
644	8	Avicula undata.	Rochester.
645	9	Avicula subplana.	Lockport.
646	10	Avicula? orbiculata.	Rochester.
647	2	Posidonomya? rhomboidea.	Lockport.
648	22	Modiolopsis? undulostriata.	Lockport.
474	19	Modiolopsis subalatus?	Wolcott.
478	4	Orthonota curta?	Wolcott.

GASTEROPODA.

		Names.	Localities.
649	2	PLATYOSTOMA NIAGARENSIS.	Lockport, Rochester, etc.
650	3	PLATYOSTOMA HEMISPHERICA.	Rochester.
651	1	ACROCULIA NIAGARENSIS.	Lockport.
652	2	ACROCULIA ANGULATA.	Lockport.

CEPHALOPODA.

653	1	GOMPHOCERAS? ———.	Rochester and Niagara falls.
654	8	CYRTOCERAS? CANCELLATUM.	Rochester and Niagara falls.
655	32	ORTHOCERAS ———.	Rochester.
656	33	ORTHOCERAS IMBRICATUM?	Lockport and Rochester.
657	34	ORTHOCERAS VIRGATUM?	Rochester.
658	35	ORTHOCERAS CANCELLATUM.	Rochester and Lockport.
659	36	ORTHOCERAS ———?	Rochester.
660	37	ORTHOCERAS UNDULATUM.	Lockport, Rochester, etc.
661	5	CONULARIA NIAGARENSIS.	Lockport, Rochester, etc.
662	6	CONULARIA LONGA.	Lockport.

CRUSTACEA OF THE CLINTON AND NIAGARA GROUPS.

663	1	CYBELE PUNCTATA.	Medina, etc.	
664	5	CALYMENE CLINTONI.	Martville, etc.	
298	2	CALYMENE BLUMENBACHII, *var.?* SENARIA.		
665	3	ACIDASPIS ———.		
666	3	PHACOPS TRISULCATUS.		
667	5	CERAURUS INSIGNIS.	Rochester.	
668	1	BEYRICHIA LATA.	New-Hartford, etc.	Cabinet.
669	1	BUMASTIS BARRIENSIS.	Lockport, etc. - -	Cabinet.
670	4	PHACOPS LIMULURUS(4).	Lockport. - - -	Cabinet.
671	7	CALYMENE BLUMENBACHII, *var.* NIAGARENSIS(1).	Lockport, Rochester, etc.	Cabinet.
503	1	HOMALONOTUS DELPHINOCEPHALUS(2).	Lockport, etc.	Cabinet.
672	1	LICHAS BOLTONI(2).	Lockport, Rochester, etc.	Cabinet.
673	1	BRONTEUS? NIAGARENSIS.	Niagara river.	
674	1	ARGES PHLYCTANODES.	Near Albion, Orleans.	
675	1	PROETUS CORYCŒUS(1).	Lockport. - - -	Cabinet.

		Names.	Localities.		
676	2	PROETUS? STOKESII.	Lockport.		
677	2	BEYRICHIA SYMMETRICA.	Lockport.	- - -	Cabinet.
678	2	CYTHERINA SPINOSA.	Lockport.		
	1	ONCHUS DEWEII.	Lockport and Rochester.		

10. CORALLINE LIMESTONE.

CORALS.

679	3	DIPLOPHYLLUM CORALLIFERUM(3).	Schoharie.	- - -	Cabinet.
680	1	COLUMNARIA INEQUALIS(1).	Schoharie.	- - -	Cabinet.
515	1	FAVOSITES NIAGARENSIS(2).	Schoharie.	- - -	Cabinet.
681	2	STROMATOPORA CONSTELLATA(1).	Schoharie.	- - -	Cabinet.
523	1	STROMATOPORA CONCENTRICA(1).	Schoharie.	- - -	Cabinet.
517	1	CATENIPORA ESCHAROIDES(1).	Schoharie.	- - -	Cabinet.

BRACHIOPODA.

682	31	ORTHIS INTERSTRIATA.	Schoharie.		
683	27	LEPTÆNA ———(2).	Schoharie.	- - -	Cabinet.
684	28	LEPTÆNA BIPARTITA(2).	Schoharie.	- - -	Cabinet.
685	2	STROPHODONTA TEXTILIS(1).	Schoharie.	- - -	Cabinet.
686	10	SPIRIFER ———(2).	Schoharie.	- - -	Cabinet.
623	6	SPIRIFER CRISPUS.	Schoharie.		
687	58	ATRYPA NUCLEOLATA(3).	Schoharie.	- - -	Cabinet.
688	59	ATRYPA LAMELLATA(1).	Schoharie.	- - -	Cabinet.
689	60	ATRYPA ———.	Schoharie.	- - -	Cabinet.

ACEPHALA.

690	10	TELLINOMYA? EQUILATERA(2).	Schoharie.	- - -	Cabinet.
691	11	AVICULA? ———.	Schoharie.	- - -	Cabinet.
692	12	AVICULA SUBRECTA.	Schoharie.		
693	13	AVICULA SECURIFORMIS(3).	Schoharie.	- - -	Cabinet.
694	14	AVICULA LIMÆFORMIS(2).	Schoharie.	- - -	Cabinet.

GASTEROPODA.

695	4	PLATYOSTOMA ———(1).	Schoharie.	- - -	Cabinet.
696	21	PLEUROTOMARIA SUBDEPRESSA(1).	Schoharie.	- - -	Cabinet.
697	17	MURCHISONIA? OBTUSA(1).	Schoharie.	- - -	Cabinet.

		Names	Localities.	
698	18	Murchisonia? terebralis(1).	Schoharie. - - -	Cabinet.
699	10	Bucania ———(3).	Schoharie. - - -	Cabinet.
700	5	Bellerophon auriculatus(2).	Schoharie. - - -	Cabinet.
		CEPHALOPODA.		
701	1	Trochoceras gebhardii(2).	Schoharie. - - -	Cabinet.
702	2	Trochoceras turbinata(1).	Schoharie. - - -	Cabinet.
703	4	Oncoceras expansum(1).	Schoharie. - - -	Cabinet.
		Orthoceras ———(4).	Schoharie. - - -	Cabinet.
		CRUSTACEA.		
704	8	Calymene camerata (5 fragments).	Schoharie - -	Cabinet.
705	3	Cytherina alta?	Schoharie.	
		Phragmoceras?(2).	Schoharie. - - -	Cabinet.

---

11. ONONDAGA-SALT GROUP.

706	4	Pentamerus occidentalis.	Galt (Canada West).
707	1	Megalomus canadensis.	Galt.
708	19	Murchisonia bivittata.	Galt.
709	20	Murchisonia longispira.	Galt.
710	21	Murchisonia boydii.	Wayne county.
711	22	Murchisonia loganii.	Galt (Canada West).
712	23	Murchisonia macrospira.	Galt.
713	24	Murchisonia turritiformis.	Galt.
714	2	Subulites ventricosa.	Galt.
715	5	Cyclonema sulcata.	Newark, Wayne.
716	22	Pleurotomaria bispiralis.	Galt (Canada West).
717	23	Pleurotomaria? ———.	Galt.
718	24	Pleurotomaria solarioides.	Galt.
719	25	Pleurotomaria perlata.	Galt.
720	11	Bucania angustata.	Galt.
721	9	Cyrtoceras arcticameratum.	Galt.
722	9	Calymene ———.	Galt.
723	4	Tentaculites niagarensis.	
724	2	Cornulites ———.	

The COLLECTION of FOSSILS made by JOHN GEBHARD junior has been purchased by the State, and is now in the State Geological Rooms at Albany, but, for want of room, is not yet arranged. The following is a synopsis of its contents, with the exception of the fossils from the Coralline limestone (mentioned on pages 28 & 29), which have been placed in the cases :

Names of Formations.		Number of Specimens.
CALCIFEROUS SANDROCK		2
CHAZY LIMESTONE		10
BIRDSEYE LIMESTONE		22
TRENTON LIMESTONE		92
UTICA SHALE		36
MEDINA SANDSTONE		9
CLINTON GROUP		33
NIAGARA GROUP, Lockport		132
HUDSON-RIVER GROUP		5
CORALLINE LIMESTONE,	Schoharie	79
TENTACULITE LIMESTONE,	"	30
PENTAMERUS GALEATUS LIMESTONE,	"	672
CATSKILL SHALY LIMESTONE,	"	4438
SCUTELLA LIMESTONE,	"	6
UPPER PENTAMERUS LIMESTONE,	"	894
ORISKANY SANDSTONE,	'	557
SCHOHARIE GRIT,	"	1162
ONONDAGA LIMESTONE,	"	373
CORNIFEROUS LIMESTONE,	"	1000
MARCELLUS SHALES and GONIATITE LIMESTONE,	"	482
HAMILTON GROUP (Lower part),	"	1423
HAMILTON GROUP (Upper part), including Chemung and uppermost rocks of Schoharie,		1313
PLASTER CASTS OF FOSSILS (mostly trilobites)		131
FISH SCALES (two species), Old Red, Pennsylvania		2
COAL PLANTS from Pennsylvania		37
COAL PLANTS from Ohio		3
FISH REMAINS from Durham, Connecticut		7
BUHRSTONE FORMATION of Georgia		11
TERTIARY, Macon, Georgia		2
TERTIARY, Banks of the Potomac		2
CRETACEOUS FORMATION of New-Jersey		5
TERTIARY FORMATIONS of Italy		46
DUDLEY ROCKS, England		48
		13064

The preceding specimens are packed in *forty-one boxes* properly labelled, and are now in the fireproof basement of the State Geological Rooms.

In addition to the above, there are, in drawers in the geological rooms, the following numbers of unique specimens, viz:

Chazy limestone, 2; Trenton, 10; Hudson-river, 9; Niagara, 4; Pentamerus galeatus, 5; Delthyris shaly, 41; Oriskany sandstone, 6; Schoharie grit, 10; Marcellus shale, 2; Hamilton group, 9. Total, 98.

FISH REMAINS: Schoharie grit, 9; Onondaga, 2; Marcellus shale, 11; Hamilton, 5 27

SPECIMENS figured for the third volume of the Palæontology, and placed in the cases 103

Which, by including the preceding list, makes a total of 13292

In addition to these, there have been placed in the cases over six hundred (600) specimens of fossils from the following formations, viz: Tentaculite limestone, Pentamerus galeatus limestone, Delthyris shaly limestone, Upper Pentamerus limestone, Oriskany sandstone, Schoharie grit, Onondaga limestone, Corniferous limestone, Marcellus shale and Hamilton group.

The collections made by Prof. HALL since the commencement of the work on Palæontology, with the exception of those enumerated in the Catalogue, are now lying in the basement story of the Geological Buildings: they consist chiefly of the following:

Ninety-six drawers in case, filled with specimens from different rocks and groups.

Nine similar drawers filled with specimens, not in case.

Three drawers with specimens.

Forty-five large drawers in close cases, filled with specimens of the fossils of the lower limestones, Helderberg limestones, Hamilton and Chemung groups. Many of these are very good and perfect specimens of fossils, intended at the time of collection to illustrate future volumes of the Palæontology.

Three boxes of the Hamilton group and Helderberg limestones.

Forty-nine boxes and two kegs of specimens mainly from the rocks and groups above the Niagara. These have been nearly all examined, and the better specimens separated from the others, and their character indicated by labels on the outside of the boxes.

Fourteen boxes of specimens of fossils and minerals, mainly of the Niagara group.

There is also a large number of slabs containing fossils, many of which are rare and valuable.

Historical and Antiquarian Collection.

HISTORICAL AND ANTIQUARIAN COLLECTION.

DONATIONS.

FROM LEWIS H. MORGAN, OF ROCHESTER.

1. *Ga-né-ga-tah* (STONE MORTAR), used by the Senecas for pounding corn, pulverizing roots, etc. : sandstone. Found near Allen's hill, Ontario county, May 9, 1843.
2. STONE PESTLE, found at Jack's reef, Onondaga county.
3. STONE PESTLE, found in the town of Middlebury, Wyoming county.
4. STONE CHISEL, from Groveland, Livingston county.
5. STONE CHISEL. Fort Hill, town of Seneca, Ontario county.
6. STONE CHISEL. Town of Coventry, Genesee county.
7. STONE CHISEL. Ontario county.
8. STONE CHISEL, used for chipping coal. Fort Hill, town of Seneca, Ontario county.
9. STONE CHISEL, from Auburn, Cayuga county.
10. STONE CHISEL, used by the Iroquois in felling trees : fire was applied near the root of the tree, and the chisel was used to cut out the coal ; after which, fire was again applied. The chisel and fire were also used to hollow out wooden vessels. From Tonawanda, Genesee county.
11. STONE CHISEL. From the town of Coventry, Genesee county.
12. STONE CHISEL. From Mendon, Monroe county.
13. STONE CHISEL. From Allen's hill, Ontario county.
14. STONE CHISEL. From Mendon, Monroe county.
15. STONE CHISEL. From Coventry, Genesee county.
16. STONE GOUGE. Found near Leroy, Genesee county.

17. SPEAR-HEAD (chert). Found at Fort Hill, Seneca, Ontario county.

18. ARROWHEAD. Town of Seneca, Ontario county.

19. ARROWHEAD. Town of Chili, Monroe county.

20. ARROWHEAD. Fort Hill, Ontario county.

21. INDIAN KNIFE (chert), used for skinning deer. Found near Avon at the site of Littlebeard's town, Livingston county.

22. TOMAHAWK, found by the skeleton of an indian, near Lima, Livingston county.

23. TOMAHAWK, found by the skeleton of an indian at Mendon, Monroe county.

24. TOMAHAWK. Town of Lima, Livingston county.

25. TOMAHAWK. Town of Ledyard, Cayuga county.

26. BRASS KETTLE, taken from an indian grave at the site of the old indian village of Gá-nun-da-sa-ga, near Geneva, 1840.

27. PART of a GUN LOCK and RIFLE BARREL found by the skeleton of an indian, in the town of Mendon, Monroe county.

28. HEAD of a *Ga-ne-ah* or WAR CLUB, fastened into the head of a club by a thong or withe. Ledyard, Cayuga county.

29. *Yuh-tah-gun-he-a-tah Geh-weh*, or MOCCASIN NEEDLE (bone of the deer). Used by the "mound-builders," and also by the Iroquois. Found at Fort Hill, near Leroy, Genesee county.

30. STONE TUBE (of variegated limestone). Town of Springport, Cayuga county. A relic of the Mound-builders, and not of the Iroquois. Similar tubes, some of which are fifteen inches in length, are found in the Ohio mounds.

31. STONE AMULET. Tonawanda, Genesee county.

32. INDIAN NECKLACE of TEETH, found near the skeleton of an indian. Genesee valley, near Avon, Livingston county.

33. *A-so-gwa-ta*, or CLAY PIPE, from Aurora, Cayuga county.

34. FRONT PART of the BOWL of a PIPE (similar to those found in the Ohio mounds). Lima, Livingston county.

35. FRAGMENT of *Ga-jeh*, or EARTHEN BASIN. Fort Hill, near Leroy, Genesee county; with a tooth found in the same place.

36. POTTERY, affected by water. Fort Hill.

37. *Gus-to-weh* : HEAD-DRESS. Seneca — Iroquois.

38. *Ga-neah*, or WAR CLUB : a species used in the war dance. Seneca — Iroquois.

39. INDIAN CALUMET. From the West (imperfect).

40. LEADEN CROSS. Found near the Tonawanda Council House, Genesee county, October, 1845.

41. FRAGMENT of the TOMBSTONE of REDJACKET, found upon his grave, four miles from Buffalo. The stone is mutilated by travellers.

42. FRAGMENT (slag?) taken from the fireplace of the old picket enclosure of Kon-non-da-sa-sa, at the foot of the Geneseo lake, in 1845. This picket was destroyed by General Sullivan.

43. STUB of the palisade at the gate or opening of the above picket enclosure. Found November 21, 1845.

44. FRAGMENT of an INDIAN PIPE. Monroe county.

45. *A-se-qua-tah*, or CLAY PIPE, taken from a Seneca burial place near Lima, Livingston county, 1848.

46 & 47. ARROWHEADS. Mendon, Monroe county.

48. ARROWHEAD of COPPER. Bend of the Honeoye creek, Monroe county.

49. PART of a GUN-BARREL, from an indian burying-ground, Ball farm, Monroe county.

50. STONE SKULL-CRACKER. From Aurora, Cayuga county. This is the vulgar name : it was fastened to the head of a club, and thus made a formidable weapon.

51. NECKLACE BEAD. From Scipio, Cayuga county.

52. UNFINISHED ARROWHEAD. From Cayuga county.

53. WHITE CHERT ARROWHEAD. From Ledyard, Cayuga county.

54. FRAGMENT of the BOWL of an Ah-so-quä-tä, or PIPE. From Scipio, Cayuga county.

55. SIX ARROWHEADS, or Gä-nuh-yä. From Ledyard and Scipio, Cayuga county.

56. FRAGMENT of a WHITE CHERT ARROWHEAD.

57. TWO TWIST ARROWHEADS. From Ontario county.

58. FRAGMENT of a Ga-jih, or EARTHEN BASIN. From Cayuga county.

59. Gä-ne-gä-tä, SENECA MORTAR, for pounding corn.

60. Gä-nih-gä-dä, POUNDER (same name as mortar). Two specimens.

61. Gä-ne-ah, BALL BAT. Two specimens.

62. Wä-a-no, INDIAN BOW. Two specimens.

63. Gä-no, FEATHERED ARROW. Six specimens.

64. Gä-wä-sä, SNOW SNAKE. Two specimens.

65. Bark tray or platter.

66. Splint basket. Two varieties.

67. A quantity of White corn. The New-York Indians cultivate this variety of corn principally, which is known, I believe, as the Tuscarora. They put it up and preserve it in bunches.

FROM SAMUEL G. EDDY, OF STILLWATER.

68. Card of indian arrowheads(17), found in immediate vicinity of the battle ground at Bemis's Heights, Saratoga county. Arrowheads of similar materials and construction are to be found, after the spring rains, on all the plowed lands between Stillwater village and Wilber's basin, a distance equal to five miles.

69. Cannon balls(2), found on the battle ground at Bemis's heights.

70. Card of military buttons(5), with the roman numerals XX distinctly visible on the faces. These buttons were worn by a soldier or soldiers of the 20th regiment of Hamilton's brigade in Burgoyne's army. The 9th, 20th, 21st, and 62d regiments were that portion of Burgoyne's army which was engaged in the bloody conflict at "Freeman's Cottage," Bemis's Heights, on the 19th day of September 1777. These buttons, together with human bones, a large pocket knife, belt buckle, pewter spoon, and a stick of healing salve, were plowed up in the month of October 1849, within the grounds enclosed by the British intrenchments.

71. Lead balls and Iron grape-shot (13 in all), found on the Freeman farm in the year 1848.

72. A Spanish silver coin (pistareen), dated 1721. This coin, together with two others of the same date and denomination, three spanish milled quarter-dollars, twelve guineas and two half joes (in all about eighty dollars), were plowed up by Mr. Ebenezer Leggett, in the fall of 1849, within the British intrenchments, and near the celebrated Freeman Cottage.

73. Piece of the plank on which Gen. Frazer died. This gallant officer was mortally wounded on the seventh of October 1777, about two miles west of the Hudson river, by a rifleman of Colonel Morgan's company. He was brought from the field of battle and taken to the "Smith House" (then used as a British hospital), which was situated on the Whitehall turnpike some six miles

north of the present village of Stillwater, and expired about eight o'clock A. M. the following day. By his own request, he was buried in the great redoubt on the hill, at six o'clock in the evening of the same day on which he expired. The Smith house was taken down in the year 1845, and the plank on which Gen. Frazer died, and of which the piece presented to the State Cabinet is a portion, was preserved by the proprietor for the antiquarians of his country.

74. PIECE of a SOLDIER'S BLANKET, dug up, with human bones, near the camp of Lord Balcarras (who was one of the commanding officers in Burgoyne's army), at Bemis's heights, seventy-one years after the battle of October 7, 1777.

75. A BOMB SHELL. This was one of the trophies taken at Bemis's heights in October 1777. The following spring, several batteaux were loaded with shells, cannon balls, etc. for shipment to Albany, one of which was sunk at Stillwater village, a short distance above the falls, in the Hudson river. During the season of low water in the summer of 1848, many of these shells and balls were dug from the bed of the river, one of which is the one here presented to the State Collection.

FROM ASA FITCH, OF SALEM.

76 & 77. SWORD and BAYONET, which belonged to Burgoyne's army.

Thomas Whiteside, one of the Cambridge (Washington county) militiamen, in service at Saratoga at the time of Burgoyne's surrender, on his return home, brought the above articles : they have been preserved in his family ever since, and were given to the State Collection by his son Thomas C. Whiteside.

78. INDIAN AXE, found at Fort Miller. From John Pattison.

79. Part of an INDIAN SPEARHEAD (made of subhyaline quartz), found at Fort Miller. From John Pattison.

80 & 81. INDIAN SPEARHEADS. Salem.

82 & 83. INDIAN ARROWHEADS. Salem.

84. RELICS of the BATTLE at Wallomsac (N. Y.), commonly called "Bennington Battle." Within the fortification thrown up by Colonel Baum, a single oak tree was left standing. The PIECE of WOOD presented to the State Cabinet, is from the decaying stump of

that tree. Sunk in it is a box containing a BULLET, found about forty rods north from the tree, in the direction whence General Stark, it is said, made his attack. The bullet is from N. Burnet, esquire, proprietor of the grounds, who picked it up when plowing about ten years ago (1838). Vestiges of this battle, formerly found in abundance, are now exceedingly rare; and all traces of the breastworks, etc. are entirely obliterated.

FROM WILLIAM J. M'ALPINE, OF ALBANY.

85. A PLASTER MODEL of the UNITED STATES DRY DOCK at Brooklyn.

86. Fourteen specimens of GRANITE, viz: six from Staten Island quarry, New-York; six from Quincy quarry, Massachusetts; and two from Bluehill quarry, Maine; being samples of the granite used in the construction of the dry dock.

87. A GLASS TUBE, hermetically sealed, containing specimens of the various SOILS through which the excavations were made, stratigraphically arranged; with figures on the tube, indicating the aggregate depth of the excavations, and the proportional thickness of the different strata of earth excavated.

88. A VIAL containing EARTH excavated at the depth of 68½ feet.

FROM JOHN GEBHARD, OF SCHOHARIE.

89. EGYPTIAN IMAGE, ten inches in length, made of the native sycamore wood, in the form of a mummy case; painted, and covered with hieroglyphics. Images of this description are frequently found in mummy cases, and appear to be a representation on a small scale of the mummy itself. It is probable that they were used as a kind of household gods by the ancient Egyptians, and in that character interred with the possessor on his decease.

90. ETRUSCAN FIGURE, representing Pallas. This figure is made of baked clay, and placed upon a marble pedestal; height eight inches.

91. BRONZE BUST of the PRINCESS LUCILLE. Height three inches above the pedestal.

92. BRONZE FIGURE of a CONSUL in his TOGA. Height five inches above the pedestal.

93. Roman figure in bronze. Height four inches.

94. Bronze figure of a cow. Height two inches above the pedestal.

95. Two bronze figures of soothsayers or oracles. Height four inches above the pedestals.

96. Bronze figure of the Egyptian Venus. Height four inches above the pedestal.

97. Three varieties of funeral lamps. These lamps are made of baked clay, and are of ancient egyptian manufacture.

FROM CHESTER C. MOORE, OF ALBANY.

98. A Medicine pouch, manfactured of deerskin, and beautifully ornamented with porcupine quills : made by the Blackfeet Indians of Oregon.

99. A string of stone beads, obtained from the Blackfeet Indians of Oregon, and supposed to have been obtained by them from the Russian traders.

100. A flint arrowhead, found in the Blackfeet country near the Rocky Mountains, where a battle had been fought between the Blackfeet and Crow tribes of Indians.

FROM CHARLES MARTIN, OF THE U. S. NAVY.

101. A mace or wand, made from the feathers of the macaw or toucan : carried in the hand by the chiefs of the Cannibal Indians of the Amazon river, eighty or ninety miles above Para a city of Brazil.

102. A tube or sheath made of woven strips of bark or reed, capable of enlargement and contraction : used for the purpose of expressing the liquid from the arrow root, in its preparation for use. From the Amazon river, 80 or 90 miles above Para, a city of Brazil.

103. Two earthen pipes, of different style, with a wooden ornamental stem. From the Amazon river above Para.

104. Gourd. From the city of Isabel, Guatemala, painted in imitation of the ruins in that country.

FROM MRS. M. ELIZABETH BALDWIN, OF SARATOGA.

105. A BELT interwoven with BEADS, and a GAME-BAG. These articles were taken from a vault in Peru, South America, in the year 1830 : they had been deposited with the remains of an indian chief a hundred years previous.

106. A BILL of the CONTINENTAL CURRENCY for sixty dollars, issued according to a resolution passed by Congress at Philadelphia, September 26, 1778.

107. A BILL of the VIRGINIA CURRENCY for seven hundred and fifty dollars, issued according to an act of the Assembly, passed March 1, 1781.

FROM THEODORE TEED, OF CORTLANDTOWN.

108. A LARGE STONE AXE.

109. A STONE CHISEL, made of greenstone.

110. An unfinished CHERT ARROWHEAD.

111. A STONE PESTLE, made of sandstone.

112. A fragment of an INDIAN BOWL, made of steatite (soapstone).

All these articles were found in Cortlandtown, Westchester county.

FROM REV. MILES BRONSON, OF ASSAM IN INDIA.

113. A SILVER COIN (one rupee), value 48 cents : issued by the East India Company, 1840.

114. A COPPER COIN (one quarter anna), value 1-48th of a rupee : issued by the East India Company.

115. A Native East-Indian COPPER COIN.

FROM RICHARD H. PEASE, OF ALBANY

116. Gä-o-wo-gus-nuh (bark canoe) : a model.

117. Gä-gä-we-sä (paddle) : four specimens.

118. Ya-ye-gwä-dä-quä (segar case).

119. Ya-yud-dos-ho-quä (card receiver) : two specimens.

120. Gä-gwih-sak-tah Yä-dä-gwah (watch case).

FROM REV. JOHN N. CAMPBELL, OF ALBANY.

121. A Cup, turned from one of the red cedar gate-posts of Fort William Henry. The posts were placed in the ground in the year 1755, and removed in 1837, and are now in the State Cabinet.

122. A Bead basket, made and presented by Peter Lepage junior, one of the pupils belonging to the New-York Institute for the Blind.

123. A specimen of "Pot Rock," from Hurlgate channel near New-York, procured and forwarded by M. Maillefert, the engineer employed in removing the obstructions to navigation in Hurlgate.

124. A piece of Copper sheeting, taken from Way's reef in Hurlgate channel. Large quantities of this were obtained while removing the reefs in Hurlgate, which had been stripped from vessels that had struck against them at different times.

FROM REV. DUNCAN KENNEDY, OF ALBANY.

125. Two Pequod stone hatchets, differing in form and material of construction. From New-England.

126. Stone axe and a Stone chisel. From Westmoreland, Oneida county.

FROM EDWIN CROSWELL, OF ALBANY.

127. Copper mexican bomb-shell, taken from the battle ground of Buena Vista by Lieut. Easterly, U. S. Army.

128. Copper mexican grape-shot, taken from the battle ground of Buena Vista, by Lieut. Easterly.

129. Cannon ball, found in excavating in front of the site of the ancient Fort Orange, Albany.

FROM JAMES MEADS, OF ALBANY.

130. A Copper mexican grape-shot, from the battlefield of Buena Vista.

131. A Mass of sparables, cemented together by heat : from the great fire in the city of Albany on the 17th day of August, 1848.

132. A Mass of tacks, cemented together by heat : from the great fire in the city of Albany on the seventeenth day of August, 1848.

FROM VARIOUS DONORS.

133. A Map of the town of North-Salem, on rollers : executed by the Donor John F. Jenkins.

134. Indian pipe, found four miles south of the village of Canandaigua.
William Case.

135. Remains of the gate-posts of Fort William Henry, at the head of Lake George. The fort was erected in 1755, and taken and destroyed by Montcalm in 1756. The posts (of cedar) were dug up in 1837, by the direction of William Caldwell the owner of the ground, and were presented to the New-York State Cabinet by John M'Gillis of St. Johns in Canada East.

136. A Piece of marble (from Maryland), of the corner stone of the Washington National Monument, laid July 4, 1848. Presented by the Board of Managers of the Washington Monument to the State of New-York.

137. Indian arrowhead (hornstone), found at Lake George.
T. Romeyn Beck.

138. Stone skinning-chisel, found in Lysander, Oswego county.
E. A. Baldwin.

139. Indian arrowhead, found in Watervliet, Albany county.
A. C. Hascy.

140. Stone pestle, used in pounding maize : found at the head of Cayuga lake, Tompkins county, by Henry Hungerford.
David Emery.

141. A Copy of an "Inquiry into the Origin of the Antiquities of America, by John Delafield junior; with an Appendix by James Lakey." 4to. Cincinnati, 1839. John Delafield.

142. Specimens of shell concretions, forming the surface rock on which the city of St. Augustine in Florida is built.
Christopher Morgan.

143. A Plate of mica, turned up by the plow several years since, in the town of Brookhaven in the county of Suffolk, at a depth of about two feet below the surface. On one side of this plate are several engravings of geometrical and other figures.
Nathaniel Miller.

144. A part of the STEM of the AGAVE AMERICANA (century plant), which flowered some years since in the greenhouse of
STEPHEN VAN RENSSELAER.

145. Two pieces of WOOD from the HULL of Commodore Perry's flag-ship, the Lawrence : obtained at Erie, Pennsylvania.
FRANKLIN B. HOUGH.

146. COPPER PICKAXE, found on the farm (in Ogdensburgh, St. Lawrence county) of HENRY VAN RENSSELAER.

147. STONE CHISEL : from Danube, Herkimer county. ASA WILCOX.

148. STONE CHISEL, made of greenstone : from Martinsburgh, Lewis county.
L. R. HOUGH.

149. LARGE SPEARHEAD, made of chert : from Martinsburgh.
L. R. HOUGH.

150. Fragments of ANCIENT POTTERY : from Martinsburgh, Lewis county.
S. A. DEWEY.

151. Four CHERT ARROWHEADS : from Martinsburgh. S. A. DEWEY.

152. STONE PESTLE, used in pounding maize : found in the town of Niskayuna, Schenectady county. PETER B. NOXON.

153. A STONE AXE, made of chlorite : plowed up in the ninth ward of the city of Albany. PETER B. NOXON.

154. Two CHERT and one WHITE QUARTZ ARROWHEADS : found in the town of Guilderland, Albany county. THADDEUS CHEESEBRO.

155. A CHERT ARROWHEAD : found in digging a cellar on the shore of Otsego lake. S. W. ROOT.

156. INDIAN ARROWHEAD : found in Croton, Westchester county.
THEODORE TEED.

157. Three fragments of INDIAN POTTERY : found in Croton. T. TEED.

158. A very singular specimen of INDIAN WORKMANSHIP, made of novaculite : found in the town of Hartford, Washington county.
HENRY B. NORTHRUP.

159. TACKS, cemented together : from the great fire in the city of Albany, on the seventeenth day of August, 1848. LEMUEL STEELE.

160. A specimen of COCOANUT-WOOD (turned) : from the Island of St. Lucia, West Indies. ROBERT REID.

161. An ANTIQUE LOOKINGLASS, set in a frame of sandal wood.
Miss CAROLINE LOVETT.

162. A Silver coin (fuang), 7½ cents, from Siam in India.
Rev. A. Hemenway.

163. A Silver coin, date 1652 : on one side "New-England," on the reverse "Massachusetts;" commonly called *Pine-tree shilling*.
Hiram H. Cooper.

164. Eleven Chert arrowheads, found in Stuyvesant, Columbia county.
Aaron Van Alen.

165. A Cannon ball, found near the junction of the Battenkill with the Hudson river, on the farm where Burgoyne erected a breast-work, etc. during the revolutionary war.
Mrs. S. M. Lansing Merchant.

166. Several Chert arrowheads; also fragments of Human bones and Indian pottery, obtained from an ancient indian burying-ground on the banks of Connecticut river. A. Marks.

167. An Indian chert arrowhead (large) : found in Bethlehem, Albany county. L. M'Mullen Selkirk.

168. A fragment of Indian pottery : found on the banks of the Hudson river, six miles above the High falls. This fragment, which is two inches long and one and a half wide, represents the head and about one half of the shell of a tortoise : it appears to have been a portion of a pipe. Ebenezer Emmons.

169. A specimen of Cloth made of the bark of the breadfruit tree, by the natives of one of the islands of the Pacific ocean.
Ferdinand Weil.

170. A piece of one of the Oak trees cut down in the town of Argyle, Washington county, in the year 1797, for the purpose of constructing a navy, under the administration of John Adams.

There were at that time two gigantic oaks which grew near together, that were cut for the abovenamed purpose. One of them was hewed, and afterwards drawn by fifteen yoke of oxen, with the forward end elevated on a huge wood-sled. When they had got out of the woods, a "stump speech" was delivered by one of the party from the forward end of the stick, as a stage. After passing the bottle around, according to the custom of the times, they moved on with shouts of overflowing patriotism that almost seemed to inspire even the dull ox with more than his ordinary ambition, and thus delivered the stick at a place then called Dumont's Ferry, a short distance below Fort Miller.

The other tree, of which the piece presented to the State Cabinet is a part, was cut and scored on two sides, and partly hewed; but owing to some small defect, it was abandoned. About twelve years subsequent to that time, it was split into rails, and laid up into fence. Only a few of the rails now remain, and it was with some trouble that a few pieces were obtained which bear the marks of the axes of those who scored and partly hewed the stick; one of which is seen on the piece presented. JAMES H. SILL.

171. Two INDIAN ARROWHEADS, made of greasy quartz; one ditto, made of yellow jasper: from Suffolk county. E. T. SMITH.

172. A STONE AXE, eleven inches in length. This relic was found several feet below the surface, in digging a well at Poughkeepsie, Dutchess county. A. HEYER BROWN.

173. A MILITARY CAP PLATE of the Revolution. DESIGN: The American Eagle with extended wings, surmounted by thirteen stars. MOTTO: "Unity is Strength," 1776.
Mrs. MERCY VALENTINE.

174. An ANCIENT MILLSTONE, plowed up in the town of Conesville, Schoharie county, in the summer of 1850. The stone is graywacke, twenty inches in diameter and two inches thick, and was used in the early settlement of the country in a hand-mill.
ABRAHAM J. WARNER.

175. A CAMP KNIFE, dug up by James Stewart, esquire, of Guy Park in the town of Amsterdam, Montgomery county, formerly the residence of Sir Guy Johnson of tory memory in the days of the revolution, and is a relic of those times.
M. S. GOODALE.

176. A CHISEL and a DEERSKIN-DRESSER, made of greenstone: found in Cherryvalley, Ashtabula county, Ohio. THEODORE MILLS.

177. A STONE AXE and a WHITE CHERT ARROWHEAD: found in Cherryvalley (Ohio). THEODORE MILLS.

178. A STONE CHISEL, and also two regularly rounded PEBBLES: found in the town of Bethlehem, Albany county. PETER G. BRADT.

179. An IRON KEY, taken from the Halls of Montezuma, Mexico, on the twelfth day of June 1848, and which originally belonged to the palace garden gate. W. A. HOTCHKISS.

180. A CLAY DRINKING CUP, in the form of a duck, from the Sandwich islands; also a HEADDRESS made of seashells.
BENJAMIN KNOWER.

181. A part of the SHOT-RACK of the British Frigate Hussar, with four CANNON BALLS; also a MUSKET, and a BAYONET and SCABBARD.

The Frigate Hussar was lost December 15th, 1780, off Stoney island on Westchester county shore, having struck Pot rock in Hurlgate. She was loaded with troops, ammunition, and supplies for the British army in this country. The troops and crew had barely time to reach the shore before she sunk, with seventy American prisoners, who were in irons and could not be rescued. These relics were obtained by Messrs. Pratt & Howe, in the month of August 1851, by the aid of Taylor's submarine armour, after having been buried over seventy years. The wreck lies seventy-six feet deep at high water. HENRY B. TODD.

182. Four MUSKET-BALLS and two BUCKSHOT, from the battlefield of Lundy's Lane, Canada West. JAMES A. HURST.

183. An IRON KEY and a BRASS BELT-SLIDE, dug up at Fort Ticonderoga in the year 1849, by WILLIAM THORN.

184. An IRON WORMER, used for drawing charges from muskets; found on the grounds near Fort William-Henry. HIRAM WOOD.

185. An ANCIENT SWORD, SCABBARD and BELT. The blade of the sword appears to be of the best of steel, mounted with brass; and on either side of the blade, in large capitals, is engraved the following: "God Bless the Province of New-York."

This sword was the property of a provincial officer who served in early French and Indian wars on the frontiers of New-York and Vermont, and who died at an advanced age more than fifty years ago. His property was sold at auction, and this sword was purchased by Mr. Francis Cobb of Cornish in Sullivan county, New-Hampshire (a remote connection of its former owner), and remained in his possession while he lived. Mr. Cobb died some two or three years since (about 1849), more than ninety years old; and when his property was inventoried, the sword was found among some rubbish in the attic of his house: it was purchased for a small sum, and presented to the New-York State Antiquarian Society by ELEAZAR JACKSON.

186. A BRICK, made from the natural soil without any admixture. Brought from the city of New-York; being a specimen of the kind used in the erection of the new building on the southwest corner of Thames-street and Broadway, near Trinity Church, and called "Trinity Building": manufactured at Buffalo, Erie county. R. SPENCER DYER.

PURCHASES.

FROM WILLIAM C. HOSMER, OF AVON.

1. INDIAN ARROWHEADS(6), picked up in the ploughed fields in the vicinity of Avon, Livingston county.
2. INDIAN ARROWHEADS of small size, used by indian boys in killing birds and inferior game(9). These arrows were inserted into the split end of tough wooden shafts, and fastened at the notches with ligatures of sinew or string bark.
3. INDIAN ARROWHEADS(4), found on a plain near Fort Niagara, and of greater antiquity than those of flint formation.
4. INDIAN ARROWHEADS(2), found on the farm of Timothy Hosmer, in the town of Porter, Niagara county, near the Lake shore ; one of them curiously twisted.
5. A HATCHET-SHAPED FLINT, obtained from Col. Jewett of Lockport.
6. BROKEN ARROWHEADS.
7. STONE DEERSKIN-DRESSERS, found on the farm of Mr. Hurlburt, in the northeast part of the town of Avon.
8. STONE DEERSKIN-DRESSER, found on the farm of Jeptha Wilber, Avon.
9. STONE DEERSKIN-DRESSER, found on the farm of James Wadsworth, near Borley's mill in the bend of the Conesus outlet, town of Livonia, Livingston county. The place where they were found was called "Fort Hill" by the early settlers ; and mound, trench, and gateway were visible in the memory of men now living.
10. STONE PESTLE, used in pounding maize ; found on the farm of Jeptha Wilber, Avon.
11. ANCIENT STONE HATCHET of rude construction, found on the site of the old village of Cannewangus (stinking waters), so called from its vicinity to the Mineral springs of Avon. After Denonville's invasion, the indians removed to the west side of the Genesee.
12. ANCIENT STONE PIPE-BOWLS(2), found in Rush, Monroe county.
13. ANCIENT STONE PIPE-BOWLS, found near Fort Hill : very rude specimens.

14. Clay pipe-stems, found in the vicinity of Avon.

15. Clay pipe-stems, found in Mendon, Monroe county, near the site of the village known in the seventeenth century to the French as "Dyen-de-haak-doh," or the Bend ; having been situated in an arm of the Hone-yah-yah (called by the whites Honeoye), or the place where the finger was left. The tradition is, that an indian, while gathering strawberries on its banks, was bitten by a copperhead on one of his fingers ; and that to prevent a spread of the venom, he severed it from his hand with a hatchet.

16. Fragments of ancient pottery, picked up at various points in the valley of the Genesee.

17. Ancient pottery found by Mr. Hosmer, together with a paint stone, in a mound of the Yemassees, near the ocean beach at San Pablo, on St. John's river, Florida.

18. Steel hatchet, found on the Wilber farm (Avon), in an old grave.

19. Bones, etc. taken from an indian grave near Fort Niagara.

20. Sword-belt plate, found near Cannewangus landing, by a workman on the Canal, many feet below the surface ; together with human bones, and a fragment of a military coat that crumbled on exposure to the air. It is perforated by a bullet. It bears the inscription, "104, New-Brunswick Regiment," surmounted by the English crown. Some luckless British soldier, taken in some distant expedition of the conquering Iroquois, may have been the victim of Indian warfare.

21. Stone implements, found on the farm of William Wadsworth near Fowlerville bridge, York, Livingston county.

22. Paint stone referred to in No. 17. The bottom of the stone, when discovered, was red with vermilion or some of the coloring matters.

23. Leaden cross, of Maltese shape, referring to missions of the Jesuits; and a bone rifle charger, found in a field that is known in song as "The Place of Bones." This field lies at the foot of a wooded ridge, in view of the village of Avon, and is supposed by some to have been the scene of conflict between Denonville and the Senecas.

24. French axes, found at an old Jesuit station on the Mendon road.

25. French axes, found on the site of a village near the dividing line between Avon and Lima, supposed to have been a famous town known to the Jesuits in the seventeenth century as Dyiu-don-sot, or Village at the spring.

26. Decoy fish, used by the Sagenaw indians, Michigan, in winter. They drop the decoy through a hole cut in the ice, to entice the trout from his watery lair below : as he approaches the surface, the expert spearman on the watch easily secures the prize.

27. Fragments of fire-arms, picked up on the supposed battle-ground of Denonville.

28. Cannon ball found by workmen, while building a bridge at Littleville, across the Conesus, four or five feet below the bed of the stream.

29. Teeth of animals, etc. found in an indian burial-place near the banks of the Genesee.

30. Large arrowhead and Stone deerskin-dresser, found on the farm of F. M. Cutler, in a field south of Gore brook, Avon, bound with bark cord of indian manufacture.

31. Heavy bar of lead, stamp still visible ; knife point ; fragment of a skull ; stone deerskin-dresser, and fragments of brazen implements, found in graves in a sidehill on the farm of Richard Wilber, Avon. A bone cross, "lined and specked," was also found, but subsequently either lost or stolen. Below the depth penetrated by the ploughshare, ashes, charcoal, and charred kernels of maize are discovered in this hill of burial. The cross would indicate that it was formerly a Jesuit station.

32. Beads of red pipe-stone ; bone elegantly polished ; glass ; variegated shell, and brass and copper, found at different points of indian occupancy in the Genesee valley.

33. A section of a circle, perforated near the rim with holes ; fragment of some unknown implement of red pipe-stone, neatly cut and polished ; and *a large bead* with a human head on one side of it, delicately carved and exquisitely proportioned : found in the old burial-place of Cannewangus.

34. Stone of octagonal shape, hollowed out : supposed to have been used by indian jugglers. Paint-stone ? Found on the Street farm (so called), which is situated three miles from Avon, in a northwest direction, on the west side of the river, in Livingston county.

35. Stone chisel (in two pieces), used in excavating canoes. Found near Spanish hill, a few miles from Athens, Tioga county, which has been occupied for purposes of fortification, and indian traces abound.

36. STONE DEERSKIN-DRESSER ; and,

37. A FRAGMENT of a PIPE (as is supposed). Found near Fowlerville bridge, in the town of Avon, on a farm of W. W. Wadsworth, after the first ploughing of a new field, about one mile from the river bed, and three and a half miles in a southwesterly direction from Avon springs.

38. A BONE FISH-SPEAR, found on the Hurlburt farm in Avon, four miles in a northeast direction from the springs, at a place known to the inhbitants as Fort Hill : it was unquestionably a Jesuit station. The place was destroyed by Denonville in 1687. Corn, in a charred state, is found commingled with the subsoil. Bone crosses have been discovered, and rosaries ; also many articles used by the French traders in Indian traffic.

39. A STONE IMPLEMENT, with a handle like a mason's smoothing trowel. This implement was found near a spring on the farm of Ira Pierson in the town of Avon, about two miles in a southeast direction from the village of West-Avon.

Mr. JOHN GEBHARD junior states, that "this unique relic is made of the *steatitic pyroxene* of Prof. LEWIS C. BECK (*rensselaerite* of Dr. EMMONS); and from its strong resemblance to the specimens of that mineral from Edwards, St. Lawrence county, the material from which it is constructed is undoubtedly from that locality. It was probably used in dressing deerskins, and for smoothing and softening the seams in manufacturing moccasins and other articles made from skins. It evidently belongs to the ante-columbian period."

40. VARIOUS BEADS. These beads were found in various places in the valley of the Genesee : at the Jesuit stations previously referred to ; the old indian burial-place, near the red bridge that crosses the river one mile west of West-Avon village ; and a few were found near Fort Niagara, and in the valley of the Susquehannah.

41. STONE DEERSKIN-DRESSER. Found on the farm of Francis M. Cutler, in West-Avon.

42. STONE DEERSKIN-DRESSER. Found on the Wilbur farm.

FROM E. G. SQUIER, OF NEW-YORK.

43. FLINT ARROWHEADS From Cayuga county, 7 specimens ; Monroe county, 2 ; Livonia, Livingston county, 2 ; vicinity of Buffalo, Erie county, 1 ; Ellisburgh, Jefferson county, 1 ; and 4 from localities not named.

44. French axes(2). From Cayuga village, Cayuga county.

45. Indian pestle. From Cayaga county.

46. Copper kettle. From an indian grave in Scipio, Cayuga county.

47. Gunbarrel. From the site of Denonville's battle with the Senecas (1687), near Victor, Ontario county.

48. Scalping-knife. From the grave of a Cayuga warrior in Scipio, Cayuga county.

49. Stone axes(4). From Springport, Cayuga county; Adams, Jefferson county; Ellisburgh, Jefferson county; and one locality not named.

50. Fragments of pottery. From the site of a Seneca village, Livonia, Livingston county.

51. Fragments of pottery. From the site of an old Seneca village in Mendon, Monroe county.

52. Pipes, pottery (5 boxes). From an ancient enclosure in the town of Ellisburgh, Jefferson county.

53. Pipes, pottery, &c. (4 boxes). As No. 52.

54. Terra-cottas. From Leroy, Genesee county, 2 specimens; Ellisburgh, Jefferson county, 7; Scipio, Cayuga county, 1; and locality not named, 1.

55. Pottery. From Ellisburgh, Jefferson county, 3 specimens; and from an ancient village of the Senecas, Livonia, Livingston county, 1.

56. Copper knives, and other metallic articles. From an old Seneca village, Livonia, Livingston county.

57. Pottery. From an ancient enclosure in Jefferson county, 2 specimens; from Scipio, Cayuga county, 2; and from Livonia, Livingston county, 2.

58. Various articles of pottery (2 boxes). From an enclosure or mound near Buffalo.

59. Various articles of pottery. From a large mound on Tonawanda island, in Niagara river: excavated by E. G. Squier, November, 1848.

60. Human remains. From the great mound on Tonawanda island.

61. Bone implements. From Ellisburgh, Jefferson county, 3 specimens; from Leray, Jefferson county, 1.

62. Stone axes. From Buffalo, 1; Livonia, Livingston county, 1; Ellisburgh, Jefferson county, 1.

63. Deposits from altar mounds of the Mississippi valley.

64. Deposits from sepulchral mounds of the Mississippi.

65. Mortar, from the old tower at Newport, Rhode-Island.

FROM LEWIS H. MORGAN, OF ROCHESTER.

ARTICLES MANUFACTURED AT SPECIAL REQUEST, BY INDIANS RESIDING IN WESTERN NEW YORK.

The name of each article is in the Seneca dialect of the Iroquois language.

[ä is sounded as in *arm;* ă, as in *at;* a, as in *ale.*]

66. Gä-no-jo-o : Indian drum (3 varieties). Used in dances.
67. Gus-dä-wa-să : Turtle-shell rattle (2 specimens). Used in dances.
68. Gus-dä-wa-să : Squash-shell rattle (4 varieties). Used in dances.
69. Gus-dä-wa-să Yen-che-no-hos-ta : Knee rattle, of deer hoofs (one pair). Used in dances.
70. Gä-geh-tä Yen-nis-hä-hos-ta : Arm-bands (1 pair).
71. Yen-nis-ho-quä-hos-ta : Wristbands (1 pair).
72. Gä-geh-tä Yen-che-no-hos-ta-ta : Knee-bands (1 pair).
73. Gä-geh-tä : Indian belt (3 varieties).
74. Ah-tä-quä-o-weh : Moccasin, for male (1 pair).
75. Ah-tä-quä-o-weh : Moccasin, for female (1 pair)
76. Gä-kä-ah : Kilt or skirt, worn in war dance.
77. Gä-kä-ah : Kilt or skirt, worn by indian women.
78. Gise-hă : Leggin, for male (1 pair).
79. Gise-hă : Leggin, for female (1 pair).
80. Gä-swhen-tä : Necklace.
81. Ya-wa-o-dä-qua : Pincushion (3 varieties).
82. Gä-yä-ah : Workbag (5 varieties).
83. Got-gwen-dä : Pocketbook (6 varieties).
84. Gä-kä : Breechcloth. Used in ball-game, foot-race, etc.
85. Gä-de-us-ha : Wampum necklace. Da-yu-yä-sont, name of a cross.
86. Ya-wa-o-dä-quä : Needlebook (5 varieties).
87. Ga-on-seh : Baby frame.
88. Gä-o-wä : Bark tray (3 specimens).
89. Ah-de-gwas-hă : Hominy blade, or Soup-stick (4 specimens).
90. Ah-was-hă : Earring (1 pair).
91. Gä-jih : Bowl, for a game with peachstones.
92. Gus-ka-eh : Peachstones (6 specimens).
93. Gus-ga-e-sa-tä : Deer buttons, for an indian game (8 specimens, or one set).
94. Gä-geh-dä : Javelin or Shooting-stick, for an indian game (18 specimens).
95. Yun-ga-sa : Tobacco pouch (4 specimens).

96. Gä-ne-gä-tä : MORTAR, for pounding corn (2 specimens).
97. Gä-nih-gä-dä : MORTAR POUNDER (2 specimens).
98. Gä-ne-ah : BALL BAT, used in playing an indian game (4 specimens).
99. Gä-wä-sä : SNOWSNAKE (4 specimens).
100. Gä-je-wä : WAR-CLUB, with ball head (4 specimens).
101. Gä-neu-ga-o-dus-ha : WAR-CLUB, with deer-horn tooth (2 specimens).
102. O-sque-sont : TOMAHAWK.
103. Ah-so-quä-ta : PIPE (made from a *cyathophyllum*).
104. Wä-a-no : INDIAN BOW (6 specimens).
105. Gä-no : ARROW (50 specimens).
106. Gä-go-shä : FALSE FACE.
107. Gä-weh-ga-ă : SNOWSHOE (3 pairs).
108. O-tä-quă-osh-ha : SNOWSHOE, of splint (1 pair).
109. Gä-sken-dä : BARK ROPE, made of slippery elm.
110. Gus-hä-ah : BURTHEN-STRAP, made of slippery elm.
111. Gus-hä-ah : BURTHEN-STRAP, made of basswood.
112. Ose-gä : SKEIN of slippery elm strings.
113. Ose-hä : SKEIN of basswood-bark strings.
114. Ah-da-dä-quä : INDIAN SADDLE.
115. Gä-na-quä : BARK BARREL. Used for beans, dried corn, etc.
116. Gä-oo-wă : BARK SAP-TUB (3 specimens).
117. O-nus-quä Ah-hose-hă : KNOT BALL (2 specimens). Used in playing a game.
118. O-no-neä Gos-ha-dä : HUSK SALT-BOTTLE (2 specimens).
119. O-je-she-wä-tä : CAKE of deer's brains and moss, for tanning deerskins.
120. Gä-nuh-sä : BREASTPLATE of shells.
121. Got-kase-hä : AXEHELVE.
122. Gä-ga-an-dä : AIR-GUN.
123. Dä-ya-yä-dă-gä-ne-at-hä : BOW and WHEEL for striking fire.
124. Gä-gis-dä : STEEL, FLINT and PUNK, for striking fire.
125. Gis-tak-he-ä : SKIN BAG (speckled fawn).
126. Gis-tak-he-ä : SKIN BAG (bearskin).
127. Tuesh-tä-ga-tas-tä : TIN BREASTPLATE.
128. Skä-wä-ka : SPLINT BROOM.
129. Ya-o-dä-was-tä : INDIAN FLUTE.
130. Ne-us-tase-ah : BASKET SIEVE. Used for sifting white corn.
131. O-ne-ose-to-wa-nes : BASKET SIEVE, coarser; for white-flint corn.
132. Ta-gase-hă : MARKET BASKET.
133. Gase-hă : COVERED BASKET.
134. O-gä-kä-ah : OPEN-WORK BASKET (3 specimens).
135. Ga-yuh : SPLINT CRADLE.

136. Gä-nose-hä : Husk and flag basket (4 specimens).

137. Ya-nuh-ta-dä-quä : Toilet basket.

138. O-gus-ha-ote : Small square basket (17 specimens). These baskets are numbered from 1 to 17 inclusive, and contain specimens of the several varieties of corn, beans, squashes, tobacco, dried corn, etc. raised and prepared by the Senecas, viz :

i. O-na-o-ga-ant : White corn.

ii. Tic-ne : Red corn.

iii. Ha-go-wä : White-flint corn.

iv. O-nä-dä : Charred, or roasted corn.

v. O-go-ou-sä : Baked corn.

vi. O-si-dä : Long-vine bean.

vii. Gweh-dä-ä O-si-dä : Red bean.

viii. Te-o-gä-ga-wä O-si-dä ; Speckled bean.

ix. Ta-gä-gä-hät : Short-vine bean.

x. Ah-wa-own-dä-go : Red-flower pole-bean.

xi. Hä-yoke : Cranberry pole-bean.

xii. O-gä-gä-ind : Gray squash.

xiii. Gä-je-ote : Big-handle squash.

xiv. Sko-ak : Toad squash.

xv. O-ne-ä-sä-ä-weh : Small squash.

xvi. O-yeh-quä-ä-weh : Indian tobacco.

xvii. O-so-wa : Parched corn pounded into flour, with maple sugar.

139. Gä-no : Arrow for air-gun (2 specimens).

140. O-sque-sont : Tomahawk. Used in the bear hunt.

141. Da-ya-no-a-quä-tä Gä-ga-neä-sä : Scalping-knife (2 specimens).

142. O-na-o-ga-ant : Two ears of white corn.

143. Tic-ne : Two ears of red corn.

144. Ho-go-wä : Two ears of white-flint corn.

145. Gus-to-weh : Head-dress.

146. Gä-ger-we-sä Dun-daque-quä-do-quä : Newyear's shovel.

147. To-do-war-she-do-wä : Ribbon for hair.

148. Gä-de-us-ha : Necklace.

149. De-con-deä-da-hust-tä : Belt for female costume.

150. Ah-de-a-dä-we-sä : Female upper dress, with silver broaches, etc.

151. Dä-yase-ta-hos-ta : Silver hatband.

152. Yen-nis-ho-quä-hos-ta : Silver wristbands (1 pair).

153. To-an-jer-go-o O-no-no-do : Groundnuts (*Apios tuberosa*), from Tonawanda.

ARTICLES MANUFACTURED AT SPECIAL REQUEST, BY INDIANS RESIDING IN CANADA WEST.

154. Gä-däs-hă : SHEAF for carrying arrows.
155. Gä-je-wä : WARCLUB, with ball head.
156. Gä-such-tä Ote-ko-ă : BELT of WAMPUM.
157. Ote-ko-ă : STRING of WAMPUM.
158. Ah-so-quä-tä : STONE PIPE.
159. Da gä-yä-sont : SILVER CROSS, 8 inches by 5.
160. Da-gä-yä-sont : do 6 inches by 4.
161. Da-gä-yä-sont : do 3 inches by 1½ (2 specimens).
162. Au-ne-as-gă : SILVER BROACH, 4 inches diameter.
163. Au-ne-as-gă : do 3 inches diameter.
164. Au-ne-as-gă : do 1½ inches diameter. There are in all 13 broaches of various sizes.
165. Au-ne-as-gă : SILVER BROACH (2 specimens).
166. Au-ne-ä-hus-hă : FINGER-RING (4 specimens).
167. Ah-was-hă : EARRINGS (1 pair).
168. Dä-yase-ta-hos-ta : SILVER HATBAND.
169. Ont-wis-tä-ne-un-dä-quä : SILVER BEADS (long).
170. O-wis-tä-no-o O-sta-o-quä : ROUND SILVER BEADS (variety).
171. Gă-ose-hă : BABY FRAME.
172. Gä-swä-hos-hă : BABY-FRAME BELT.
173. Gă-nose gă : BABY-FRAME BELT (2 specimens).
174. Da-ya-he-gwä-hus-ta : HATBAND of BROACHES.
175. Gä-yä-ah : SATCHEL.
176. Gä-ya-äh : WORKBAG.
177. Ya-wa-o-dä-qua : PINCUSHION (2 specimens).
178. Gä-kä-ah : KILT, made of fawn skin.
179. Got-ko-on-dä Gise-hă : DEERSKIN LEGGIN.
180. Da-yunt-wä-hos-tä : DEERSKIN WAIST-BELT.
181. Yunt-ka-to-dä-tä : DEERSKIN SHOULDER-BELT.
182. Ah-tä-quä-o-weh : MOCCASIN (3 specimens).
183. HAIR ORNAMENT.
184. SHOT-POUCH.
185. Gät-go-ne-as-heh : HOMMONY BLADE (2 specimens).
186. Gät-go-ne-as-heh : do a chain cut on the end of the handle.
187. Ya-ă-go-jen-ta-quä : BREAD-TURNER.
188. Ah-do-gwä-seh : WOODEN LADLE (4 specimens).
189. Ah-do-gwä-seh : BARK LADLE.

190. Ah-do-gwä-seh : Wooden spoon.
191. Gä-na-quă : Bark barrel (3 sizes).
192. Gä-o-wä : Bark tray (6 sizes).
193. Gä-oo-wä : Bark sap-tub.
194. Gă-te-as-hă : Glass beads.
195. Gă-no-sä : Conch-shell breast-plate.
196. Ah-dä-dis-hă : Cane (2 specimens).
197. Ah-so-quä-tä : Pipe, made of Missouri stone.
198. Ah-so-quä-tä : Pipe, made of black stone.
199. Ah-so-quä-tä : Pipe, made of nodule.
200. Ah-so-quä-tä : Pipe, made of wood and lead.
201. Gä-gä, ne·as-heh : Belt and knife.
202. Gus-dä-wah-să : Turtleshell rattle (2 specimens).
203. O-no-gä Gus-dä-wah-să : Horn rattle.
204. Gus-to-weh : Headdress.
205. Gä-wă : Moccasin awl.
206. Bunch of sumac.
207. O-yeh-quä-ä-weh : Indian tobacco.
208. Gis-tät-he-o Gä-yä-ah : Fawnskin bag.
209. Gus-dä-wa-sä Yen-che-no-hos-ta : Knee-rattle, of deer-hoofs.
210. Spear used in the war of 1812.
211. Gä-ne-a-ga-o-dus-ha : War-club.
212. Ya-o-dä-was-tä : Indian flute (2 specimens).
213. Wä-a-no : Indian bow.
214. Gä-ne-ah : Ball-bat.
215. Gä-no : Arrow, pointed with deer's horn.
216. Gä-no : Feathered arrows (18 specimens in sheaf).
217. O-dä-da-one-dus-tä : Eye-showerer.
218. Yun-ga-sa : Tobacco-pouch, made of the foot and leg of the snapping turtle.
219. Gä-go-sä : False face.
220. O-ä-ta-ose-kä : Moosehair burthen-strap.
221. Gus-hä-ah : Moosehair and bark burthen-strap.
222. Gus-hä-ah : Burthen-strap (bark thread and worsted).
223. Gus-hä-ah : Burthen-strap (bark, with moosehair figures).
224. Gä-te-äs-hă Gä-a-o-tä-ges : Grass shoulder-ornament.
225. Yout-kä-do-quä : Basket fish-net.
226. Husk moccasins (one pair).
227. Gä-a-sken-dä : Bark rope, made of basswood filaments.
228. Gä-a-sken-dä : Bark rope (2 specimens from Tonawanda).
229. Ose-gă : Skein of slippery-elm thread.
230. Ose-gă : Skein of ditto, colored.

231. Ose-gă : TWISTED INTO STRINGS.
232. Ose-gă : STRIPS of SLIPPERY ELM BARK.
233. O-să : SKEIN of BASSWOOD FILAMENTS.
234. O-să : STRIPS of BASSWOOD BARK.
235. Go-yo-ga-ace : FINGER-CATCHER.
236. BIRD-TRAP, for catching quails.
237. Gus-hä-ah : DEERHAIR BURTHEN-STRAP.
238. Gus-hä-ah : BASSWOOD BURTHEN-STRAP.
239. Ne-us-tase-ah : BASKET SIEVE.
240. Gase-hă : COVERED BASKET.
241. O-gä-kä-ah : OPEN-WORK BASKET.
242. Ta-gase-hă : MARKET BASKET.
243. Gä-geh dä : JAVELIN, or SHOOTING-STICK.
244. Ah-de-gwas-hă : HOMINY BLADE.
245. PADDLES (6 specimens).
246. Yun-des-ho-yon-dä-gwat-hä : POP-CORN SIEVE.
247. An-ne-us-gă : SILVER BROACH (9 specimens on a card).
248. An-ne-us-gă : do (20 small specimens on a card).
249. Gä-ka-ah : SKIRT.
250. Gise-hă : LEGGINS for female (one pair).
251. Ah-de-a-dä-we-să : FEMALE OVERDRESS.
252. E-yose : BROADCLOTH BLANKET.
253. O-sta-o-quä : BEAD NECKLACE.
254. Gä-ka-ah : SKIRT for female.
255. Gise-hă : LEGGINS for female (one pair).
256. Ah-de-a-dä-we-să : OVERDRESS for child.
257. Yen-nis-ho-quä-hos-ta : WRISTBANDS of BEADS (one pair).
258. O-ha-dä : PORCUPINE QUILLS.
259. DEER'S HAIR, used for making burthen-straps, etc.
260. Da-ya-no-tä-yen-dä-quä : SNOW-BOAT.
261. Gä-wä-sä : SNOW-SNAKE (5 specimens).
262. Gä-ne-ko-wă-ah : BURTHEN FRAME.
263. Gä-no-sote : BARK HOUSE.
264. Gä-snä Gä-o-no : BARK CANOE.

FROM VARIOUS PERSONS.

265. Gä-yä-ah : WORKBAG (2 specimens).
266. Da-ya-he-gwă-hus-tä : HATBAND of BROACHES.
267. An-yus-gă : SILVER BROACH (large variety).
268. An-yus-gă : SILVER BROACH (smaller variety).

269. An Indian pipe, manufactured from the *steatitic pyroxene* of Prof. Lewis C. Beck. Found near Fort George, Warren county.

This relic presents the best specimen of indian design and sculpture ever found in this State. It is three inches in height, and represents an indian in a sitting posture, with his arms resting upon his knees. The back constitutes the bowl of the pipe, at the lower extremity of which there is a hole for the insertion of the stem.

270. An Indian relic, plowed up at the depth of a foot beneath the surface of the soil, in the town of Commerce, Oakland county, Michigan, in the year 1848.

This relic is made of *novaculite,* and in the form of an axe with two edges, with a hole in the centre for the insertion of a handle.

271. Tomahawk, which formerly belonged to the celebrated Indian Chief Cornplanter.

COLLECTION

OF THE LATE

H. CASIMIR DE RHAM, JUNIOR:

PRESENTED BY HIS PARENTS,

MR. AND MRS. H. C. DE RHAM.

5—1

THE DE RHAM COLLECTION.

MAMMALIA.

ORDER CARNIVORA.

FAMILY SORECIDÆ.

	Latin Names.	English Names.
1	CONDYLURA CRISTATA.	*Starnose Mole* (male, female, and two young).
2	SOREX DEKAYI.	*Dekay's Shrew.*

FAMILY URSIDÆ.

3	PROCYON LOTOR.	*Raccoon.*

FAMILY MUSTELIDÆ.

4	MEPHITIS AMERICANA.	*Skunk.*
5	MUSTELA FUSCA.	*Brown Weasel.*
6	PUTORIUS NOVEBORACENSIS.	*New-York Ermine.*
7	PUTORIUS VISON.	*Mink.*

FAMILY CANIDÆ.

8	VULPES FULVUS.	*Red Fox.*

FAMILY FELIDÆ.

9	LYNCUS BOREALIS.	*Northern Lynx.*

ORDER RODENTIA.

FAMILY SCIURIDÆ.

10	SCIURUS LEUCOTIS.	*Little Grey Squirrel* (male and female).
11	SCIURUS VULPINUS.	*Fox Squirrel.*
12	SCIURUS NIGER.	*Black Squirrel* (male and female).
13	SCIURUS HUDSONICUS.	*Red Squirrel* (male and female).
14	SCIURUS HUDSONICUS.	*Red Squirrel* (albino).
15	SCIURUS STRIATUS.	*Striped Squirrel.*
16	PTEROMYS VOLUCELLA.	*Flying Squirrel.*

FAMILY ARCTOMIDÆ.

Latin Names.	English Names.
17 Arctomys monax.	*Woodchuck.*

FAMILY GERBILLIDÆ.

18 Meriones americanus. *Deermouse.*

FAMILY CASTORIDÆ.

19 Fiber zibethicus. *Muskrat*, or *Musquash* (m. and f.).

FAMILY MURIDÆ.

20 Mus leucopus. *Jumping Mouse.*
21 Arvicola rufescens. *Tawny Meadow-mouse.*

FAMILY LEPORIDÆ.

22 Lepus nanus. *American Grey Rabbit.*
23 Lepus americanus. *Northern Hare* (m., f. and y.).

24 Erinaceus europæus. *Hedgehog* (old and young), from England.
25 Capra ibex (Linneus). Skull and horns of the male, from the Alps.

BIRDS.

ORDER ACCIPITRES.

FAMILY VULTURIDÆ.

1 Cathartes gryphus. *Condor* (male), from the Andes.
2 Cathartes aura. *Turkey Buzzard* (male).

FAMILY FALCONIDÆ.

3 Aquila chrysætos. *Golden Eagle* (male).

This fine specimen was shot a few years since at Islip, Suffolk county, and is the identical one referred to by Dekay in his Zoology of New-York, Part II, page 4.

4 Hallætos leucocephalus. *Bald Eagle* (male and female).
5 Pandion carolinensis. *American Fish-hawk* (male), with a fish in the beak.
6 Buteo sancti-joannis. *Rough-legged Buzzard* (m. and f.).

Latin Names.	English Names.
7 Buteo borealis.	*Red-tailed Buzzard* (male).
8 Nauclerus furcatus.	*Swallow-tailed Hawk* (male).
9 Falco columbarius.	*Pigeon Hawk* (male and female).
10 Astur atricapillus.	*American Goshawk* (male).

FAMILY STRIGIDÆ.

11 Surnia funerea.	*Hawk Owl.*
12 Surnia nyctea.	*Snowy Owl* (male).
13 Bubo asio.	*Little Screech-owl* (male and female).
14 Otus palustris.	*Short-eared Owl* (male).
15 Ulula nebulosa.	*Barred Owl* (male and female).
16 Ulula acadica.	*Acadian Owl* (male).

ORDER PASSERES.

FAMILY CAPRIMULGIDÆ.

17 Caprimulgus vociferus. *Whippoorwill* (male).

FAMILY HIRUNDINIDÆ.

18 Hirundo purpurea.	*Purple Martin* (male).
19 Hirundo fulva.	*Cliff Swallow* (male and female).

FAMILY AMPELIDÆ.

20 Bombycilla carolinensis. *Cedar-bird* (female).

FAMILY ALCEDINIDÆ.

21 Alcedo alcyon. *Belted Kingfisher* (young male).

FAMILY CERTHIDÆ.

22 Troglodytes ædon.	*House Wren* (male).
23 Troglodytes ludovicianus.	*Mocking Wren* (male).
24 Troglodytes palustris.	*Marsh Wren* (male).

FAMILY PARIDÆ.

25 Parus bicolor. *Crested Tit* (two males).

FAMILY SYLVIADÆ.

26 Regulus satrapa.	*Golden-crested Kinglet* (male).
27 Sialia wilsoni.	*Bluebird* (male and female).

FAMILY MERULIDÆ.

	Latin Names.	English Names.
28	Orpheus polyglottus.	*Mockingbird* (male).
29	Orpheus rufus.	*Brown Thrush* (male).
30	Orpheus carolinensis.	*Catbird* (male and female).
31	Merula migratoria.	*American Robin* (male and female).

FAMILY SYLVICOLIDÆ.

32	Trichas philadelphia.	*Mourning Warbler* (male and female).
33	Vermivora pennsylvanica.	*Worm-eating Warbler* (m. and f.).
34	Vermivora solitaria.	*Blue-winged Warbler.*
35	Vermivora chrysoptera.	*Golden-winged Warbler* (male).
36	Vermivora peregrina.	*Tennessee Warbler* (male).
37	Vermivora celata.	*Orange-crowned Warbler* (young male).
38	Sylvicola maculosa.	*Spotted Warbler* (male).
39	Sylvicola pardalina.	*Spotted Canada Warbler* (male).
40	Sylvicola blackburniæ.	*Blackburnian Warbler* (male).
41	Sylvicola castanea.	*Bay-breasted Warbler* (male).
42	Sylvicola striata.	*Blackpoll Warbler* (male).
43	Sylvicola discolor.	*Prairie Warbler* (male).
44	Sylvicola canadensis.	*Black-throated Blue Warbler* (young male).
45	Sylvicola æstiva.	*Summer Yellowbird* (male and young).
46	Sylvicola pinus.	*Pine Warbler* (female).
47	Sylvicola icterocephala.	*Chestnut-sided Warbler* (male).
48	Sylvicola parus.	*Hemlock Warbler* (two males).
49	Sylvicola formosa.	*Kentucky Warbler* (male).
50	Wilsonia mitrata.	*Hooded Warbler* (female).
51	Wilsonia pusilla.	*Green Black-capped Warbler* (male).

FAMILY MUSCICAPIDÆ.

52	Culicivora cærulea.	*Blue-grey Gnatcatcher* (male).
53	Muscicapa ruticilla.	*American Redstart* (male and female).
54	Tyrannus crinitus.	*Great-crested Kingbird* (male).

FAMILY VIREONIDÆ.

55	Vireo olivaceus.	*Red-eyed Greenlet* (male).
56	Icteria viridis.	*Yellow-breasted Chat* (male).

FAMILY LANIIDÆ.

57	Lanius septentrionalis.	*Northern Butcherbird* (two males).

FAMILY CORVIDÆ.

	Latin Names.	English Names.
58	GARRULUS CRISTATUS.	*Blue Jay* (male).
59	GARRULUS CANADENSIS.	*Canada Jay* (male).
60	PICA CAUDATA.	*Magpie* (male).
61	CORVUS AMERICANUS.	*Common Crow* (male).
62	CORVUS CORAX.	*Raven.*

FAMILY QUISCALIDÆ.

63	QUISCALUS VERSICOLOR.	*Common Crow Blackbird* (m. and f.).
64	STURNELLA LUDOVICIANA.	*Meadow Lark* (male and female).
65	ICTERUS BALTIMORE.	*Golden Oriole* (male).
66	ICTERUS PHŒNICEUS.	*Red-winged Oriole* (male).
67	MOLOTHRUS PECORIS.	*Cow Bunting* (female).
68	DOLICHONYX ORYZIVORUS.	*Bobolink* (male and female).

FAMILY FRINGILLIDÆ.

69	COCCOBORUS CERULEUS.	*Blue Grosbeak* (male).
70	COCCOBORUS LUDOVICIANUS.	*Rose-breasted Grosbeak* (male).
71	STRUTHUS HYEMALIS.	*Snowbird* (male and female).
72	FRINGILLA ILIACA.	*Fox-colored Sparrow* (male).
73	FRINGILLA PENNSYLVANICA.	*White-throated Sparrow* (m. and f.).
74	FRINGILLA LEUCOPHRYS.	*White-crowned Sparrow* (male).
75	EMBERIZA SAVANNA.	*Savannah Bunting* (female).
76	AMMODRAMUS PALUSTRIS.	*Swamp Finch* (female).
77	CARDUELIS TRISTIS.	*Yellowbird* (male).
78	ERYTHROSPIZA PURPUREA.	*Crested Purple-finch* (male and female).
79	PITYLUS CARDINALIS.	*Cardinal Grosbeak* (male).
80	PIPILO ERYTHROPHTHALMUS.	*Chewink*, or *Ground Robin* (male).
81	SPIZA CYANEA.	*Indigo-bird* (male).
82	PYRANGA ÆSTIVA.	*Redbird* (male, young male and female).
83	PYRANGA RUBRA.	*Black-winged Redbird* (male).
84	PLECTROPHANES LAPPONICUS.	*Lapland Snowbird* (female).
85	PLECTROPHANES NIVALIS.	*White Snowbird* (male and female).
86	ALAUDA CORNUTA.	*Horned Lark* (male and female).
87	CORYTHUS ENUCLEATOR.	*Pine Bulfinch* (male, young m. and f.).
88	LOXIA LEUCOPTERA.	*White-winged Crossbill* (male).

FAMILY PICIDÆ.

89	PICUS PILEATUS.	*Crested Woodpecker* (female).
90	PICUS ERYTHROCEPHALUS.	*Redheaded Woodpecker* (male).

	Latin Names.	English Names.
91	Picus villosus.	*Hairy Woodpecker* (male).
92	Picus pubescens.	*Downy Woodpecker* (male).
93	Picus varius.	*Yellow-bellied Woodpecker* (male).
94	Picus carolinus.	*Red-bellied Woodpecker* (male).
95	Picus arcticus.	*Arctic Woodpecker* (male).
96	Picus auratus.	*Golden-winged Woodpecker* (2 males and 1 fem.).

FAMILY COLUMBIDÆ.

97 Ectopistes migratoria. *Wild Pigeon* (male).

ORDER GALLINÆ.

FAMILY PHASIANIDÆ.

98 Meleagris gallopavo. *Wild Turkey* (male).
Also young of the domestic fowl.

FAMILY TETRAONIDÆ.

99 Ortyx virginiana. *American Quail* (m., f., and 3 young).
100 Tetrao umbellus. *Common Partridge* (m., f., & 3 young).
101 Tetrao cupido. *Pinnated Grouse* (male and female).
102 Tetrao canadensis. *Spruce Grouse* (male and female).
103 Argus giganteus (Temminck). *Argus Pheasant.* From Sumatra.
104 Phasianus nycthemerus (Linneus). *Silver Pheasant.* From China.

ORDER GRALLÆ.

FAMILY CHARADRIDÆ.

105 Charadrius semipalmatus. *American Ring Plover* (male and fem.).
106 Charadrius melodus. *Piping Plover.*
107 Charadrius vociferus. *Kildeer Plover* (male).
108 Charadrius virginicus. *Golden Plover* (male and female).
109 Strepsilas interpres. *Turnstone.*

FAMILY GRUIDÆ.

110 Ardea herodias. *Great Blue Heron* (adult with a fish in the beak, and an immature male).
111 Ardea ludoviciana. *Louisiana Heron* (male).
112 Ardea virescens. *Green Heron* (male and female).

	Latin Names.	English Names.
113	Ardea exilis.	*Small Bittern* (male).
114	Ardea minor.	*American Bittern* (male and female).
115	Ardea discors.	*Black-crowned Night-heron* (male).

FAMILY SCOLOPACIDÆ.

116	Numenius longirostris.	*Long-billed Curlew* (male).
117	Numenius hudsonicus.	*Jack Curlew* (male).
118	Heteropoda semipalmata.	*Semipalmated Sandpiper* (male).
119	Tringa maritima.	*Purple Sandpiper* (male).
120	Tringa rufescens.	*Buff-breasted Sandpiper* (female).
121	Tringa cinclus.	*Black-breasted Sandpiper* (male).
122	Tringa schinzi.	*Schinz's Sandpiper* (male).
123	Tringa pectoralis.	*Pectoral Sandpiper* (male and female).
124	Tringa canutus.	*Redbreasted Sandpiper* (male and fem.).
125	Tringa pusilla.	*Wilson's Sandpiper* (male).
126	Calidris arenaria.	*Sanderling* (two males and one female).
127	Totanus macularius.	*Spotted Sandlark* (male).
128	Totanus bartramius.	*Grey Plover* (male).
129	Totanus flavipes.	*Yellowlegs* (male).
130	Totanus melanoleucus.	*Varied Tatler* (male and young).
131	Totanus semipalmatus.	*Willet* (male).
132	Scolopax wilsoni.	*Common American Snipe* (2 m. and f.).
133	Rusticola minor.	*American Woodcock* (m., f., & 2 young).

FAMILY RALLIDÆ.

134	Rallus crepitans.	*Saltwater Meadowhen* (male).
135	Ortygometra carolina.	*Sora Rail* (male).
136	Gallinula galeata.	*Florida Gallinule* (male).

FAMILY RECURVIROSTRIDÆ.

137	Himantopus nigricollis.	*The Lawyer* (male and female).

ORDER LOBIPEDES.

FAMILY PODICIPIDÆ.

138	Podiceps rubricollis.	*Rednecked Grebe* (male).
139	Hydroka carolinensis.	*Dipper*, or *Pied Dobchick* (male).

ORDER NATATORES.

FAMILY ALCIDÆ.

	Latin Names.	English Names.
140	Mergulus alle.	*Sea Dove* (male).
141	Alca torda.	*Razorbill* (male).

FAMILY COLYMBIDÆ.

142	Colymbus glacialis.	*Great Loon* (male and female).
143	Colymbus septentrionalis.	*Red-throated Loon* (female).

FAMILY PROCELLARIDÆ.

144	Thalassidroma wilsoni.	*Wilson's Petrel* (male).

FAMILY PELECANIDÆ.

145	Sula americana.	*American Gannet* (male).

FAMILY LARIDÆ.

146	Rhynchops nigra.	*Black Skimmer* (male).
147	Sterna hirundo.	*Common Tern* (male).
148	Sterna cayana.	*Cayenne Tern* (male).
149	Sterna nigra.	*Black Tern* (male and young).
150	Larus argentatus.	*Winter Gull* (male and female).
151	Larus atricilla.	*Laughing Gull* (male).
152	Larus bonapartii.	*Bonaparte's Gull* (male and female).
153	Larus sabini.	*Fork-tailed Gull* (male).
154	Lestris buffoni?	*Arctic Hawk-gull* (male).
155	Lestris richardsonii.	*Richardson's Hawk-gull* (male).

FAMILY ANATIDÆ.

156	Mergus merganser.	*Buff-breasted Sheldrake* (male).
157	Mergus cucullatus.	*Hooded Sheldrake* (male and female).
158	Fuligula valisneria.	*Canvasback* (male).
159	Fuligula marila.	*Broadbill* (female).
160	Fuligula rufitorques.	*Bastard Broadbill* (male).
161	Fuligula labradora.	*Pied Duck* (male).
162	Fuligula rubida.	*Ruddy Duck* (male and female).
163	Fuligula glacialis.	*Oldwife* (male in winter plumage, and male and female young).
164	Fuligula albeola.	*Buffleheaded Duck* (male and female).
165	Fuligula clangula.	*Whistler* (male).
166	Fuligula histrionica.	*Harlequin Duck* (male).

	Latin Names.	English Names.
167	Fuligula mollissima.	*Eider Duck* (male).
168	Fuligula perspicillata.	*Surf Duck* (immature male).
169	Fuligula americana.	*Broadbilled Coot* (male).
170	Fuligula fusca.	*White-winged Coot* (male).
171	Anas sponsa.	*Wood Duck* (male and young male).
172	Anas carolinensis.	*Green-winged Teal* (male and female).
173	Anas acuta.	*Pin-tailed Duck* (male and female).
174	Anas clypeata.	*Shoveller* (male in winter plumage, and male and female in summer plumage).
175	Anas strepera.	*Grey Duck*, or *Gadwall* (male).
176	Anas americana.	*American Widgeon* (male and female).
177	Anser canadensis.	*Wild Goose* (male).
178	Anser albifrons.	*White-fronted Goose* (male).
179	Anser bernicla.	*Brant Goose* (male).

AMERICAN BIRDS DESCRIBED BY AUDUBON, WHICH HAVE NOT BEEN OBSERVED IN THE STATE OF NEW-YORK.

180	Ictinia plumbeus.	*Mississippi Kite* (male).
181	Falco peregrinus.	*Great-footed Hawk* (male, with *Golden-winged Woodpecker* under foot).
182	Milvulus tyrannus.	*Fork-tailed Flycatcher* (male).
183	Helinaia protonotarius.	*Prothonotary Swamp-warbler* (m. & f.).
184	Sialia occidentalis.	*Western Bluebird* (male).
185	Sialia arctica.	*Arctic Bluebird* (male).
186	Turdus nævius.	*Varied Thrush* (female).
187	Coccothraustes vespertina.	*Evening Grosbeak* (male and female).
188	Pyranga ludoviciana.	*Louisiana Tanager* (male and female).
189	Icterus bullockii.	*Bullock's Hangnest* (male).
190	Garrulus stelleri.	*Steller's Jay* (male).
191	Sitta pusilla.	*Brown-headed Nuthatch* (male).
192	Picus principalis.	*Ivory-billed Woodpecker* (male and fem.).
193	Picus querulus.	*Red-cockaded Woodpecker* (m. and f.).
194	Picus torquatus.	*Lewis's Woodpecker* (male).
195	Picus mexicanus.	*Red-shafted Woodpecker* (male).
196	Centurus carolinensis.	*Carolina Parrot* (young).
197	Columba passerina.	*Ground Dove* (male).
198	Ortyx plumifera.	*Plumed Partridge* (male).
199	Ibis rubra.	*Scarlet Ibis* (male).

FOREIGN BIRDS.

Latin Names. English Names.

200 Upupa epops, Linneus. *Hoopoe.* Africa.

201 Epimachus magnificus, Oken. *Rifleman* (male and female). New South Wales.

202 Oriolus galbula, Oken. *Golden Blackbird.* Europe.

203 Gracula rosea, Oken. *Rose-colored Thrush.* East Indies.

204 Edolius malabaricus, Oken. *Drongo.* Africa.

205 Galbulus viridis, Oken (two specimens). Africa.

In addition to these, there are twenty-two specimens of foreign birds whose specific names have not been determined.

MINERALS, FOSSILS, SHELLS, &c.

ROCKS.

1 to 50 inclusive. Rock specimens, from Cumberland.

MINERALS.

51 Carbonate of barytes, incrusted with copper pyrites and carbonate of lime.

52 Crystallized sulphate of barytes (crystals in the form *épointée* of Haüy). From Devonshire, England.

53 Calcareous concretion. From the Lago de Tartari, near Rome.

54 Carbonate of lime, in botryoidal concretions.

55 Botryoidal magnesian limestone. From Durham.

56 Fibrous limestone; edges polished.

57 Fibrous sulphate of lime. Derbyshire, England.

58 Fibrous gypsum. Nova-Scotia.

59 Compact fluor spar.

60 Crystallized fluor spar, polished.

61 Crystallized fluor, on blende. Matlock, England.

62 White crystallized fluor, upon zinc ore. Derbyshire, England.

63 FLUOR SPAR, crystallized in cubes of a beautiful bluish tint. From Cumberland, England.

64 FLUOR SPAR, crystallized in cubes of a beautiful green. Cumberland.

65 FLUOR SPAR, crystallized in cubes; colorless.

66 FLUOR SPAR, incrusted with crystals of carbonate of lime.

67 VEINED FLUOR, polished. Derbyshire.

68 VEINED FLUOR, called by the miners *blue john.*

69 GROUP of QUARTZ CRYSTALS, incrusted with transparent terminated six-sided prisms of heavy spar.

70, 71 Two six-sided prisms of QUARTZ, with six-sided pyramids of a beautiful brownish tinge.

72 PSEUDOMORPHOUS QUARTZ, sprinkled with blende. From Alston, Eng.

73 TALC. 74 GREEN TALC. 75 BLACK SPINELLE.

76 BROWN GARNET: crystals with twenty trapezoidal faces.

77 GREEN FELSPAR. Siberia.

78 GLASSY FELSPAR. Near Bonn.

79 CHRYSOBERYL. Near Saratoga-springs.

80 BERYL. Acworth, New-Hampshire.

81 BERYL (imbedded). Acworth, N. H.

82 STAUROTIDE. Litchfield, Massachusetts.

83 STAUROTIDE. Franconia.

84 BRUCITE, in carbonate of lime. Warwick, New-York.

85 ONYX AGATE. Siberia.

86 CHRYSOPRASE. Baumgarten.

87 OLIVINE. Habichtwald.

88 CYANITE. Chesterfield.

89 ASBESTUS. Greenwood furnace, Orange county, New-York.

90 GOLD ORE. Charlotte, North-Carolina.

91 SILVER ORE. Siberia.

92 MURIATE of SILVER. Siberia.

93 COPPER ORE. Franklin, New-Jersey.

94 ARSENIATE of COPPER, on arsenical iron. Amity, New-York.

95 RED OXIDE of COPPER. Siberia.

96 RED OXIDE of COPPER, incrusted with green carbonate of copper and quartz. Siberia.

97 BLUE CARBONATE of COPPER. Siberia.

98 MALACHITE. Siberia.

99 VEINS of LEAD ORE. From the Odin mine.

100 SLICKENSIDE GALENA. From the Odin mine.

101 ARSENIATE of LEAD. From Caldbeck-fells, Cumberland.

102 ARSENICAL PYRITES? incrusting quartz crystals. Caldbeck-fells.

103 Molybdena. Caldbeck-fells.
104 Uranite. Cornwall, England.
105 Oxide of tin. Cornwall.
106, 107 Axinite. Cornwall.
108 Volcanic basalt. Cassel.
109 Mineral caoutchouc. England.
110 Elastic bitumen. 111 Carbonate of lead.
112 Sulphuret of zinc and tin. Hartz, Germany.
113 Crystallized brown oxide of iron. Cornwall.
114 Massive garnet. 115 Semiopal.
116 Porphyry, containing bronzite.
117 Lepidolite and rubellite. Paris, Maine.
118 Drusy quartz.
119 Auriferous pyrites. North-Carolina.

FOSSILS.

120 Calymene senaria (folded), Hall. Trenton limestone.
121 Head and post-abdomen of *Calymene senaria*, Hall. Trenton limestone.
122 Cephalic shield of *Trinucleus concentricus*, Hall. Trenton limestone.
123 Matrix of *Calymene senaria*, Hall. Trenton limestone?
124 Bellerophon bilobatus, *var.* corrugatus, Hall. Trenton limestone.
125, 126, 127 Chætetes lycoperdon, Hall. Trenton limestone.
128 Calymene blumenbachii (in two positions), Brongniart. Dudley, England.
129 A Slab covered with small bivalves, fragments of crustaceans, corallines, etc. From Dudley, England.
130 Post-abdomen of an *Asaphus* (not described by Murchison). Dudley.
131 Euomphalus pentangularis. From the Mountain limestone of Semplough, Cumberland, England.
132 Spirifer obtusis. From Egalsfield, Cumberland.
133 Spirifer attenuatus. From Semplough, Cumberland.
134, 135 Bivalve (Genus Allorisma of King). From Parkhead, Cumberland.
136 Spirifer glaber. From the Mountain limestone of England.
137 Spirifer lynx. Mountain limestone of England.
138, 139 Orthis resupinatus. Mountain limestone of England.
140 Favosites (polished). Mountain limestone.

141 SPIRIFER. Mountain limestone of England.

142 ACROCULIA. From Oriskany sandstone.

143, 144 CORNULITES ARCUATUS. Niagara limestone.

145 CAST of LEPTÆNA. From Schoharie grit.

146 CRINOIDAL COLUMN. Mountain limestone of England.

147 CORALLINE (silicified). Corniferous limestone.

148 ENCRINAL MARBLE (polished). Derbyshire, England.

149 ENCRINAL MARBLE (polished). Peak Castle, England.

150 PECTEN? From the top of one of the mountains of the Jura chain, Switzerland.

151, 152 CALAMITES. Cumberland, England.

153 CALAMITES ——? Workington, Cumberland.

154 CALAMITES ——? Parton, Cumberland.

155 STIGMARIA ——. Cumberland.

156, 157, 158 LEPIDODENDRON ——. Cumberland.

159 ODONTOPTERIS ——. Parton, Cumberland.

160 NEUROPTERIS ——. Somerset, England.

161, 162 PECOPTERIS MANTELLII. Near Whitehaven, Cumberland.

163 ODONTOPTERIS ——. From Whitehaven, Cumberland.

164 SPHENOPTERIS AFFINIS? Whitehaven.

165, 166 SPHENOPTERIS ——. Whitehaven.

167 ASTEROPHYLLITES PARKINSONI. Parton, Cumberland.

168 ASTEROPHYLLITES ——. Parton, Cumberland.

169, 170 VERTEBRA of the ICHTHYOSAURUS. Lyme in Dorsetshire, Eng.

171 LEFT HIND-PADDLE of the ICHTHYOSAURUS PLATYODON. From the Lias, England.

172 RIGHT FORE-PADDLE of ICHTHYOSAURUS PLATYODON. From the Lias, England.

173 COPROLITE. One of the sides is polished, exhibiting a fish-scale, and the enamelled portions of fishes that remain undigested by the ICHTHYOSAURUS. From the Lias, England.

174 FOSSIL FISH. Scotland.

175, 176 FOSSIL TEETH of ICHTHYOSAURUS. From the Blue Lias of Lyme, Dorset, England.

177 AMMONITES OBTUSUS. From the Lias, England.

178 AMMONITES NODOSUS? From the Lias, England.

179, 180 AMMONITES. Matlock, England.

181, 182, 183 AMMONITES. From the Lias, England.

184 AMMONITE. From Whitby, England.

185, 186 GRYPHÆA INCURVA. Clifton, Somerset, England.

187 GRYPHÆA COLUMBA. Beds of the Tiverlane.

188 Ammonite. From the Oolite, England.

189 Gryphæa? (13 specimens). Lias? England.

190 Shark's tooth. From the Oolite, England.

191, 192 Terebratula. From the Oolite, England.

193 Ichthyodorulite (mineralized by sulphuret of iron). From the Lias, England.

194 Shark's tooth (imbedded in chalk). From the Cretaceous formation, England.

195 Turrelites costatus. Chalk marl.

196 Belemnites mucronatus, Cretaceous formation, Yorkshire, England.

197 Exogyra costata. From the Greensand, New-Jersey.

198, 199, 200 Gryphæa mutabilis. From the Greensand, New-Jersey.

201 Galerites. From the Cretaceous formation, Yorkshire, England.

202 Ananchytes ovatus. From the Cretaceous formation, Yorkshire.

203 Scutella. From the Cretaceous formation, England.

204 Murex (Fusus) contrarius, Sowerby. Given to H. C. De Rham junior, by Prof. Sedgwick, at the Woodwardian Museum, Cambridge, March 6, 1837. From the Redcrag, England.

205 Fusus (covered with Balanæ). From the Redcrag, England.

206 Fossil wood. From Alabama.

207 Petrified wood. From near Utica.

208 Nautilus truncatus. From the Lias of England.

209 Cast of Pleurotomaria. Lias, England.

210, 211 Casts of a univalve. Lias, England.

ZOOLOGICAL FRAGMENTS.

212, 213 Skull of the Skunk (*Mephitis americana*).

214 Skull of the Fisher (*Mustela canadensis*).

215, 216 Skull of the American Sable (*Mustela martes*).

217 Skull of the North-American Otter (*Lutra canadensis*).

218 Upper mandible of the Albatross. From South America.

FISHES.

ORDER PLECTOGNATHI.

FAMILY GYMNODONTIDÆ.

219 Diodon pilosus (*Hairy Balloonfish*). New-York bay.

FAMILY OSTRACIONIDÆ.

220 Lactophrys derhamii? Taken on the shore of Long Island. Not described in Dekay's Zoology.

Characteristics. No orbital spines; back elevated in the form of a crescent longitudinally, with two spines centrally situated on the periphery of the crescent, and distant one-third of an inch from each other; three spines on each side of the abdomen: length four inches.

Should this prove to be an undescribed species, it is proposed to name it *derhamii*, in honor of the late Henry C. De Rham junior.

SHELLS.

[Arranged according to the System of Lamarck.]

CLASS ANNELIDES.

ORDER SEDENTARIA.

FAMILY SERPULACEA.

221, 222, 223 Serpula vermicularis.

CLASS CIRRIPEDES.

ORDER SESSILE CIRRIPEDES.

224 Tubicinella balænarum. The Tubicinellæ are found with nearly the whole shell buried in the thick skin of the whale.

225 Coronula balænaris.

226 Coronula balænaris (6 specimens), on a piece of whaleskin.

CLASS CONCHIFERA.

ORDER C. DIMYARIA.

FAMILY CONCHACEA (*marine*).

227 Cytherea maculata.

228 Cytherea dione.

229 Cytherea ——.

230 Cytherea ——.

FAMILY CARDIACEA.

231 Cardium ——.

232 Cardium ——.

233 Cardium ——.

234 Isocardia moltkiana.

FAMILY ARCACEA.

235 Arca ——.

FAMILY NAJADES.

236 Unio ——.

ORDER MONOMYARIA.

FAMILY MYTILACEA.

237 Pinna squamosa?

FAMILY PECTINIDES.

238 Pecten ——.

239 Pecten ——.

CLASS MOLLUSCA.

ORDER GASTEROPODA.

FAMILY PHYLLIDINA.

240 Chiton ——(5 specimens).

241 Chiton ——.

242 Chiton ——.

FAMILY BULLÆANA.

243 Bulla ampulla.

ORDER TRACHELIPODA.

FAMILY COLIMACEA.

244 Helix pomatia. England.
245 Helix aspersa(3). England.
246 Helix melanotragus. Africa.
247 Helix nemoralis. England.
248 Helix ——(2). England.
249 Helix ——. West Indies.
250 Helix ——. West Indies.
251 Helix ——. West Indies.
252 Carocolla ——. West Indies.
253, 254 Bulinus rosaceus. W. I.
255 Bulinus rosaceus (young).
256, 257 Pupa ——. West Indies.
258 Auricula ——. West Indies.

FAMILY LIMNEANA.

259 Limnæa stagnalis.

260 Planorbis corneus.

FAMILY PERISTOMATA.

261 Ampullaria fasciata(3).

262 Ampullaria guinaica. W. I.

263 Paludina ——(2).

FAMILY NERITACEA.

264 Neritina spinosa.
265 Neritina ——.
266 Natica mamilla(2).
267 Natica ——.
268 Natica ——.
269 Natica ——(2).
270 Nerita peloronta(2).
271 Nerita versicolor.
272 Nerita ——.

FAMILY MACROSTOMATA.

273 SIGARETUS CONCAVUS.
274 HALIOTIS TUBERCULATA.
275 HALIOTIS CANALICULATA.
276 HALIOTIS ——(5).

FAMILY TURBINACEA.

277 SOLARIUM GRANULATUM.
278 ROTELLA (not figured or described by Kiener). Seas of Tropical climates.
279 ROTELLA (not figured or described by Kiener).
280 ROTELLA (not figured or described by Kiener). The three preceding species would be considered by Kiener as varieties of *Rotella lineolata.*
281 TROCHUS MACULATUS.
282 TROCHUS ——(2).
283 TROCHUS ——.
284 MARGARITA ——(2).
285 MARGARITA ——.
286 PLANAXIS ——.
287 TURBO ——.
288 TURBO ——.
289 TURRITELLA DUPLICATA. Ceylon.
290 TURRITELLA CINGULATA, Sowerby. Pacific ocean.

FAMILY CANALIFERA.

291 CERITHIUM TUBERCULATUM.
292 TURBINELLA CORNIGER.
293 TURBINELLA POLYGONA.
294 FASCIOLARIA AURANTIACA?
295 FUSUS MORIO (*varietas*).
296 PYRULA MELONGENA.
297 PYRULA CARICA.
298 PYRULA MELONGENA (*varietas*).
299 RANELLA BECKII, Kiener.
300 MUREX REGIUS(4).
301 MUREX BRASSICA(2).
302 MUREX RADIX(3).
303 MUREX BRANDARIS(2).
304 MUREX PINNATUS, Swainson.
305 MUREX ELONGATUS.
306 MUREX ERINACEUS.
307 MUREX CALCAR, Kiener.
308 MUREX CRASSILABRUM? Gray.
309 TRITON VARIEGATUM.
310 TRITON SUCCINCTUM.
311 TRITON SUCCINCTUM (young shell).

FAMILY ALATÆ.

312 ROSTELLARIA PES-PELICANI(2).
313 STROMBUS LENTIGINOSUS(2).
314 STROMBUS CANARIUM.
315 STROMBUS PUGILIS(2).
316 STROMBUS GRANULATUS, Sowerby.
317 STROMBUS GRACILIO, Sowerby.
318 STROMBUS GIBBERULUS. Molucca.
319 STROMBUS FLORIDUS. Moluccas.
320 STROMBUS VINTATUS. Moluccas.

FAMILY PURPURIFERA.

321 CASSIDARIA ——.
322 CASSIS TESTICULUS(3).
323 CASSIS ERINACEUS.
324 RICINULA HORRIDA.
325 PURPURA HÆMASTOMA(2).
326 PURPURA MARGINALBA, Blainville; *varietas*, Kiener.
327 PURPURA INTERMEDIA, Kiener.
328 PURPURA DELTOIDEA.
329 PURPURA PATULA.
330 PURPURA TEXTILOSA (young).
331 PURPURA COSTATA, Blainville.
332 PURPURA CHOCOLATUM, Duclos.
333 PURPURA SERTUM(2).
334 MONOCEROS CRASSILABRUM.
335 MONOCEROS ——.
336 DOLIUM VARIEGATUM (young).
337 DOLIUM VARIEGATUM.
338 DOLIUM PERDIX.
339 BUCCINUM PAPILLOSUM(7).
340 BUCCINUM UNDATUM(3).
341 BUCCINUM RETICULATUM.
342 BUCCINUM QUOYII, Kiener.
343 TEREBRA CŒRULESCENS(2).

FAMILY COLUMELLATA.

344 COLUMELLA MELEAGRIS, Duclos.
345 MITRA MELONGENA.
346 VOLUTA MUSICA.

FAMILY CONVOLUTÆ.

347 OVULUM OVUM. From the hole pierced in the outer lip of this shell, it was undoubtedly worn by a native female of one of the South Sea islands as an ear ornament.
348 CYPRÆA NUCLEUS. Pacific ocean.
349 CYPRÆA TIGRIS(3).
350 CYPRÆA MAURITIANA.
351 CYPRÆA HISTRIO(2).
352 CYPRÆA TALPA.
353 CYPRÆA ADUSTA.
354 CYPRÆA ACHATINA. N. Holland.
355 CYPRÆA LURIDA.
356 CYPRÆA LYNX(3).
357 CYPRÆA CAPUT-SERPENTIS.
358 CYPRÆA ZIGZAG.
359 CYPRÆA CAURICA(4).
360 CYPRÆA VITELLIS.
361 CYPRÆA CARNEOLA(2).
362 CYPRÆA EROSA. Indian ocean.
363 CYPRÆA —— (young shell).
364 CYPRÆA RUVEI(3). N. Holland.
365 CYPRÆA XANTHODON.
366 OLIVA PORPHYRIA.
367 OLIVA INFLATA(2).
368 OLIVA ANGULATA.
369 OLIVA SAYII(3).
370 OLIVA EPISCOPALIS.
371 OLIVA PERUVIANA.
372 OLIVA UTRICULUS (*varietas*).
373 OLIVA DACTYLEA(3).
374 OLIVA SUBULATA.
375 OLIVA RETICULATA.
376 OLIVA UTRICULUS(2).
377 OLIVA ——.
378 OLIVA ——.
379 OLIVA ——.
380 CONUS NEBULOSUS.
381 CONUS MUSTELINUS, Bruguière.
382 CONUS ACHATINUS, Bruguière.
383 CONUS COLUMBA, Bruguière.
384 CONUS MONILE, Bruguière.
385 CONUS TEREBRA, Bruguière.
386 CONUS VERRICULUM.

RADIATA.

CLASS ECHINODERMATÆ.

387 ASTERIAS ACULEATA.

389 ECHINUS SPHÆRA.

388 ASTERIAS —— (GONIASTER of Agassiz).

CLASS POLYPI.

390 FUNGIA AGARICIFORMIS.

391 FUNGIA ——.

392 OCULINA RAMEA.

393 OCULINA ——.

394 MADREPORA MURICATA.

395 MADREPORA ——.

396 NULLOPORA ——.

397 SPONGIA —— (attached to an ARCA).

ADDED TO THE COLLECTION DURING THE PRINTING OF THE CATALOGUE.

1 DIDELPHUS VIRGINIANA. *American Opossum* (female).

2 PUTORIUS NOVEBORACENSIS. *New-York Ermine* (spring plumage). Presented by HERMAN WENDELL, M.D.

3 VULPES FULVUS. *Red Fox* (male).

4 HYSTRIX HUDSONIUS. *North-American Porcupine* (male). Very large.

5 NUMENIUS LONGIROSTRIS. *Long-billed Curlew* (male).

6 PODICEPS RUBRICOLLIS. *Red-necked Grebe* (male).

7 SALAMANDRA SUBVIOLACEA. *Violet-colored Salamander* (male).

www.ingramcontent.com/pod-product-compliance
Lightning Source LLC
LaVergne TN
LVHW010249110826
845151LV00004B/1425